THE EMERGENCE OF ARAB NATIONALISM

THE EMERGENCE OF ARAB NATIONALISM

With a Background Study of Arab-Turkish Relations in the Near East

ZEINE N. ZEINE
American University of Beirut

CARAVAN BOOKS
Delmar, New York

The Emergence of Arab Nationalism
First published under the title
Arab-Turkish Relations and the
Emergence of Arab Nationalism

First Edition 1958
Second Edition 1966
Third Edition 1973

Third Edition Published by Caravan Books, Inc.,
Box 344, Delmar, New York 12054

Printed in Lebanon by Imprimerie Catholique

Library of Congress Cataloging in Publication Data

Zeine, Zeine N
The emergence of Arab nationalism.

First ed. published in 1958 under title: Arab-Turkish relations and the emergence of Arab nationalism.
Bibliography: p.
1. Nationalism – Arab countries. 2. Turkey – Foreign relations – Arab countries. 3. Arab countries – Foreign relations – Turkey. I. Title.
DS63.6.Z44 1973 327.496'1'056 76-39576
ISBN 0-88206-000-7

CONTENTS

	Preface to the Third Edition	vii
1.	The Ottomans and the Ottoman Conquest of the Middle East	1
2.	Ottoman Government in Arab Lands	17
3.	Independence Movements in Arab Lands	30
4.	Arab Revolutionary Activities and the Young Turks, 1865-1909	46
5.	The Emergence of Arab Nationalism Part One — Under the Young Turks, 1909-1914	73
6.	The Emergence of Arab Nationalism Part Two — The War Years, 1914-1918	101
7.	Conclusion and Postscript	125
	Appendixes	140
	Bibliography	169
	Index	186

PREFACE TO THE THIRD EDITION

THE PURPOSE of this work is to study the genesis and history of Arab nationalism, and to set forth and reinterpret Arab-Turkish relations in the Arab provinces of the Ottoman Empire. The work also attempts to remove certain fallacies and misconceptions concerning the origin and evolution of Arab nationalism, as well as the relations between Arabs and Turks. Those relations constitute a most important background to the awakening of Arab political consciousness during the second half of the nineteenth and the beginning of the twentieth centuries.

Since the first publication of this book in 1958, no less than twenty-five books have appeared on the subject of Arab nationalism, written in Arabic by Muslim Arab authors. They are all in agreement with the principal theme of this study, namely, that Arab nationalism in its genesis and growth has been inseparable from Islam. These books have now been added to the bibliography.

It is impossible to thank individually all those from whose advice, assistance and encouragement I have benefited in writing this book. The list of their names is too long to be recorded in this Preface. However, I would like to express my deep gratitude for the help received from the following eminent Arab leaders — all of whom are, alas, no longer living : Fāris Nimr Pasha, Nūrī Pāsha al-Sa'īd, 'Alī Jawdat al-Ayyūbī, Fāris al-Khūrī, Shaikh 'Ārif al-Zain, Tawfīq al-Nāṭūr, Sa'īd Ḥaidar, the Emīr 'Ādil Arslān, Sāṭī' al-Ḥuṣrī, and Shaikh 'Abd al-Qādir al-Maghribī. They all had personal experiences and an intimate knowledge of the Ottoman Empire. They were also contemporary with the birth of Arab political nationalism and independence.

I owe special thanks to two distinguished Turks: General 'Ali Fuad Pasha, Chief-of-Staff of the Fourth Army Corps under Djemal Pasha, in Syria; and Enver Ziya Karal, Professor of Modern History in the Faculty of Languages, History, and Geography at Ankara University: the former for his assistance in clarifying certain important issues, with his first-hand knowledge of Arab-Turkish relations during World War I, and the latter for kindly reading the entire manuscript of the first edition of this work and making valuable suggestions.

Several friends and colleagues have also helped in one way or another, and I am grateful to them for their kind advice and assistance. I would like to mention, in particular, Professors Albert Hourani, Charles Issawi, George Kirk, Leslie W. Leavitt and Christopher H. O. Scaife, Ambassador Abdu'l Rahman Adra, and Dr. Fuad Sarruf. But in all fairness to them all, it must be stated I hold myself responsible for the views and opinions expressed in this work.

A number of new documents, some in the original Arabic and hitherto unpublished, will be found in the text and in the Appendixes of this work. I am deeply indebted to Dr. Salah Munajjid for his generous permission to reproduce and publish four documents belonging to his private library.

I am also grateful for the help and courtesies received from the Staffs of the Public Record Office in London, the Archives du Ministère des Affaires Étrangères and the Bibliothèque Nationale in Paris, the British Museum Library, and the Royal Institute of International Affairs (Chatham House).

ZEINE N. ZEINE

American University of Beirut
Beirut, Lebanon
February, 1973

CHAPTER ONE

THE OTTOMANS AND THE OTTOMAN CONQUEST OF THE NEAR EAST

THE TURKS are one of the three principal Islamic peoples of the Middle East, the other two being the Arabs and the Persians. But they established the largest and strongest Muslim Empire, known as the Ottoman Empire, since the rise of Islam. At one time, the Ottoman Empire stretched from the gates of Vienna to the straits of Bāb al-Mandib, and from the Caucasus across North Africa nearly to the Atlantic Ocean. A series of decisive victories in a long chain of conquests led the Turks to the zenith of their military power and glory.[1] An unbroken succession of ten brilliant and great Sultans led the Ottomans to acquire in the fourteenth, fifteenth, and sixteenth centuries a vast empire: Uthman ("Osman"), at the time of whose death in 1326 the city of Brusa fell in Ottoman hands; Orkhan, the founder of the Janissaries (the Yeni-Cheri) and the conqueror of Nicomedia, Nicaea, and Pergamum; Murad I, who crossed the

1. "... l'Empire ottoman est resté durant tout le XVIe siècle et le XVIIe siècle une des plus grandes puissances du monde occidental, sinon la plus grande de toutes. Régnant sur plusieurs millions de kilomètres carrés, disposant de ressources budgétaires plus stables et plus larges que n'importe quel État européen (y compris l'Espagne et ses mines d'or), servis par une administration méthodiquement organisée et dévouée au bien public, sûrs de la fidélité d'un peuple chez lequel la discipline compte au premier rang des vertus traditionnelles, ayant les meilleures troupes régulières, la meilleure artillerie, une marine qui dominait toute la Méditerranée, les sultans obligeaient alors l'Europe entière à compter avec eux: Louis XIV, rappelait récemment F. Grenard d'une manière très opportune, si arrogant à faire respecter du Saint-Père des privilèges contestables, souffrait que son ambassadeur à Constantinople fut bâtonné et emprisonné, et tous les voyageurs européens au Levant étaient alors pénétrés, devant le spectacle de Stamboul, de cette admiration respectueuse qu'inspirent les grands foyers de civilisation." Jean Sauvaget, *Introduction à l'histoire de l'Orient musulman* (Paris: Adrien-Maisonneuve, 1943), 1: 164-65.

Hellespont and won several victories in Europe, particularly at Adrianople in 1361, which henceforth became the capital of the Ottoman dominions, and at Kossovo in 1389; Bayezid I, the great victor at the famous battle of Nicopolis (1396)[2] and the conqueror of Greece (Athens fell in 1397); Muḥammad I, who through his wisdom and courage reunited the Empire at the beginning of the fifeteenth century when it seemed to have fallen into irretrievable ruin; Murad II, who won the decisive battle of Varna in 1444 against a Christian army which was "the most splendid that had been assembled since the French chivalry and the Hungarians advanced against Bajazet at Nicopolis;"[3] Muḥammad II, surnamed *Abū'l Fatḥ* or *Al-Fātiḥ*, "the Conqueror," who captured Constantinople in 1453 and made that city "the centre jewel in the ring of the Turkish Empire;" Bayezid II, during whose reign (1481-1512) the Turkish navy became, in the words of Edward Creasy, "the terror of the Christian fleets..., contending skilfully and boldly against the fai superior fleets of the Pope, of Spain and of Venice"; Selim I, who led his victorious army southwards and in less than two years added Syria, Egypt, and Arabia (1516-17) to the Ottoman dominions, and, finally, Sultan Sulaiman, "the Magnificent," "the Law-Giver," "the Lord of his Age," "the Perfecter of the Perfect Number,"[4] who captured Belgrade, invaded Hungary

2. After the battle of Nicopolis, Sultan Bayezid sent to the Mamlūk Sultan of Egypt (Zāhir Saif-ud-Dīn Barqūq) a number of the heavily armed prisoners which his army had captured and they were paraded in the streets of Cairo. Then again, after the battle of Varna, Sultan Murād II sent some Hungarian prisoners, this time to the Sultan of Herat in Afghanistan! The Sultan kept them and used them in his army as a "tank division." These giant warriors of the North must have produced a great impression in Egypt, in Afghanistan, and in the Muslim world in general as the Ottomans were considered the champions of Islam. (Lecture by Professor Paul Wittek, School of Oriental and African Studies, University of London, 8 March 1951.)

3. Edward S. Creasy, *History of the Ottoman Turks from the Beginning of their Empire to the Present Time* (London, 1878), p. 64. "One hundred thousand paladins, the flower of the chivalry of France and Germany, nobles not a few from England, Scotland, Flanders, and Lombardy, and a large body of the Knights of St. John responded to the Papal call, and enlisted under the banner of Sigismund. In the battle of Nicopolis (1396) the forces of Christendom were overthrown by the Ottomans .... The triumph of the Ottomans was complete.." John A. R. Marriott, *The Eastern Question*, 4th ed. (Oxford, 1951), p. 66.

4. "Solayman was the Tenth Sultan of the House of Othman; he opened the Tenth century of the Hegira; and for these and other decimal attributes he was styled by his countrymen 'the Perfector of the Perfect Number.'" Creasy, *History of the Ottoman Turks*, p. 160.

and won the decisive battle of Mohács (1526), occupied Budapest, besieged Vienna (1529), and added Mosul and Baghdad (1535) to the Ottoman Empire. In his time, the Turkish dominions formed "an empire of more than forty thousand square miles, embracing many of the richest and most beautiful regions of the world ... and which under no subsequent Sultan maintained or recovered the wealth, power, and prosperity which it enjoyed under the great lawgiver of the House of Othman."[5]

The conquest of Constantinople in 1453 followed by the extraordinary expansion of Ottoman power in Europe and in the Near East during the second half of the fifteenth and the first quarter of the sixteenth centuries struck the whole of Christendom in the West — the Pope, the College of Cardinals, and all the Christian princes — with the magnitude of the danger which threatened them. One Council after another was held in Rome to discuss the Turkish danger and to propose that "something must be done" against the Turk.

Emperor Charles V wrote to his Ambassador in England on 16 April 1523: "We are sending you special credentials addressed to Henry and Wolsey, which you will first give them... you will point out to the King and the Cardinal the great danger to Christendom which has arisen from the fall of Rhodes. The Turk almost certainly intends to attack Christendom this year, either in Italy or in Hungary, or on both sides at once. It is very likely that his first blow will be at Italy, and will fall on us and our kingdoms at Naples and Sicily, and consequently on the States of the Church and so on all Christian princes, but wherever the Turk attacks Christendom, it will be little to our honour as emperor, and protector of the Church, or that of our brother, as Defender of the Faith, to permit such attacks in our lifetime, and if we do so it will be to our eternal shame, besides the present evils we may suffer.... For our part, we are reluctant to abandon the war which we have prepared against France, but in view of the great present necessity of resisting the Turk and the peril to all Christendom for which we would be responsible, we ask them to consider whether the best expedient would not be a truce for a considerable period of years.... On the conclusion of this truce, a treaty should be arranged if possible for

5. Ibid., p. 197; Joseph von Hammer-Purgstall, *Histoire de l'empire ottoman depuis son origine jusqu'à nos jours*, trans. J. J. Hellert, 18 vols. (Paris, 1935-41), 1: 11, 55-75.

the defense of Christendom against the Turk...."[6]

No wonder then if Richard Knolles wrote:

"... At this present if you consider the beginning, progress and perpetual felicity of this the Ottoman Empire, there is in this world nothing more admirable and strange; if the greatness and lustre thereof, nothing more magnificent and glorious; if the Power and Strength thereof, nothing more Dreadful and Dangerous, which... holdeth all the world in scorn thundering out nothing but Blood and War, with a full persuasion in time to Rule over all, prefixing unto itself no other limits than the uttermost bounds of the Earth, from the rising of the Sun unto the going down of the same."[7]

The origin of the Turks who established such an empire, their arrival from central Asia in Anatolia in the middle of the thirteenth century and their employment by the Seljukid Sultans, are all wrapped up in legend and obscurity.[8] We know that Osman (1288-1326) or Uthman, son of Ertoghrul, was the founder of the Turkish dynasty which gave the name Ottoman[9] to the Empire that it established and which lasted for nearly six hundred years, under thirty-seven Sultans. This Empire, however, could not have been the work of a group of adventurers or a band of nomads, "flying from the highlands of Central Asia before the fierce onset of the Mongols." M. F. Köprülü criticizes H. A. Gibbons for accepting the legendary history of the Ottomans in his work, *The Foundation of the Ottoman Empire*, and believes that it is a mistake to

6. Garett Mattingly, ed., *Further Supplement To Letters, Despatches and State Papers, Relating to the Negotiations Between England and Spain, Preserved in the Archives at Vienna and Elsewhere (1513-1542)* (London, 1940-47), p. 206.

7. Sir Richard Knolles and Sir Paul Rycaut, *The Turkish History, From the Original of that Nation to the Growth of the Ottoman Empire, to the present year, with the lives and conquests of their princes and emperors, with a continuation MDCLXXXVII whereunto is added The Present State of the Ottoman Empire, by Sir Paul Rycaut*, 3 vols., 6th ed. (London, 1687-1700), 1: Preface.

8. See H. A. Gibbons, *The Foundation of the Ottoman Empire: A History of the Osmanlis up to the Death of Bayezid I (1300-1403)* (Oxford, 1916); V. V. Barthold, *Histoire des Turcs d'Asie Centrale*, trans. M. Donskis (Paris, 1945); Mehmed Fuad Köprülü, *Les origines de l'empire ottoman* (Paris, 1935); Paul Wittek, *The Rise of the Ottoman Empire* (London, 1938).

9. The current usage of the word "Turk" appeared towards the end of the Ottoman Empire. Originally, it was used to denote Anatolian peasants (corresponding to the word "fellāḥ" in Arabic). To call an Istanbul gentleman a Turk was an insult: he was a subject of the Ottoman Empire.

attribute the establishment of this Empire to the Muslim zeal and enthusiasm of a tribe of 400 tents which settled in the thirteenth century in the northwest corner of Anatolia. It is Köprülü's opinion that in the first half of the fourteenth century, the Seljukid Empire had reached its political and cultural climax, and had already one of the most advanced economic and social organizations of the Middle Ages. The Ottoman Empire grew out of the political and social synthesis of all the Turkish elements in Anatolia during the thirteenth and fourteenth centuries.[10]

As to the Islamization of the Ottomans, there seems to be little agreement among historians concerning the exact time and circumstances which made the Ottoman Turks adopt Islam. Gibbons says that there is no historical evidence that the tribe to which Uthman belonged was Muslim. These new arrivals in Anatolia became Muslim in the thirteenth century only after settling among the Seljukid Turks, who were already Muslims. Köprülü thinks that it is unwise to conclude from legends that Uthman was converted to Islam. He dismisses the question of the Islamization of the Ottomans by saying: "These Turkish tribes were in general Muslims but free from all fanaticism. The precepts of religion were too complicated and impossible for them to observe, so they remained faithful to their national traditions, covered with a light varnish of Islamism...."[11] It is believed that Islam first penetrated among the Turkish tribes in Transoxiana sometime, approximately, between A.D. 820 and 1000[12] when the Arabs first came in contact with the Turks. Al-Manṣūr, the second Abbasid Caliph (745-775), was the first Caliph to have a small corps of Turkish soldiers in his army. Moreover, as a result of the Muslim wars in Turkestan, such cities as Bokhārā, Samarkand, Farghanah, and Ashrusnah were in the habit of sending "as part of the poll-tax" children of the nomads of Turkestan, ordinarily taken captives and so made slaves, according to the custom of those days. But it was actually during the reign of Al-Mu'taṣim (833-842), the third son of Harūn al-Rashīd, that large numbers of Turks entered into the household of a Caliph[13]. Afraid of the Persians who

10. Köprülü, *Les origines de l'empire ottoman*, pp. 29, 33, 78.
11. Ibid., p. 58.
12. Barthold, *Histoire des Turcs d'Asie centrale*, p. 47.
13. Sir William Muir, *The Caliphate: Its Rise, Decline, and Fall* (London, 1899), pp. 437, 515-20. Charles Diehl and Georges Marçais, *Histoire générale: Histoire du moyen âge*, vol. 3, *Le monde oriental de 395 à 1081* (Paris, 1936), pp. 378-79, 572-73.

had become so influential in the days of his brother Amīn, and having no confidence in the Arabs "whose chauvinism had departed, and who, spoiled by the luxury of town life, had lost their vigour," he turned towards the Turks to gain their support and protection, his own mother being one of them. In the thirteenth century, large numbers of Turks entered the Muslim Empire, especially into Persia, Iran, and Syria in the days of the great Turkish dynasty of the Seljukids. But it remained for the Ottomans to be the first Turks to conquer the Arab lands of the Near East from the Mamlūks of Egypt who then ruled those lands.

At the beginning of the sixteenth century, the three Powers which ruled the Middle East were the Ottomans, the Persians, and the Mamlūk Sultans of Egypt and Syria. Persia's power was expanding under the Safawid ruler, Shāh Ismā'īl. The Mamlūks, on the other hand, weakened in war, particularly against the Mongols, had lost their vigor and their army was inferior to the Ottomans in equipment and discipline. With the coming of *Yavūz* Sultan Selim — the Stern and Inflexible — to the throne, the balance of power in the Middle East turned in favor of the Ottomans. In addition to various political and territorial reasons which had caused several wars between the Persians and the Turks, there was the old religious conflict between Shi'ism and Sunnism. Persia was a Shi'ite country, and Shāh Ismā'īl, who supported a vigorous Shi'īte policy, had made Shi'ism the state religion. He had also made a treaty with the Mamlūks in 1514 as a result of which the latter had broken their diplomatic relations with Sultan Selim. Sultan Selim, on the other hand, considered himself as the champion and protector of Sunnism and had massacred thousands of Shi'ites in his domains. In 1514, Sultan Selim undertook a new campaign against Persia and defeated Shāh Isma'īl's army on the plain of Chalderan, between Lake Urmia and Tabriz. As a result of this victory, Eastern Anatolia and Upper Mesopotamia, including Kurdistan, were added to the Turkish Empire.

The next concern of Sultan Selim was to get rid of the power of the Mamlūks who had made a treaty with Shah Ismā'īl and broken their diplomatic relations with the Ottoman Government. At the head of a large army, Selim advanced towards Syria in the latter part of 1516. But, meanwhile, the Mamlūk Sultan Qansaw al-Ghawrī had left Cairo with a strong army and moved to the north of Syria. On 24 August 1516, the two armies clashed on the plain of Marj Dābiq, north of Aleppo. The Mamlūk forces were decisively defeated by the Ottoman army. The battle lasted only a few hours — from sunrise till late afternoon. Qansaw al-Ghawrī himself was killed. His cavalry was thrown into disorder by the gunfire of the Turks and fled in panic. Ḥama fell on 20 September, Ḥoms on 22 September, Damascus on 9 October. On 22 January 1517, having crossed the Sinai desert on their way to Cairo, the Ottoman troops fought and won the decisive battle of Raydaniyyah. Ten days later, Cairo was in Ottoman hands, and on 17 April, Tumān-Bay, the last of the Mamlūk Sultans, perished at the hands of Sultan Selim's executioners. Egypt became a part of the Ottoman Empire and that extraordinary dynasty of Mamlūks or slave kings, which had ruled Egypt and the Arab lands in the Near East since 1250, came to an end. "Thus," wrote Ibn Iyās, "the rule of al-Ashraf al-Ghawrī came to an end, in the twinkling of an eye, as though he had never been. Praise be to Him whose Kingdom never wanes, and who never changes! Thus he and his kingdom came to an end together; the kingdom of Egypt and the Dominion of Syria, over which he had reigned for fifteen years, nine months and twenty days...."[14]

It is not possible to know for certain what the Arab-Turkish relations were in the early days of Ottoman rule. But all the generalizations and sweeping statements made during the second half of the nineteenth and the beginning of the twentieth centuries about the antipathy between those two races, such as: "the Arab hated and mistrusted the Turk, the Turk hated and mistrusted the Arab," are greatly exaggerated and certainly do not apply to the early centuries of Ottoman administration. Most of those who have written on Turkish history have not only been ignorant of the vast amount of sources that exist for such a task but have generally clung to one prejudice or another. "For various obvious reasons," wrote the late Harold Bowen, "Turkey and the Turks have aroused passionate feelings in those who have written about them. Exaggerated denunciation has been answered by indignant defence. Those

14. Abu al-Barakat Muḥammad ibn Aḥmad Ibn Iyas, *Badā'i' al-Zuhūr fī Waqā'i' al-Duhūr* [Wondrous Flowers Culled from the Annals of Time], 3 vols. (Cairo, A.H. 1312 [A.D. 1894]), 3: 58, 68.

For an account of the Ottoman conquest of Syria and Egypt see Ibn Iyas, *An Account of the Ottoman Conquest of Egypt in the Year A.H. 922 (A.D. 1516)*, trans. W. H. Salmon (London, 1921), and George W. F. Stripling, *The Ottoman Turks and the Arabs, 1511-1574* (Urbana: University of Illinois Press, 1942), pp. 43-58. See also Arnold J. Toynbee, *A Study of History*, 12 vols. (London, 1934-61). 1: 347-88.

who have suffered from Turkish ruthlessness and prevarication have been contradicted by others subjected by Turkish magnificence, courtesy and charm. Misunderstandings have been countless; and on any fact capable of being variously interpreted controversy has raged. In the realm of generalisation it is quite evident that many of the writers knew little of what they were talking about, or were blinded by prejudice of one kind or another."[15] In their introduction to *Islamic Society and the West*, H.A.R. Gibb and Harold Bowen have stated: "Current views on Turkey and Egypt in the eighteenth century so abound with misconceptions, which we ourselves shared at the oustet of our study, that it is our first duty to marshal for others the data which have led us to very different conclusions."

The Turks made no attempt to assimilate the non-Turkish elements in their Empire and the Arabs were the largest of these elements.[16] Indeed, in the Arab provinces of their Empire, the Turks remained "strangers." Very few of them settled in those lands. Only their government officials and their soldiers went there, and not for long. The Turkish officials were continuously changed and replaced by others. As George W. F. Stripling has pointed out: "The Mamelukes, after all, had practically been brought up in Syria and Egypt, and consequently they had some interest in the appearance and reputation of their home. The Turks, however, were sent for a term, none too long to familiarize themselves with the conditions of their charges, and very frequently, after a brief sojourn amongst the Arabs, they returned to Turkey for the rest of their lives, or were assigned to some other posts remote from the Arabs, or at best in other parts of the Arab lands where conditions were quite different from those with which they were familiar.... Assimilation could not take place under such conditions."[17]

But there are a number of important points to remember in connection with the relations between Arabs and Turks. The Ottomans did not conquer the Arab lands from the Arabs. They fought the Mamlūks, not the Arabs. Indeed, there is no evidence that, at first, the Arabs took much interest in their new masters. The Arab fortunes as well as the institution of the Caliphate had

15. Harold Bowen, *British Contributions to Turkish Studies* (London: Longmans, Green & Co., for the British Council, 1945), p. 8.

16. See the population statistics in Appendix A.

17. Stripling, *The Ottoman Turks and the Arabs*, p. 59.

long passed their lowest ebb as a result of a long period of decay and disintegration which had set in since the tenth century. "The line of Abbasid Caliphs in Cairo were mere court functionaries of the Mamlūk Sultans. The Egyptian historian Maqrīzī (d. 1442) remarks: 'The Turkish Mamlūks installed as Caliph a man to whom they gave the name and title of Caliph. He had no authority and no right to express his opinion. He passed his time with the commanders, the great officers, the officials and the judges, visiting them to thank them for the dinners and parties to which they had invited him.'"[18] It is safe to say that Ottoman rule protected the Arab world and Islam from foreign encroachments for nearly four hundred years and, in general, accorded a wide measure of local autonomy to the Arab provinces, except during the last years of 'Abdul Ḥamīd's despotic and corrupt administration and the brief period of the Young Turk's Turanian chauvinism. Although Turkish was the official language of administration and government and the majority of the Turks never learned Arabic, yet not only numerous Arabic words found their way into their language but prayers and readings from the Qur'ān in the mosques of Constantinople and other Turkish towns were always in Arabic. The Arabs were proud that the Arabic language — their most cherished and precious heritage, after Islam — remained the spiritual language of the Turks.

The Muslim Arabs played, also, an important role in the judicial system of the Ottoman Empire and thus wielded much power in the internal administration of that Empire. Indeed, the backbone of Ottoman Government — the Muslim sacred *Sharī'ah* — could not be maintained, without a knowledge of the Arabic language. After all, the Qur'ān and all other sources of Muslim jurisprudence are all in Arabic. The University of Al-Azhar in Cairo and the Sunni religious schools of Damascus, Tripoli, and Aleppo trained a large number of 'Ulamās, Qādīs, and Muftīs well versed in Muslim law and jurisprudence. They were appointed to various religious courts throughout the Empire and thus occupied positions of great influence and importance.[19] The *Shaikh al-Islām*

18. Cited by Bernard Lewis, *The Arabs in History* (London, 1950), p. 155.

19. "The task of maintaining intact the traditions of the Mahommedan faith, and of insuring their observance by the successors of the Prophet, devolves upon the 'Ulemas,' the Moslem doctors-in-law, whose functions are sacerdotal, juridical, and scholastic, and from whose ranks the Mullahs, the Imams and the Judges of the Cheri Courts are recruited." Great Britain, Foreign

was the head of the Muslim legislature and the authoritative, exponent of the Sacred Law. It seems that the title originated with Muḥammad II, the *Shaikh al-Islām* being originally the Grand Mufti of Constantinople. "Here is the authorized interpreter of the Kuran, and strictly speaking, no legislative or executive act can be valid without his sanction pronounced by an authoritative decree (*fetva*) declaring that it is in conformity with the Sacred Law."[20] The importance of his office was so great that he could demand the obedience of even the Sultan himself. Indeed, to remove a Sultan from the throne, the sanction of *Shaikh al-Islām*, in the form of a *fetva* was necessary in order to, at least, "legalize" that action in the eyes of the Muslims. Such a *fetva* was issued when the following Sultans were deposed: Selim III (1808), 'Abdul 'Aziz (1876), Murad V (1876), and 'Abdul Ḥamīd II (1909). The *Shaikh al-Islām* was appointed by the Sultan himself and resided in Constantinople. He and the Grand Vizier were the two highest and most influential officials of the Empire.[21]

Many visible signs and symbols expressed the Islamic nature of the Ottoman Empire and the importance of the Arabic language in that Empire. To begin with, it must be noted that with the exception of Orkhan, all the remaining thirty-six Sultans have Arabic names and almost all their Imperial seals — *Mührü Humayun* — have Arabic engravings on them. The large collection of seals in the Museum of Topkapi Palace at Istanbul contains "the most ancient seal... the golden seal-ring which, by command of Selim I (A.D. 1512-1520), was used to seal the door of the *Enderun* (inner) Treasury of the Palace." The words "*Sultan Selim Shah*" are inscribed

Office, *British Documents on the Origins of the War, 1898-1914*, ed. G. P. Gooch and Harold W. V. Temperley, 11 vols. (London, 1926-54), vol. 5, *The Near East, 1903-9*, p. 6.

20. Ibid., p. 6. See also George Young, ed., *Corps de Droit Ottoman*, 7 vols. (Oxford, 1905), 1: 6. "He had the right to appoint and promote all the other muftis of the empire, and in later times he appointed the qadis also; his department included the Fatwa-Khanah, a bureau for the promulgation of formal legal decisions, either on matters of State, such as the declaration of war or peace, the validity of a proposed legislative enactment & c., or on matters of personal law, concerning private individuals." *Handbooks Prepared Under the Direction of the Historical Section of the Foreign Office*, No. 96a & b, *The Rise of Islam and the Caliphate; The Pan-Islamic Movement*, p. 31.

21. The sultans considered all their wars with the Christian powers in Europe as Holy Wars but the *Shaykh-al-Islām* alone had the right to declare a war to be a Holy War.

in the middle of a gem, surrounded by an Arabic inscription: "*tawakkulī 'alā Khāliqī*" [My trust is in my Creator].[22] Many mosques in Istanbul have verses from the Qur'ān written in Arabic on their walls and inside their domes. The old Topkapi Palace of the Sultans has many Qur'anic citations on its walls and on the top of its gates. High up above the middle-gate or *Orta Kapi* one reads in Arabic: "*La ilāha illa allāh, Muḥammad rasūl allāh*" [there is no god but God, Muhammad in the Messenger of God]. In the Austrian Army Museum (Arsenal) in Vienna, there are eleven Ottoman flags which were captured from the Ottoman armies after their unsuccessful attempt to capture Vienna in 1683. These war standards are of different sizes and colors — red and white or crimson and green. But they all have one characteristic in common. Embroidered on each one of them is an Arabic statement from the Qur'an such as *Bi'sm allāh al-raḥman al-raḥīm* [in the name of God, the most merciful, the most compassionate], or *La ilāha illa allāh, Muḥammad rasūl allāh* or *Enna fataḥnā laka fatḥan mobīnā* [we have given you a perspicuous victory] or *Naṣr min allāh wa fatḥ qarīb* [victory is from God and a speedy conquest]. There is nothing *Turkish* about these flags; indeed, everything about them is Muslim.

Another "evidence," if further evidence be needed, to demonstrate the importance of the Arabic language and of Islam in Ottoman history is provided by the name plates of Ottoman ships. There are today about thirty such plates in Istanbul, all with Arabic names inscribed on them, such as "*Salīmiyyah,*" "*Fatḥiyyah,*" "*Majīdiyyah,*" and "*Maḥmūdiyyah.*" It seems also that Sulaiman the Magnificent's ships carried two green flags: one on top of the mainmast in the middle of the ship and the other on top of the sail boom attached to the middle of the mainmast, diagonally. The first flag had a long double-bladed sword painted on it in white, with the following Arabic inscription above it: *La ilāha illa allāh, Muḥammad rasūl allāh,* and on the four corners of the flags, there were written the names of the four caliphs: *Abū Bakr, 'Uthmān, 'Umar,* and *'Ali.*

The most important factor which bound the Arabs and the Turks together for nearly four centuries was undoubtedly Islam. The Ottoman Turks were Muslims, and the Ottoman Sultans

22. See Seal No. 4819 in Ismail Hakki Uzunçarşili, *Topkapi Sarayi Müzesi Mühürler Seksiyonu Rehberi* [A Guide to the Seals Section in the Topkapi Saray Museum] (Istanbul, 1959), pp. 13-20. For Illustrations of some of these seals, see Figs. 6 and 7 in Appendixes K and L.

were *Ghāziz*, i.e., the champions of Islam, the "warriors of the Faith," the "Sword of God" and the "protector and the refuge of the believers."[23] The Arab lands found themselves part of the most powerful Muslim Empire that had existed since the rise of Islam. Although the circumstances which led the last puppet Caliph under the Mamlūks in Egypt, Al-Mutawakkil, to transfer — if there was a transfer — the office of the Caliphate to Sultan Selim, are obscure and are not discussed by any contemporary historian,[24] the fact remains that for four hundred years the Ottoman Sultans fell heir to the institution of the Caliphate.[25] They

23. Wittek, *The Rise of the Ottoman Empire*, pp. 14, 18, 45.

24. "The popular account at the present day of the relations between Sultan Selim and the Khalifah Mutawakkil is that the Caliph made a formal transfer of his office to the conqueror, and as a symbol of this transference handed over to him the sacred relics, which were believed to have come down from the days of the Prophet—the robe, of which mention has already been made as being worn by the Abbasids of Baghdad on Solemn state occasions—some hairs from his beard, and the sword of the Caliph 'Umar. There is no doubt that Selim carried off these reputed relics to Constantinople (where they are still preserved in the mosque of Ayyub), as part of the loot which he acquired by the conquest of Egypt; but of the alleged transfer of the dignity of the Khilafat there is no contemporary evidence at all." Sir Thomas W. Arnold, *The Caliphate* (London, 1924), pp. 142-43.

25. "As the claim to the Caliphate on the ground of descent from the Quraish was, in the case of an Ottoman Sultan, impossible, his assumption of the title was defended by complaisant jurists on the ground that the Moslems must have an *imām*, and that the office must be in the hands of a sovereign powerful enough to exercise the functions proper to it—the defence of religion and the government of the state—in accordance with Qur'an IV, 58: 'Obey God and the Prophet and those who have rule over you.' The theological and legal defence for the Caliphate being in the possession of the Sultans of Turkey was based on the following considerations: (1) the possession of power, (2) election, (3) nomination by the last Abbasid Caliph, (4) guardianship of the Holy Cities, and (5) possession of the relics of the Prophet." Great Britain, Foreign Office, *Handbooks Prepared under the Direction of the Historical Section of the Foreign Office*, No. 96 a & b, *The Rise of Islam and the Caliphate* and *The Pan-Islamic Movement*, pp. 43-44.

The opening line of a *Fatwa* issued by *Shaykh al-Islām* 'Abdul Raḥīm Effendi during the reign of Sultan Aḥmad III (1703-1730) begins thus: "Padishah-i-Islam whose Caliphate will endure until the Day of Judgement. . . ." See Document 22 in *Topkapi Sarayi Muzesi arşivi Kilavuzu* [A Guide to the Archives of the Topkapi Saray Museum], 2 vols. (Istanbul, 1940), vol. 2.

As to the earliest instance known of a sultan with the title of "Amīr al-Mu'minīn," Hamilton A. R. Gibb writes: "It occurs in the protocol of a 'waqfnama,' recently published at Istanbul, where the sultan is called 'Amīr-ul-Muminīn wa Imāmul-Muslimīn, sayyidul-ghuzāt wal-mujāhidīn, al-muayyad bitayidi rabbil-ālamīn, . . . shamsu samais-saltana wal-khilafa wad-dawla

also became the "Protectors" of the twin Holy Cities of Mecca and Medina in Arabia, assuming the title of *Khādim al-Ḥaramain al-Sharifain*, after Sultan Selim had received from Sayyid Barakāt, the Sharīf of Mecca, the keys of that city as a symbol of obedience and loyalty.

Consequently, up until the beginning of the twentieth century when the Arabs became politically nation-conscious, the fact that the Ottoman Empire was "Turkish" did not matter so much as the fact that it was Muslim. The Turks and the vast majority of the Arabs were members of one great Muslim Community united by their faith and their allegiance to a Muslim sovereign — the Ottoman Sultan: the *Pādishāh*-Caliph who was "the Vicar of God on earth," "the Successor of the Prophet," *Imām al-Muslimīn*, the Pontiff of Muslims, *'Alam Panāh*, "the Refuge of the world," *Zill-Allāh*, "the Shadow of God," *Khādim al-Ḥaramain al-Sharifain*, "the Servant of the two Holy Sanctuaries," and "the Protector and Governor of Holy Jerusalem."[26] The capital of their Empire, Constantinople, had been renamed "*Islambul*" (instead of *Istanbul*, probably from the Greek word *Eis-ten-Polin* meaning "into the

wad-dunya wad-dīn, abul-fatḥ wan-naṣr, as-Sulṭān Muḥammad Khān.'" Hamilton A. R. Gibb, *Studies on the Civilization of Islam*, ed. Stanford J. Shaw and William R. Polk (Boston: Beacon Press, 1922), p. 147.

26. "When a new Sultan was proclaimed to be the ruler of the Ottoman Empire, he was girt with the sword of Osman, the founder of the dynasty. The ceremony corresponding to the Coronation of Christian Kings in Europe, took place in the Mosque of Eyyub, situated at the end of the Golden Horn, outside the walls of Constantinople. It was traditionally performed by the Head of the Mowlawi Derwishes, called Chelebi Effendi." Sir Edwin Pears, *Forty Years in Constantinople, 1873-1915* (New York: Henry Holt, 1917), p. 176.

The treaty of 25 February 1597, between Henry IV of France and Sultan Muhammad III begins: "Moy qui suit par les infinies graces du juste, grand et tout puissant créateur et par l'abondance des miracles du chef de ses Prophètes, Empereur des victorieux Empereurs, Distributeur des couronnes aux plus grands princes de la terre, serviteur des deux très sacrées et très augustes villes, Meque et Médine, Protecteur et Gouverneur de la Sainte Jérusalem . . . Seigneur des Mers blanches et noires . . . ." France, Ministère des Affaires Étrangères, *Turquie*, vol. 1, 1494-1644.

In the capitulations granted in 1675, Sultan Muhammad IV spoke of himself as: "Moi qui suis le puissant Seigneur des Seigneurs du monde, dont le nom est formidable sur Terre, Distributeur de toutes les couronnes de l'Univers, Sultan Mahomet Ḫan . . . . Cette Haute Porte Impériale qui est le refuge des Princes du monde, et la retraite des Rois de tout l'Univers." Frank E. Hinckley, *American Consular Jurisdiction in the Orient* (Washington: Lowdermilk, 1906), p. 7.

City"), i.e., the city where "Islam abounds."[27] It is interesting to note that in the minds of European writers on the Ottoman Empire, the word Turk included all the Muslim inhabitants of that Empire, regardless of their race or nationality.[28] The word "Arab" was specifically reserved for Bedouins and the nomads of the desert.

It is not true to say that the Arabs were for four hundred years powerless under the Turks, or that the Arab lands were depleted and despoiled by Turkish occupation. Nor is it true to say that the Muslim Arabs were not allowed to bear arms or serve in the Ottoman armies. High Arab army officers and Arab troops have distinguished themselves in the Turkish armies.[29] Many Arabs served in very important and influential positions in the Ottoman Empire but it is not possible to compile a full list of them because often their religion, their Turkish education and their names identified them, thoroughly, with the Turks. General Nūrī Pasha as-Sa'īd, several times Prime Minister in modern Iraq, has written: "In the Ottoman Empire, Arabs, as Muslims, were regarded as partners of the Turks. They shared with the Turks both rights and responsibilities, without any racial distinction: the higher appointments in the State, whether military or civil, were open to the Arabs; they were represented in both the upper and the lower houses of the Ottoman Parliament. Many Arabs became Prime Ministers, *Shaikh al-Islam*, Generals and Walis, and Arabs were always to be found in all ranks of the State services."[30] Indeed, the Arabs were referred to, by the Turks, as *Qawm nejib* (a noble

27. "Les Grecs Modernes avaient donné à leur capitale le nom mutilé de Istambol; les Turcs lui ont donné celui d'Islambol (réservoir de l'islamisme)." Alexandre Mazas, *Les hommes illustres de l'Orient*, 2 vols. (Paris, 1847), 2: 383, n. 1.

28. In Rev. William Jowett, *Christian Researches in the Mediterranean from 1815-1820* (London, 1822), p. 421, is quoted a letter from Rev. James Connor, dated 23 February 1820, who wrote: "Our Consul told me that the population of Beirut amounts to about 10,000 souls. Of these about 3,000 are Turks and the remainder Christians of various denominations." The word "Turk" here, obviously, stands for "Muslim." Very few Turks ever inhabited the Arab provinces of their Empire.

29. To mention only some outstanding examples: Gen. 'Ali Fuad Pasha Cebesoy told the author that Arab troops from the regions of Damascus, Aleppo, and Jerusalem distinguished themselves highly under Osman Pasha at Plevna, between July and December 1877, and again in 1915 at Gallipoli and in 1916 in Romania, at the Battle of Argostoli.

30. Gen. Nūrī as-Sa'īd, *Arab Independence and Unity* (Baghdad: Government Press, 1943), p. 2.

people) and the Arabic-speaking provinces were "regarded by the Ottoman ruling class, at least in the beginning, with a certain deference which they did not accord to the rest of the Sultan's dominions — for the very reason that its inhabitants did speak the sacred language, while most of them at the same time professed the dominant religion."[31]

There is no historical evidence to support the popular view, current in the twentieth century, that the Turks were mainly responsible for Arab "backwardness" and cultural retardation for four hundred years. On the contrary, the Arab lands seem to have profited from the Turkish occupation. "Syria," Gibb and Bowen have written, "had probably benefited materially more than any other Asiatic province from incorporation in the Ottoman Empire, as a result of the commercial connexions thus formed and enjoyed a fairly flourishing social and economic life."[32] It may well be that the Arabs, up to the reign of 'Abdul Ḥamīd, suffered not from too much Turkish Government but actually from too little of it! It must also be said in all fairness that the Turks did not attempt to assimilate or Turkify the Arabs until the coming to power of the Committee of Union and Progress in 1908. Generally speaking, up until the middle of the nineteenth century, the Arabs seem to have suffered more from their own feudal lords, their feuds and rivalries and their conflicts with the Pashas, than from the central authority at Constantinople. Their internal dissensions, their tribal organizations and feudal institutions, their dynastic rivalries and their extreme individualism continued to keep them divided and weak. Moreover, the Muslim Arabs' belief in the perfection of the religious principles underlying their political and social institutions and in the sacredness of their language, as well as the memory of their "glorious past" and of their military conquests in the early days of Islam, had developed in them a feeling of "Arab" superiority. This "superiority complex" had rendered them aloof and, therefore, unwilling to change their ideas and their way of life for what they considered to be new-fangled and heretical innovations originating in non-Muslim lands, i.e., in *Dār al-Ḥarb* or the "House of War."[33]

31. Hamilton A. R. Gibb, *Islamic Society and the West: A Study of the Impact of Western Civilization on Moslem Culture,* 1 vol. in 2 (London (1950-57), vol. 1, pt. 1, p. 160.

32. Ibid., p. 218.

33. According to Muslims, the world is divided into two Houses or Domains, the "House of War" (Dār al-Ḥarb) inhabited by non-Muslims, and the

In the words of Professor Bernard Lewis:

"From its foundation until its fall, the Ottoman Empire was a state dedicated to the advancement or defence of the power and faith of Islam. For six centuries the Ottomans were almost constantly at war with the Christian West, first in the attempt — mainly successful — to impose Islamic rule on a large part of Europe, then in the long drawn out rearguard action to halt or delay the relentless counter-attack of the West.... For the Ottoman, his Empire was Islam itself. In the Ottoman chronicles, the territories of the Empire are referred to as 'the lands of Islam,' its armies as 'the soldiers of Islam,' its religious head as 'the Sheikh of Islam.' Its people thought of themselves first and foremost as Muslims. 'Ottoman' was a dynastic name like Umayyad or Abbasid, which only acquired a national significance in the nineteenth century under the influence of European liberalism...."[34]

"House of Peace" (*Dār al-Salām*) which is, in reality, the domain of Islam (*Dār al-Islām*), inhabited by Muslims or true believers. (One of the duties of true believers is to enlarge the latter at the expense of the former.)

34. See Bernard Lewis, "Islamic Revival in Turkey," *International Affairs*, vol. 28, no. 1 (January 1952): 47. See also Sulaiman Faiḍi, *Fī Ghamrat al-Nidāl*: *Mudhakkirāt Sulaimān Faiḍī* [In the Throes of the Struggle: Memoirs of Sulaimān Faiḍī] (Baghdad, 1952), pp. 208-19; Amin Shakir Sa'īd al-Iryan and Muḥammad Muṣṭafa 'Aṭā, *Turkiyya wa'l-Siyāsah al-'Arabiyyah* [Turkey and Arab Politics] (Cairo, 1954), pp. 5-8, 90-91; Muḥammad Jamīl Baihum, *al-'Arab wa'l-Turk* [The Arabs and the Turks (Beirut, 1957), p. 80; 'Abd al-Karīm Maḥmud Ghrāybah, *Muqaddamat Ta'rīkh al-'Arab al-Ḥadīth*, 1500-1918 [An Introduction to the modern history of the Arabs, *1500-1918*) (Damascus, 1960), vol. 1, pp. 88-89; idem, *Al-'Arab wa'l-Atrāk* [The Arabs and the Turks] (Damascus, 1961), Preface and pp. 281-83.

CHAPTER TWO

OTTOMAN GOVERNMENT IN ARAB LANDS

To UNDERSTAND the nature of Ottoman administration whether in Arab lands, or in the rest of the Ottoman Empire, one must remember, first, that the principles and the spirit of Ottoman government were typically Muslim and, secondly, that it was necessary to have a special category of laws to govern and regulate the affairs of the non-Muslim subjects and of the foreign communities living in the Ottoman Empire. It is not within the scope of this work to describe the elaborate system of government which operated in the Ottoman Empire: the "Ruling Institution," its complicated pattern of central administration — apart from the Sultan himself, his Imperial Household and his vezirs — with a large body of secretaries and "recorders" (*Ahl al-Qalam*); the army and the navy or "Men of the Sword" (*Ahl al-Saif*); and the "Religious Institution" headed by the *Shaikh al-Islam* who was almost of equal rank with the Grand Vezīr, supported by a vast concourse of '*Ulema* as guardians of the Sacred Law.[1] But it is important to recall briefly the main features of this Government.

The Government of the Ottoman Empire was based, essentially, on Muslim principles embodied in the *Sharī'a*, the Canon Law or the Sacred Law of Islam, administered by religious courts under the supreme authority of *Shaikh al-Islam*. The supreme legislator (*Shāri'*) in Muslim society is God himself. He revealed His laws directly to the Prophet who transmitted them to mankind, first,

1. See 'Abd al-Raḥmān Sharaf, *Ta'rīkh-i Dawlat-i-Osmaniyyeh* [Ottoman history] (Istanbul, A.H. 1309 [A.D. 1893]), vol. 1, pp. 281, 300; Gibb, *Islamic Society and the West*, vol. 1, pt. 1, pp. 107-99, and vol. 1, pt. 2, pp. 70-113; and Albert H. Lybyer, *The Government of the Ottoman Empire in the time of Suleiman the Magnificent* (Cambridge: Harvard University Press, 1913).

through the Qur'an and, secondly, through his customary conduct and practices — the *Sunnah*. Hence *Sharī'a* law is "sacred, infallible and immutable" and the Muslim government is the direct government of God. It is the supreme religious and social duty of every Muslim to submit to this Law before which all Muslims are equal. "The principle of unity and order which in other societies is called *civitas*, *polis*, State, in Islam is personified by Allah: Allah is the name of the supreme power acting in the common interest. Thus the public treasury is 'the treasury of Allah,' the army is 'the army of Allah,' even the public functionaries are 'the employees of Allah'."[2]

Nearly three hundred years after the death of the Prophet, four schools of the interpretation of Tradition and the Qur'an became well established. The interpreters were four great Muslim jurists and Imams whose teachings and legal explanations became the basis of the understanding and application of the *Sharī'a* Law in different parts of the Muslim world. These four schools bear the name of their founders. They are the *Ḥanafī*, the *Mālikī*, the *Ḥanbalī*, and the *Shāfi'ī* schools. When the *Sharī'a* became the fundamental Law of the Ottoman Empire, the Ottomans officially adopted its *Ḥanafī* interpretation and closed the door to fresh interpretations.[3]

The Sultans enacted from time to time certain *Irādés* and *Firmans*, or Royal Commands, and issued certain regulations and laws known as *Qanūns*.[4] These *Qanūns* — the only "secular" legislation

2. Sir Thomas Arnold and Alfred Guillaume, eds., *The Legacy of Islam* (London, 1931), p. 286.

3. "In a famous phrase it was said, 'the Gate of Interpretation has been shut.' The final touches of the immutable edifice of the Law were given, as far as the Hanefi section of Ottoman society was concerned, in the fifteenth and sixteenth centuries, with the composition of two books. 'The Pearls' and 'The Confluence of the Seas,' in which were collected and reduced to order of a sort the opinions of all the most celebrated Hanefi doctors of times gone by." Gibb, *Islamic Society and the West*, pp. 22-23.

Concerning these early schools of law and Muslim jurisprudence, see Noel J. Coulson, *A History of Islamic Law* (Edinburgh: Edinburgh University Press, 1964), pp. 36-73.

4. "All Ottoman society was divided into clearly defined groups and it was by virtue of their membership of such groups that the relationship of individuals to the government was conditioned. In order, therefore, to define the obligations entailed by this relationship, and also the status, the emoluments, the dress, & c., of persons actually in the government service, regulations were issued by the Sultans under the name *Kanun*." Ibid, p. 23. See also Lybyer, *The Government of the Ottoman Empire in the time of Suleiman the Magnificent*, pp. 157-59.

which existed in the Ottoman Empire — could in no way be opposed to the principles of the Sacred Law but had to be in harmony with it. They were often based on three secondary sources of Muslim jurisprudence: the *Ijmāʿ* or "Consensus" of the Muslim community, the *Qiyās* or "the analogical deductions of jurists," and the *Ijtihād*. In its broad and general sense, *Ijtihād* is the decision which the Muslim judge is forced to reach as his personal opinion or at his discretion if he finds no guidance in the Qur'an or in the Sunna of the Prophet. These *Qanūns* belonged to the second category of laws ruling the subjects of the Ottoman Empire.[5]

A third category of laws was embodied in the *Capitulations* ("Droit Capitulaire") which regulated the relations of non-Muslim and foreign communities in the Ottoman Empire and were of an international character. Except in very special cases, the non-Muslim communities in the Ottoman Empire were not subject to the *Sharīʿa* law as they could not be within the pale of Muslim jurisdiction. When Muḥammad II conquered Constantinople, he found that the Christians and other non-Muslim communities had their own legal systems and tribunals in which justice was administered by the spiritual heads of those communities or their representatives. Their laws were based partly on Græco-Roman laws and partly on the Byzantine Civil Law of Justinian. He also found "a large number of foreign colonies, each with a well defined legal status, which had been conceded to them by the Byzantine Emperors, and with distinct courts and court machinery and laws, and enjoying privileges and immunities."[6]

Immediately after the conquest of Constantinople, the "Conqueror," by confirming the practices of his predecessors, established the principle of religious autonomy and extra-territorial jurisdiction for his non-Muslim subjects in the administration of their own affairs.[7] He also granted commercial privileges to large foreign

5. For a detailed account of the laws of the Ottoman Empire, see George Young, *Corps de Droit Ottoman*, 7 vols. (Oxford: Clarendon Press, 1905).

6. Ibrahim A. Khairallah, *The Law of Inheritance in the Republics of Syria and Lebanon* (Beirut, 1941), p. 149.

7. In this connection, it is interesting to note the following policy of Great Britain in India: "Muhammadan law was applied to Muslims in British India as a matter of policy. This policy was the result of the adoption of a tradition inherited from the Mughal rulers of India, who applied the Hindu and Muhammadan laws to their subjects conformably with their own views, to safeguard and guarantee to each of these communities the practice of its own religion."

trading communities established in the Ottoman Empire. The economic interests of the Empire necessitated the presence of these communities.[8] These immunities or privileges came to be known as Capitulations.[9] The Egerton Manuscript No. 2817 in the British Museum shows the grant of "special privileges for residence and trade" to the Genoese inhabitants of Galata (a suburb of Constantinople) after the fall of that city on 29 May 1453. This Grant is dated 1 June of that same year.[10] Other Capitulations followed, the most famous among them being the one granted to Francis I of France, the first European King thus favoured by Sultan Sulaiman, the Magnificent, in 1535, according to which the French obtained considerable trading privileges in the Ottoman Empire.[11] Eight years later, Francis I actually "cooperated with

Asaf A. A. Fyzee, *Outlines of Muhammadan Law* (Oxford: Oxford University Press, 1949), p. 42.

8. "Au moyen âge, le commerce avec l'Orient se développa grâce à la concession aux étrangers de certains quartiers des villes les plus importantes dans lesquels il leur était permis de s'administrer eux-mêmes. Ce système était appliqué déjà dans l'empire byzantin et dans les royaumes fondés par les Croisés. . . ." Albéric Cahuet, *La Question d'Orient dans l'Histoire Contemporaine* (*1821-1905*) (Paris, 1905), p. 5.

9. "The Sultan (Muḥammad II) had to regulate the judicial status of the non-Moslem population which formed the majority of the subjects of his new Empire. This he effected by a series of conventions with the chiefs of the various religious communities. To the Christians he conceded freedom of worship, the application of their own laws, and the administration of justice among themselves. At Constantinople, he invested a Greek Patriarch as the Supreme Judge in all the civil and religious affairs of the Greeks. To the Armenians, he accorded similar privileges." G. Pelissié du Rausas, *Le régime des capitulations dans l'empire ottoman* (Paris, 1910), p. 10, cited in Khairallah, *The Law of Inheritance in the Republics of Syria and the Lebanon*, p. 150, n. 45. "Mehmed the Conqueror himself went so far to meet the susceptibilities of his non-Muslim subjects that one of his first acts after his capture of Constantinople was to invite the clergy of the Orthodox Church to elect a new Œcumenical Patriarch; and, when they presented George Scholarius as their candidate, the Ottoman Master of the Orthodox Christian World took care to ratify the election in accordance with the procedure that had been customary under the East Roman Imperial regime." Toynbee, *A Study of History*, 6: 203, n. 4.

10. The Grant is in Greek but carries on top of it the monogram (Tughra) of Sultan Muhammad II—The Conqueror—and, at the bottom, the name or signature, in Arabic script, of *Zaghanus*.

11. "1535—Le Sr de la Forest a été le premier ambassadeur de France à la Porte Ottomane, il obtint en 1535 du G. S. Sultan Soliman une capitulation très avantageuse pour les Français et fit en 1537 une alliance très étroite entre le Roy son maître et le Sultan." France, Ministère des Affaires Étrangères, *Turquie, 1451 à 1643, Supplément*, vol. 1.

Sulaiman the Magnificent in naval operations against the Habsburg Power in the Mediterranean."[12] The English obtained formal capitulations in 1580 during the reign of Queen Elizabeth when William Harborne was appointed as the first English Ambassador to the Sublime Porte.

As far as the machinery of justice was concerned in the Ottoman Empire, the Capitulations necessitated the establishment of special Consular courts having complete jurisdiction over the nationals of the countries represented by those consuls. Non-Muslim nationals of foreign countries living in Turkey enjoyed extra-territorial privileges and were not subject to Ottoman law. In these Consular Courts, the Consul himself generally acted as Judge of First Instance with two assessors. The sentences passed were executed on Turkish territory. Hence, the plea of the British Consul in Cyprus in 1844 that Her Majesty's Government allow him to build a small prison near his Consulate.[13]

In 1593, King Henry IV of France wrote to Sultan Murad III begging him not to listen to anyone who might come to him on behalf of the King of Spain who was waging an unjust war ("l'Injuste guerre") against him. In his letter, Henry IV addressed the Sultan in the following words:

"Très haut, très puissant, très excellent, très magnanime et Invincible Prince, le Grant Empereur des Mousoulmans, Sultan Murad han en qui tout honneur et vertu abonde—nostre très cher et parfait amy." Ibid.

On 25 February 1597, the Treaty of Alliance (Capitulations of 1535) was renewed between Henry IV, "Empereur de France" and "Sultan Mehemet (III) Empereur des Musulmans." A new privilege was granted, at this time to the King of France: his ambassador was to have precedence over all the other ambassadors at Constantinople. This privilege is found in the following excerpt of the above-mentioned treaty:

"Et parceque je dui Empereur de France est envertues les autres Rois et Princes le plus noble et de plus haute famille, le plus parfait ami que nos ayeux ayent jamais eu, Comme il s'est vu par les effets de sa fermeté et persévérance, Nous voulons et commandons que Son Ambassadeur qui résidé à Nostre heureuse Porte, venant à Notre Grand et Superbe Divan ou allant au Palais de Nos Grands Vizirs ou autres de Nos Conseillers, cheminent devant et précédent l'Ambassadeur du Roi d'Espagne et ceux des autres Rois et Princes Conforme la coutume ancienne." Ibid.

12. Toynbee, *A Study of History*, 2: 181, n. 2.

13. Great Britain, Foreign Office, 78/580, *Turkey*, Despatch No. 13, dated Cyprus, 6 August 1844, and addressed to the Earl of Aberdeen by Niven Kerr, states: "My Lord, . . . I have to state to your Lordship that the British Consulate here is, I believe, the only one that has not a Prison attached to it. . . . I am induced respectfully to submit to your Lordship's consideration my earnest hope that I may be authorized to construct a small Prison in the vicinity of this Consulate in which British subjects might be confined in conformity with the

In the absence of any new evidence, it seems that the Arab lands which were conquered from the Mamlūks by Sulan Selim were not directly administered from Constantinople — as is shown "from a study of the bureaus and from the separate listing of the revenues from Syria, Mesopotamia, and Egypt in contemporary estimates."[14] Moreover, Arabia, the cradle of Islam, was hardly ever under the direct or rigid control of the Ottomans. "The Holy Cities of Mecca and Medina, far from paying tribute, received a large annual subsidy at the cost of Egypt."[15]

Almost complete local and internal independence was left to the feudal Emirs and the local chiefs in Arab lands, particularly in Lebanon. Afrer the conquest of Egypt, Sultan Selim returned to Damascus and confirmed in office Al-Ghazālī as the *Vali* of Syria, annexing to that vilayet, Jerusalem, Gaza, Safad, and al-Karak. In "Southern Syria," which included Lebanon, all the feudal lords paid homage to him except the Tanūkhī emirs who refused to appear before him, having remained faithful to the Mamlūks when the latter fought against Sultan Selim at Marj Dābiq. He was much impressed by the dignity and personality of Emir Fakhr-al-Dīn whose title in those days was *Sultan al-Barr* [the king of the land] and *Emir Lubnan*. Selim confirmed him in office as the Emir of the district of Shūf.Other principal Emirs who were confirmed in their fiefdoms were Emir 'Assāf Mansūr al-Turkumānī in Kisirwan and Jubail and the Banū Sifas in 'Akkar and Tripoli.[16] The remaining lands were, in the same way, left to their feudal lords. Sultan

instructions lately sent me . . . . A suitable prison might be erected here for a sum not exceeding £ 30 . . ."

"The whole judicial, and even administrative problem was infinitely complicated by the capitulations, under which the various Great Powers possessed Courts, post offices and special privileges of their own." R. W. Seton-Watson, *The Rise of Nationality in the Balkans* (London: Constable, 1917), p. 101.

14. Lybyer, *The Government of the Ottoman Empire in the time of Sulaiman the Magnificent*, p. 173.

15. Ibid., p. 30. "Parts of the mountain lands of Albania and Kurdistan, and the desert of Arabia, though nominally under direct administration, were in very slight obedience; they retained their ancient tribal organizations, under hereditary chieftains who were invested with Ottoman titles in return for military service, and whose followers might or might not submit to taxation." Ibid.

16. See Mār Istefān al-Duwaihī, *Ta'rīkh al-Tāifah al-Mārūniyyah* [A history of the Maronites] (Beirut, 1890), pp. 152-53, and *Ta'rīkh al-Amīr Ḥaidar Aḥmad Shihāb* [History (written) by Amīr Ḥaidar Aḥmad Shihāb] (Cairo, 1900), vol. 1, pp. 561-62. See also Philip K. Ḥittī, *Lebanon in History, from the Earliest Times to the Present* (London, 1957), pp. 357-59.

Selim also appointed governors for Aleppo, Homs, Tripoli and other coastal towns. "The keynote of Ottoman administration," wrote Gibb and Bowen, "was conservatism, and all the institutions of government were directed to the maintenance of the *status quo*. Since the *Qanūns* of Selim and Suleyman were regarded as the embodiment of the highest political wisdom, amelioration could have no meaning except the removal of subsequent abuses."[17] But the keeping of the *status quo* meant also the keeping of all the internal troubles and feuds among the Emirs owing to their rivalries and jealousies, leading to rebellions and internecine wars. The Ottoman Sultan asserted his authority in the last resort by armed intervention. The system of local feudal government in Syria and Lebanon, superimposed by a loose Turkish administration headed by a Turkish Governor General and supported by a Turkish Army, continued down to the latter part of the nineteenth century.

In the nineteenth century, because of the increasing impact of Western thought upon the Ottoman Empire and of the political pressure of the European Powers, and as a result of various attempts to reform Ottoman institutions, particularly the *Ṭanzīmāt*, a system of secular jurisdiction was introduced throughout the Empire. Only the Personal Status law remained under the *Sharī'a* Law. At the beginning of the century, in order to make it possible for native merchants to compete successfully with foreign businessmen who enjoyed the privileges and the protection conferred upon them by the Capitulations, the Ottoman Government created a Corporation of merchants under Charter ("*Beratli*") which had the same privileges accorded to the foreigners.[18] In 1840, a new Penal Code was adopted based on the French penal code. In the same year, a special tribunal called *Majlis-i Aḥkām-i Adliye* was instituted to deal with the cases of high state functionaries. A Commercial Code was promulgated in 1850, and in 1861 special Tribunals of

17. Gibb, *Islamic Society and the West*, vol. 1, pt. 1, p. 200.

"Enfin, il faut noter ce fait qu'il est exceptionnel de voir les Ottomans imposer à une nouvelle province incorporée dans leur Empire, les lois décrets ou règlements purement Ottomans; au contraire, ils s'attachent toujours à maintenir en place les institutions anciennement établies, afin d'éviter de troubler la structure économique, sinon sociale du pays—la domination militaire et politique étant assurée." Robert Mantran and Jean Sauvaget, comps., *Règlements fiscaux ottomans: les provinces syriennes* (Beirut, 1951), p. x.

18. Young, *Corps de Droit Ottoman*, 1: 224.

Commerce were established to administer that code. One more civil law to be added to the foregoing list was the Ottoman law of nationality, issued on 19 January 1869, and specifying the conditions under which Ottoman nationality could be gained or lost. According to the first article of this law, every individual born of an Ottoman father and mother or of an Ottoman father only, was an Ottoman subject ("sujet Ottoman").[19]

In 1869, the Ottoman civil laws were collected and codified into a Register called "*Majallah al-Aḥkām al-'Adliyyah*" by a special committee of 'Ulemas and non-'Ulemas appointed for that purpose and called the "*Majallah Jam'iyyati*,"[20] This Ottoman Civil Code contains a total of 1,851 articles.Finally, in 1879, there was a whole reorganization of the judical system by the creation of a Ministry of Justice and of "regulated tribunals" or *Mehākim-i-Nizāmiye*.[21] This judicial reorganization was based on French jurisprudence and was an important step in the direction of the modernization of the Ottoman Empire.

The Porte started, also, a reorganization of the administrative units of the Empire. The Ottoman administrative system which borrowed its fundamental lines from Persian, Byzantine, Seljukid, and Mamlūk administrations resembled a pyramid at the top of which stood the smallest unit, the village or *kariye* and the broad base of which rested on the *eyalet* or province, known later, in the nineteenth century, as *vilayet* (from the two Arabic words "*iyālah*" and "*wilāyah*"). A number of villages[22] formed a *nāḥiyah* under a *Mudīr*, and a number of *nāḥiyas* constituted a *kaza* (Arabic *qadā*)

19. Ibid., 2: 223-29.

20. See Subḥī Maḥmassānī, *Falsafat al-Tashrī' fi'l-Islām* [The philosophy of legislation in Islam] (Beirut 1946), pp. 70-75.

21. "... The Nizamie Tribunals [were] composed of local and provincial Courts of First Instance and Appeal, with a Court of Cassation at Constantinople for the hearing of criminal and civil cases. At the same time, the Court of Appeal was divided into three Chambers, dealing with penal, civil, and commercial cases, respectively, and the Commercial Courts and Commercial Court of Appeal were transferred from the control of the Ministry of Commerce to that of the new Ministry of Justice." Great Britain, Foreign Office, 371/345, "Extracts from the Annual Report for Turkey for the year 1906." Cited in Great Britain, Foreign Office, *British Documents on the Origins of the War, 1898-1914*, 5: 3.

22. Towns and villages were, in turn, divided into quarters called *mahalle*, at the head of which was a *Mukhtar*—usually for every 20 or 25 houses. The number of *Mukhtars* in every town and village depended upon the number of their inhabitants.

ruled over by a *Qā'im-Maqām* (or lieutenant-governor). Two or more *kazas* composed a *sanjak* (or *liwa*), governed by a Mutaṣarrif. All the above subdivisions were part of the province over which the *Vāli*, generally with the title of Pasha, was the supreme governor-general and had wide judicial powers. He "united in himself the supreme military and civil authority, and was responsible for public order and security, for the collection of taxes and the remittance of the stipulated annual tribute or contribution to Istanbul and for the public administration generally."[23]

The reorganization of the *vilayets* was due principally to Midhat Pasha's successful reforms in the *vilayet* of the Danube when he was its *Vali* (1865-1868) and resembled France's administrative units. The *vilayet* corresponded to the French *Department*; the *sanjak* to *l'Arrondissement*; the *kaza* to *le Canton*, and the *nāḥiya* to *la Commune*. Midḥat Pasha's reforms were incorporated in the vilayet law of 1864, revised in 1871.[24]

Up until the first half of the nineteenth century, the Arab *vilayets* in the Near East were Mosul, Baghdad, "*Ḥaleb*" (Aleppo), Saida, and "*Shām*" (Damascus) with a total estimated population of 500,000 in the chief towns.[25] In Arabia, there were the *vilayets* of Ḥijāz and the Yemen. After the civil war in Mount Lebanon and Damascus in 1860, the *vilayet* of "*Shām*" did not include, anymore, the Lebanon. According to the "Protocole" for the Lebanon, submitted to the Porte by the Ambassadors of Five Powers — Great Britain, Russia, France, Austria, and Prussia — and accepted by

23. Gibb, *Islamic Society and the West*, vol. 1, pt. 1, p. 201. The other important officials in the government of a province were the *defterdar* or "book-keeper" and the *Ketkhuda* or steward (called vulgarly *Kakhya* or *Kikhya*), appointed on annual tenure, who held in his hands the other branches of administration. The "Kadi and the other religious dignitaries" administered justice according to Muslim *Sharī'a* law and had the right of "sending protest and memorials direct to Istanbul." Ibid.

24. For a detailed account of these laws and the administrative units of the Ottoman Empire, see Young, *Corps de Droit Ottoman*, 1: 29-69.

25. J. Lewis Farley, *The Resources of Turkey, Considered with Special Reference to the Profitable Investment of Capital in the Ottoman Empire* (London, 1863), p. 5. Farley gives the following statistics for populations: "Mosul 65,000, Baghdad 105,000, Aleppo 100,000, Beyrout 50,000 and Damascus 180,000.

The *vilayet* of Aleppo included four *sanjaks*: Marash, Urfa, Zor, and Aleppo.

In the sixteenth and the beginning of the seventeenth centuries, the number of *eyalets* in the whole of the Ottoman Empire stood at 35 or 36; in the third quarter of the seventeenth century at 39. Gibb, *Islamic Society and the West*, vol. 1, pt. 1, p. 142.

the latter, Mount Lebanon was detached from Syria and became an autonomous sanjak ruled by a Mutaṣarrif.[26] The "Protocole" embodied the "Règlements Organiques" of 9 June 1861, replaced by that of 6 September 1864, and amended by the Protocol of 28 July 1868.[27]

In 1887, because of the growing importance of Jerusalem, the Porte created the new administrative unit of the independent *sanjak* of Jerusalem in the south of Palestine. This *sanjak* was detached from the *vilayet* of "*Shām*" and put under the direct control of the Porte. Meanwhile, the town of Beirut was expanding, and its commercial prosperity increasing rapidly. Consequently, the Porte decided to establish, in 1888, the new *vilayet* of Beirut to which the four *sanjaks* of Lattakia, Tripoli, Acre, and Nablus were attached. Thus, from 1888 onwards, the province of Syria was divided into three *vilayets* (Aleppo, "*Shām*", and Beirut) and two detached *sanjaks* (Lebanon and Jerusalem).

Although the "Nationality Law" was a significant change in the Turkish concept of nationality, nevertheless, the individual was not a citizen of the Empire but a subject of the Sultan, and in certain cases, a "Consular protégé" of one of the Foreign Powers.[28] The subjects of the Sultan were either Muslims or non-Muslims. The non-Muslims, particularly the Christians, were considered as *Dhimmis*, i.e., as the "tolerated" and "protected" people because they were *Ahl al-Kitāb* (i.e., the People of the Book). They were known, however, as the *ra'iyyah*, i.e., as the "shepherded people."[29]

26. "Its governor was necessarily a Christian and its administrative Council consisted of four Maronites, three Druses, two Greek Orthodox Christians, one Greek Catholic, one Moslem and one Metwali. The sanjak was divided into seven Kazas, of which four were Maronite, one Greek Catholic and one (Shuf) Moslem. . . . The head of the police was always a Maronite. The Province enjoyed a system of taxation of its own." Great Britain, Admiralty, *A Handbook of Syria* (*including Palestine*) (London, 1919), p. 243. See also Great Britain, Foreign Office, *Correspondence Relating to the Affairs of Syria, 1860-61* (London, 1861), pt. 2, p. 314.

27. For the full texts of the protocols and the "Règlements Organiques", see Young, *Corps de Droit Ottoman,* 1: 139-54.

28. For an account of the significance of the Ottoman Nationality Law, see Paul Ghali, *Les nationalités détachées de l'Empire Ottoman à la suite de la guerre* (Paris, 1934), pp. 61-71.

29. It is to be noted that in the Old Testament, God is represented as a Shepherd and the people as his sheep or his flock and in the New Testament, Christ speaks of himself as the "good shepherd".

The word *ra'iyyah* in its original meaning is a respectable word. It is derived from the Arabic *ra'ā*, "to shepherd," hence *rā'ī*, a shepherd, i.e., "him who leads to pasture lands." Thus the *ra'iyyah* are "those (cattle or other animals) under the guidance of a *rā'ī*."

In Ottoman parlance, however, the word *ra'iyyah*, which included at one time all the subjects of the Sultan,[30] denoted, when applied to the Christians, particularly during the years of the weakness and decline of the Empire, an inferior and humiliating position compared with the Muslims. The Christians were tributary people whose life and property were under "*amān*," i.e., safe only by the good pleasure of the Turkish authorities. In principle, the Christian was not allowed to ride a horse[31] or to carry arms, nor could he join the Ottoman army or be admitted into the civil service. He was outwardly distinguished by the color of his dress, his headwear and his shoes. The dress itself was to be different from the clothes "worn by men of learning, piety and nobility."[32] There

30. P. Rizzis was a Maltese who wanted to change his British nationality and become Austrian, while still living in Port Sa'id (considered Ottoman territory). In taking up his case, the British Consul in Port Sa'id wrote to the Foreign Office: "In the Ottoman Dominion, every man is either a Consular protégé (Ḥimāya) or a native subject (Ra'iya). If I inform the Egyptian Government that I have withdrawn protection (Ḥimaya) from Mr. P. Rizzis, the latter at once becomes a Ra'ya until he can obtain other Consular protection." Great Britain, Foreign Office, 78/5238, *Turkey, Egypt*, Letter of D. A. Cameron, British Consul in Port Sa'id dated 10 June 1902 to the Marquess of Lansdowne. See also *Al-Manār* (Cairo), vol. 17, pt. 7 (23 June 1914): 534-39.

31. "During the early nineteenth century these old rules were disregarded, and says Cevdet Paşa, 'even some of the non-Muslim subjects, without authorization, could be seen in public places on caparisoned horses'. Such unauthorized horse-riding by infidels, 'being unseemly in the eyes of the people', was banned . . . . " Bernard Lewis, *The Emergence of Modern Turkey* (Oxford University Press, 1961), pp. 389-390.

Many Christians sought the favor and privilege of finding employment in a foreign Consulate or Embassy in the Ottoman Empire and of becoming a Consular or Embassy protégé. See Francis Rey, *La protection diplomatique et consulaire dans les Echelles du Levant et de la Barbarie* (Paris, 1899).

32. "Christians must not mount on horseback in the towns: they are prohibited the use of yellow slippers, white shawls and every sort of green colour. Red for the feet and blue for the dress, are the colours assigned them. The Porte has just renewed its ordinances to reestablish the ancient form of their turbans; they must be of a coarse blue muslin, with a single white border." Christian-François Volney, *Travels in Syria and Egypt During the Years 1783, 1484 and 1785 . . .*, trans. from the French, 2 vols. (Perth, 1801), 2: 263.

When Mr. John Barker was appointed British Consul in Aleppo in 1803, the Sultan issued a *Firman* recognizing him as Consul. Part of that *Firman* reads

could be no real equality between him and the Muslim. Although the inequalities were formally, i.e., "on paper," abolished by the *Hattī-Humayūn* of 1856,[33] nevertheless, in practice, the old "*Millet* system" continued throughout the nineteenth century.

The word *Millet* is an Arabic word for which there is no equivalent in Western political terminology.[34] The *Millets* were actually the members of the non-Muslim religious communities living in the Ottoman Empire who had already been granted a wide scope of cultural and civil autonomy by Muḥammad the Conqueror. First, in importance, among these *Millets* was the *Millet-i-Rūm* which comprised all the Greek Orthodox Christian subjects of the Sultan. The next, in importance, were the Armenian *Millet* and the Jewish *Millet*. The "nationality" of every "*ra'iyyah*" in these *Millets* was the particular religious denomination to which his *Millet* belonged. "In Syria," wrote Chevrillon, "individuals of the same race under the influence of different religious ideas are separated in distinct groups which are rightly called *Nations* and which are as different one from the other as the peoples of Europe are."[35] Writing to Sir Henry Bulwer from Beirut on 25 April 1861, Lord Dufferin noted: "... All over the Turkish Empire religious communities (Millets) are considered as individual nationalities."[36] In the French *Correspondances Diplomatiques* concerning the Asiatic provinces of the Ottoman Empire, there are many references to "la nation maronite," "la nation Grecque catholique." The Maronite parriarch is called "le Chef de la nation Maronite."[37] Indeed, M. de

thus: "And if he shall wish to travel by land or by sea, no one shall . . . annoy him about his *riding on horseback, nor for his costume* . . . . And in places which may be unsafe, it shall be lawful for him *to wear a white turban, gird on a sword, have and carry bows and arrows* . . . spurs to his boots . . . . Without being hindered by an Kadee, Beylerbeg, or other person" [author's italics]. Edward B. Barker, *Syria and Egypt under the Last Vice Sultans of Turkey, Being Experiences During 50 Years of Mr. Consul-Gen. Barker*, 2 vols. (London, 1876), 2: 322-23.

33. The word *ra'iyah* was abondoned and replaced by the word *tab'ah* (from the Arabic "*tabi'a*", meaning literally to follow).

34. The Arabic word *Millah* means *Sharī'ah* or religion. The Qur'an speaks several times of the *Millah of Ibrahim*, i.e., the religion of Abraham. (See Sura 2, *Al-Ba'ara* [The cow] and Sura 3, *Al-'Imrān* [The family of 'Imrān]. Later, the word was used to denote the people of the same religion.

35. André Chevrillon, *Conférence sur la Syrie* (Rouen, 1897), p. 18.

36. Great Britain, Foreign Office, *Correspondence Relating to the Affairs of Syria*, 1860-61, pt. 2, p. 191.

37. The Patriarchs of the various Christian denominations were called by the Turks *Millet Bashi*, i.e., literally, the head of the nation.

Petiteville, the French Consul General in Beirut, wrote in one of his despatches: " ... cette Syrie ou le mot religion est synonyme du mot nation, voire même du mot Patrie."[38] Thus the line of demarcation was not along racial but along religious lines. The political identity of the Sultan's subject was Ottoman (Osmanli) and his "nationality" was the *religion* of the Community to which he belonged, i.e., his *Millet.* The idea of nationality in the West European nineteenth century sense was almost non-existent in the Ottoman Empire.[39]

38. Paris, Archives du Ministère des Affaires Étrangères, *Turquie: Beyrouth.* 1888, Despatch No. 13 of 25 March 1888: "Notes sur la Syrie". Among other particulars which an Osmanli had to fill in his *Tezkere* or Passport, was the nature of his *Millet.*

On 19 August 1856, the French Consul-General in Syria, E. de Lesseps, enclosed in his despatch a report written by M. Blanche, the French Vice-Consul in Tripoli. M. Blanche wrote, in part: "Le fait le plus saillant qui se présente à l'observation dans l'étude de ces contrées, c'est la place qu'occupent les idées religieuses dans l'esprit des peuples, la haute autorité qu'elles exercent dans leur existence. La religion apparaît partout, est mêlée à tout dans la société orientale. Les mœurs, la langue, la littérature, les institutions tout en porte l'empreinte; tout a un caractère éminement religieux. L'Oriental n'est pas attaché au pays où il est né—il n'a pas de *patrie* . . . il a une *religion.* Il est attaché à sa religion comme ailleurs on est attaché à la patrie. Sa *Nation*, c'est l'ensemble des individus qui professent les mêmes croyances que lui, qui pratiquent le même culte: tout autre est pour lui un étranger." Paris, Archives du Ministère des Affaires Étrangères, *Turquie*, vol. 11, *1856 à 1859*, no. 32.

39. "The Ottoman Empire began as the very opposite of a national State. It is not called after any people who inhabit it, but after the prince who founded it—Osman. It is true that Osman and his tribe were Turks; but they were only one out of a dozen Turkish States in Anatolia, and their Turkish neighbours were their most formidable rivals and enemies. . . .

"The cultivation of national consciousness by the Ottoman Turks was partly an imitation of older nationalist movements in Europe and partly the spontaneous product of similar conditions . . . . " Great Britain, Foreign Office, *Handbooks Prepared under the Direction of the Historical Section of the Foreign Office*, No. 96 c & d, *The Rise of the Turks; The Pan-Turanian Movement* (London, February 1919), pp. 16-17.

CHAPTER THREE

INDEPENDENCE MOVEMENTS IN ARAB LANDS

THE OTTOMAN EMPIRE entered the most decisive phase of its history in the nineteenth century. The once great Empire of the Ottomans which stretched from the gates of Vienna to the shores of the Caspian Sea and from the Persian Gulf to Aden and through the Red Sea and North Africa to almost the Atlantic Ocean, entered its last stages of decline and ruin.[1] All the evils of its autocratic regime were unveiled. Only through a proper knowledge of this background is it possible to understand the full significance of the awakened consciousness of the Arabs as to their fate and future destiny. The Empire was moving speedily towards final disintegration unless immediate steps were taken to infuse a new life into its internal organization and administration. From the first quarter of the nineteenth century onwards, a group of enlightened Turks were becoming increasingly aware of the necessity of rejuvenating the old and out-moded institutions and administrative machinery of their Empire. They were called the "New Ottomans." The period during which these "New Ottomans" struggled to achieve reforms in their country is known as the period of the *Tanzimāt* or the *Tanzimāt-i-Khayriyyah* ("Beneficent Legislation"), an expression which was apparently first used in the days of Maḥmūd II (1808-1839). The basic reform projects, however, were not carried out.[2]

1. "Sous Mahmoud et aux débuts du règne d'Abdul-Mejid, la Turquie était à peu près, selon l'image connue, comme un navire dont il faut renouveler la carène, la mâture, les voiles et l'équipage." Edouard Philippe Engelhardt, *La Turquie et le tanzimat: ou histoire de réformes dans l'Empire Ottoman depuis 1826 jusqu'à nos jours*, 2 vols. (Paris, 1884), 2: 4-5.

2. It must not be supposed that between 1839 and 1876 no changes took place in the Ottoman Empire. Life in Europe was undergoing a great transfor-

The truth is that none of the Sultans who issued the *Hatti-Humayuns* ever seriously considered becoming constitutional monarchs, nor did they want any intervention by the European Powers in their internal affairs. Indeed, how could any Sultan agree to any check on his sovereignty, whose official titles included such prerogatives and honorifics as "the Prince of the Faithful," "the Shadow of God on Earth," "the Vicegerent of the Prophet," "the Ruler of the Two Seas," "the Monarch of the Two Lands,"

mation: the slow moving tempo of the eighteenth century was being replaced by a fast moving pattern of progress based on industrialization and technology and new political doctrines inspired by the French Revolution. The flotsam and jetsam of western ideas, fads and fashions and new ways of living reached the Golden Horn, the western shores of Asia Minor and the Near East. Moreover, Ahmet Emin Yalman has recorded in his book *Turkey in the World War* (New Haven: Yale University Press, 1930), p. 26, that "in 1848, the era of revolution in Europe brought the Ottoman Empire a rich harvest of able men." "They came as fugitives," continues Yalman, "Turkey refused to give them up, even though Austria and Russia threatened war. Many of them became Turks and entered the Turkish public service." Thus, in many ways contacts increased with the Western world. But still at this time, introducing "Western civilization" in Turkey meant, on the whole, imitating and adopting the external trappings of that civilization. Stephen Panaretoff wrote in his *Near Eastern Affairs and Conditions* (New Haven, 1922), p. 130: "European usages and customs found their way into the capital. The Sultan set the example of European dress, gave in his palace dinners, concerts and balls as any European ruler would have done." These and other superficial changes did take place here and there in Turkey and mainly in Constantinople. But they must not be confused with the reforms that men like Rashid Pasha and Midhat Pasha had in mind. They both wanted *constitutional reforms* of far-reaching character by adopting the Western constitutional system of Government which, in the words of Midhat Pasha, has been "one of the principal causes of the progress of nations," for "Turkey," he added, "ranks among the Great Powers and in order to obtain this object and to march on a footing of equality with its neighbours in the progress of sciences, she must need follow the same method." 'Ali Haydar Midḥat, *The Life of Midhat Pasha, A Record of His Services, Political Reforms, Banishment, and Judicial Murder, Derived from Private Documents and Reminiscences, by His Son, Ali Haidar Midhat Bey . . .* (London: J. Murray, 1903), p. 80.

See also Enver Ziya Karal, *Osmanli Tariḫi* [History of Turkey], 18 vols. (Ankara, 1962), vol. 6, *Islahat Fermani Devri, 1856-1861* [The period of reform decrees, 1856-1861] (Ankara, 1954); Baron Ludovic de Contenson, *Les réformes en Turquie d'Asie, la question arménienne, la question syrienne*, 2d ed. (Paris, 1913); Frank Edgar Bailey, *British Policy and the Turkish Reform Movement, 1826-1853* (Cambridge: Harvard University Press, 1942); and Roderic H. Davison, *Reform in the Ottoman Empire, 1856-1876* (Princeton: Princeton University Press, 1963).

and "One by whose birth creation had been honoured and the moon of happiness had risen"?[3]

Harold Temperley wrote: "The health of the Turkish Empire depended on three factors: on the ability of the Turks to reform; on the willingness of the Christian subjects to acquiesce in the process; and on the readiness of the Great Powers to help or hinder this evolution. No one of these factors sufficed by itself.... But the Great Powers could not save Turkey. She alone could save herself, and reconcile her Christian subjects to her by reform. As will be seen, the Turks in fact waxed weaker and weaker, and the Christians stronger and stronger...."[4]

Anti-Turkish sentiment in Arab lands in the nineteenth century was a product of diverse causes. The immediate causes were due

3. Salim Sarkis, *Sirr Mamlakah* [The secret of a kingdom] (Cairo, 1895), p. 5. "The Ottoman Government, when it undertook to place the Empire on a new foundation, was neither entirely sincere in its professions, nor did it clearly understand what it was about. It accepted the announcement of great, immense and sudden reforms, less with a desire to reinvigorate Turkey than to gain Europe. It was less occupied with the laws it was to make than with the newspaper articles it would produce. It consequently undertook too much, too suddenly, and got confused amidst the novelties it promulgated. An uncertainty between the old and the new everywhere prevailed, and still prevails. A Pasha said to me the other day, 'What am I to do? I govern a province, and the great Vizier sends me an order which is framed on the new ideas that we profess. The Sheikh-ul-Islam complains against me because I do not act upon the old laws, which with him are still sacred. I say the two things are incompatible; and I am told I must follow our own usages, but I must give them a new dress. I don't know what I am about.'" Sir Henry Bulwer, British Ambassador in Constantinople, in a Report on the Finances of the Turkish Empire, August 1861; cited by Richard Robert Madden in *The Turkish Empire in its Relation with Christianity and Civilization* (London, 1962), pp. 407-8.

In September 1830, M. Michaud wrote from Pera (Istanbul) on the subject of *La Réforme en Turquie*: "... Pour arriver d'ailleurs à une civilisation quelconque, il faudrait en avoir au moins une première idée et savoir ce que c'est; ici notre civilisation est tout à fait comme une terre inconnue, comme un monde nouveau; il est difficile de marcher droit vers un but qu'on ne connaît pas, et de marcher vite lorsqu'on ne connaît pas précisément où l'on va. Il n'y a point de véritable zèle parce qu'il n'y a point de conviction; le sultan, lui-même, ne croit pas toujours à sa propre révolution; de là ces hésitations qui ressemblent au découragement et qui font encore quelquefois que tous les projets de réforme sont abandonnés." M. Poujalet, *La France et la Russie à Constantinople* (Paris, 1853), pp. 148-49.

4. Harold Temperley, *England and the Near East: The Crimea* (London, 1936), p. vii.

to the rapid increase in the deterioration of the Turkish Government and to Western influences of various kinds. Under the impact of Western education, the infiltration of Western political ideas, the intercourse of commerce, the introduction of the material goods of life, as well as through travel abroad and personal contacts with the West, the inhabitants of the Near East were slowly waking up to a new world of progress and power which was taking shape in the West, in sharp contrast to the state of ignorance and weakness in which the Ottoman Empire was submerged.

But in the nineteenth century, there was as yet no "Arab Question" in international politics. Indeed, the word "Arab" itself as a designation for the inhabitants of the Arab provinces of the Ottoman Empire rarely occurs in the books and documents of the period. It was reserved mainly for the Bedouins of the desert and for all the non-town dwellers in the Near East. The general terms "Muslim" and "Christian" were used to describe the two principal classes of inhabitants in this area. As to the great majority of the Muslim subjects of the Sultan, whether Turks or Arabs, they were "brothers in the Faith," i.e., they were Muslims before being Turks or Arabs.[5] Moreover, "the various races of which the subject populations were composed were not to be welded into a nation; and this, for the reason that the ruling class... on the one hand represented the political domination of Islam, and on the other was isolated by its constitution from all the ruled of whatever faith."[6] At the same time, the ruled and subject populations were in turn organized into semi-independent bodies, and as Gibb and Bowen have pointed out, "any wider allegiance

5. Rashīd Riḍā, founder of the Arabic periodical *Al-Manār*, wrote in an article entitled "Races in the Ottoman Empire" that Arab unity is based on Islam and on the Arabic language and that the Arabs have been the last among all peoples to develop race consciousness and race prejudice, for the vast majority among them are Muslims and as Muslims they are conscious only of their "religious nationality." *Al-Manār* (Cairo), vol. 17, no. 7 (July 1914): 534.

"Islam is the fatherland of the Muslim" ("*Al-Islām watan al-Muslim*"), see 'Abd al-Raḥmān 'Azzām, *Al-Risālah al-Khālidah* [The eternal message] (Cairo, 1946), p. 105. 'Azzam adds, on p. 141: "The Muslim's fatherland ("*watan*") has no geographic boundaries, it expands with the spreading of his faith."

6. Gibb, *Islamic Society and the West*, vol. 1, pt. 1, p. 159.

that the individual members of these units might entertain was religious rather than political."[7]

However, the desire for autonomy did appear in different parts of the Ottoman Empire, principally in Arabia, in Egypt, in the Lebanon, and in Syria, but for very different reasons. The steps taken and the methods used were according to the exigencies of the time and the circumstances of the day. In Arabia, the successfull attempt which was made to throw off the Turkish domination was the work of the Wahhabis. The anti-Turkish agitation was an entirely Muslim movement, and for certain reasons entirely anti-Western. The wrath of the Wahhabis was directed against what they considered to be the religious laxity and corruption of the Ottoman Government and the Ottoman Sultan himself, "including its ungodly inclination towards the filthy devices of the Frankish infidels," i.e., towards introducing reforms on Western lines.[8] The study of the origins of anti-Turkish sentiment in Arabia has hitherto been one of the neglected chapters of modern Arab history. It is often forgotten that a great blow to the already weakened foundations of the Ottoman Empire was delivered by the Emīr Muḥammad al-Sa'ūd when he triumphantly entered Mecca in 1806 and had the public prayers read in his name instead of in the name of Sultan Selim III. Jean Raymond who was at the time the French Consul in Baghdad reported: "L'esprit de conquête s'est répandu dans tous les rangs, et le souvenir de l'ancienne puissance des Arabes semble avoir fait revivre jusque dans le cœur le plus faible le doux espoir de se voir encore gouverner par les princes de sa nation. Le passage suivant vient à l'appui de ce que j'énonce: l'autre jour un Wahaby disait d'un ton prophétique, 'le temps s'approche où nous verrons un Arabe assis sur le

7. Ibid.

"Islam is a faith that has never encouraged the growth of nationality. Its universal character has toned down, rather than accentuated, racial and cultural differences that might have hardened into national qualities . . . the only common factors in the Arab World (in Turkish days) were unity of language and unity of subjection. The Syrian and the Egyptian, the nomad and the fellah, the learned and the populace, were too much divided by customs, by ideas, by tradition, to be at all willing to recognize anything common but religion. . . . " Henry H. Dodwell, *The Founder of Modern Egypt: A Study of Muḥammad 'Ali* [Cambridge: At the University Press, 1931], pp. 127-28.

8. Arnold J. Toynbee and Kenneth P. Kirkwood, *Turkey* (New York, 1927), p. 42.

trône des Califes; nous avons assez longtemps langui sous le joug d'un usurpateur.'"[9]

Alhough temporarily defeated between 1810 and 1817 by Muḥammad 'Alī Pasha, the Wahhabīs continued to grow in strength, though less aggressive than before, and completely regained their power at the beginning of the twentieth century, once more capturing Mecca in 1924, this time from King Ḥusain.

The next move to separate the Arab world from Turkish sovereignty came from Muḥammad 'Alī Pasha of Egypt between 1830 and 1841 when his forces occupied Syria and advanced as far as Kutahiya in Asia Minor. There is no historical evidence, however, to support any nationalistic aspect in this struggle. The goal of Muḥammad 'Alī Pasha who, himself, was of Turkish origin, was not the establishment of an *Arab* Empire in opposition to the Ottoman Empire, much as he may have professed, for ulterior motives of his own, pro-Arab sympathies and pro-Arab support. "An Arab racial movement in Egypt and Syria a hundred years ago would have been contrary to the whole trend of Oriental thought in those days. The world in which Muḥammad 'Alī found himself was medieval in the widest and most inclusive sense of the world. All true believers were members of one big fraternity and they were all equal."[10]

Muḥammad 'Alī Pasha's dominating and ambitious personality aimed at making Egypt independent of the Sultan and, possibly,

9. Jean Raymond, *Mémoire sur l'origine des Wahabys, sur la naissance et sur l'influence dont ils jouissent comme nation* (1806) (Cairo, 1925), p. 34.

10. Asad J. Rustum, *The Royal Archives of Egypt and the Origins of the Egyptian Expedition to Syria, 1831-1841* (Beirut: American Press, 1936), p. 85. Dr. Rustum adds, however, that "through his contact with Europe and European officers, Ibrahim Pasha seems to have been personally convinced of the soundness of the nationalistic philosophy . . . . In this sense Ibrāhīm Pasha certainly deserves the place of honour in the history of nationalism in the Arab East." Ibid., p. 96.

It seems that in France, a number of deputies believed in the policy of supporting Muḥammad 'Ali Pasha and helping him to break the Ottoman Empire into two halves, one Turk and the other Arab and thus forming a "*Royaume Arabe.*" But Freycinet adds that while such a policy was a sign of the times, it was that of a "romantic school" and the conception itself was "un peu chimérique." Charles de Freycinet, *La question d'Egypte*, 2d ed. (Paris: P. Brodard, 1904), p. 76.

"It is certain that Mehmet Ali never meant to be a pan-Arab, but . . . he meant to increase his power." Temperley, *England and the Near East: The Crimea*, pp. 96, 419-22.

at the actual conquest of the Ottoman Empire. While for nearly ten years he occupied and ruled the *vilayet* of Syria, he failed in his ultimate purpose and was finally compelled by British naval and military intervention to withdraw into Egypt. However, by the Firman of 1 June 1841, and the second Treaty of London of 13 July 1841, Muḥammad 'Alī was confirmed as the hereditary Pasha of Egypt. It is true that the Pasha was to be under the suzerainty of the Sultan, but in actual practice, Egyptian administration politically, economically, and even militarily became almost completely autonomous. The Pasha was master of his own house.

In the Lebanon, anti-Turkish sentiment was fostered by several factors such as Western education, the political ideals of the French Revolution, revival of Arabic language and literature, the printing press, the publication of Arabic newspapers, travel abroad, and the return of Lebanese emigrants from the United States. But this sentiment was primarily due to the fact that the Christians considered themselves like an alien island in the ocean of Turkish Muslim sovereignty. They simply did not feel "at home" under the Turkish Government. It was not *their* Government. Towards the middle of the nineteenth century, they were provided with an additional reason to work for their independence: the civil war of 1860. Naturally, after the tragic massacres of that year, the Maronites of Mount Lebanon never ceased to work for their complete separation from the Ottoman Empire. At the same time some foreign protection was necessary and it was obvious that in the case of Lebanon, that protection had to come either from Austria or from France, preferably from the latter, the traditional protector of the Maronites in the Near East. But the conclusion reached, that the upheaval of 1860 was "the decisive event of the nineteenth century" and that as a result of it "the seed of patriotism was sown, and a movement came into being whose inspiration was Arab and whose ideal was national instead of sectarian,"[11] is misleading and entirely unwarranted. The anti-Turkish sentiment which grew in Mount Lebanon was mainly a Maronite-Lebanese affair and cannot be considered in any way as a national rising of the Arabs in the Arab Near East against Turkish rule. The vast majority of Muslims living in territories governed by the Sultan did not desire at that time to overthrow and destroy his government.

11. George Antonius, *The Arab Awakening: The Story of the Arab National Movement* (London: Hamish Hamilton, 1938), p. 60.

It must also be remembered that the Christians of Lebanon had more frequent and more numerous contacts with the West than the rest of the Arab Near East had; hence, Lebanon acted as a gateway for the entry of Western influences into the Asiatic provinces of the Ottoman Empire. It was natural that the process of Westernization should have been fostered by them. As Christians, they looked upon their co-religionists of the West and particularly upon the French as the leading lights in the progress of Western civilization.

Another important reason why the Lebanon was the principal channel through which the impact of the West on the Arab Near East was felt more strongly than, perhaps, through any other channel, was commercial intercourse with the West. This was particularly true in Lebanon because of its geographic location and its past history when in the days of the Phœnicians the country was the foremost trading center between the Near East and the West. It is also important to note that under the Turks, "before 1856 Jews and Christians could not legally acquire land in Syria and until 1867 a similar prohibition applied to the case of all foreigners."[12] As a result, many Christians lived in towns and engaged in trade. In the long run, most of the prosperous merchants all over the Empire were the Christians. Consequently, as Professor Arnold Toynbee has so correctly pointed out, "as merchants on the grand scale, they entered into commercial relations with the Western World and acquired a first-hand knowledge of Western manners and customs and Western languages."[13] There is no doubt that the growth of commercial prosperity accelerated the process of Westernization in Arab lands. Speaking of Beirut, in the middle of the nineteenth century, Gregory Wortabet[14] wrote: "Its shops and stores are well provided from the factories of Europe and America. The produce of the Indies, he (the traveller) finds in almost every street. Suspended on a rope from the verandahs of the various shops, he will see exposed for sale New England drills, Manchester greys, Scotch zebras, French silks, Swiss handkerchiefs, etc., and all bearing the stamps of the various factories where they

12. Great Britain, Admiralty, *A Handbook of Syria (including Palestine)*, p. 250.

13. Toynbee, *A Study of History*, 2: 224.

14. Gregory M. Wortabet, *Syria and the Syrians, or Turkey in the Dependencies*, 2 vols. (London: James Madden, 1856), 1: 35-43.

are manufactured. . . . Those who knew Bayroot twenty years back and the condition of its inhabitants, will acknowledge the midnight and midday difference between 1835 and 1855."[15]

"A few years ago," Lewis Farley, who lived in Beirut, wrote in 1863, "our principal merchants were foreigners, now they are natives; they now do all the exporting and importing business, and to them foreign ships come consigned. A few years ago, they lived in small houses, dingy and gloomy... but now they have built new houses, spacious and splendid, with garden lots, and furnished them in Europeo-Oriental style. . . . A few years back, men and women, beyond the circle of near connexions never associated, but now a more European life is being introduced in that respect. . . . A few years ago, all the shipping of the place was the lateen-sailed boats, which went up and down the coast with fish or fruits, or some other produce of the country. . . . But now look at the roadstead of Bayroot and see its tonnage; gaze on the almost daily steamers that touch there from all parts of Mediterranean. . . ."[16]

One more illustration of the type of change and improvement which was taking place in Lebanon is worth recording here. It is taken from the "Report for 1893-94," entitled *Lebanon Schools*, written by the Reverend Dr. Carslaw of the Foreign Mission of the Church of Scotland. Dr. Carslaw in his capacity as a medical missionary had been transferred to the village of Shwair in Lebanon. The above-mentioned Report was written soon after his return — on 30 April 1894 — from a lecture tour in Scotland. Dr. Carslaw writes:

> "On our way up the mountain, we noticed a great improvement in the villages we passed through. Building operations were going on in many of them. Houses were having the old clay roofs taken off, and new roofs of Marseilles tiles put on. The outside shutters of windows, too, were getting a coat of green paint, and

15. Seven years later, Lewis Farley wrote: "For some years past, a very extraordinary improvement in the commercial prosperity of Syria has been everywhere apparent. . . . At Alexandretta, Lattakia, Tripoli, Sidon, Kaiffa and Jaffa, signs of an increasing commerce have been also evident. . . . " Farley, *The Resources of Turkey*, p. 206.

16. "No longer than fifteen years ago, there was scarcely any steam communication between Beyrout and Europe, now . . . English steamers run regularly between Beyrouth and Liverpool . . . . The line of steamers belonging to the Messageries Imperiales . . . and Austrian Lloyd's Company has also been increasing." Ibid., pp. 209-10.

everything spoke of comfort and prosperity. In Shweir itself, too, we found things in the course of being changed; new houses are being built — those that are finished are roofed with tiles. Eighteen years ago there was not a tiled roof in the whole district, and at Shweir at that time there were only two houses that had glass windows; now glass windows are common, being looked upon as a necessity. Shweir has now a municipality, which has been working wonders. Streets have been paved, the fountains have been opened up, and their channels altered where necessary in order to avoid impurities, and iron pipes have been put in all of them. Quite recently, too, the municipality have fixed up four kerosene lamps to light up the principal street, and we saw them lighted one night. Workmen and labourers will no longer work for the same wages as they did a few years ago, and as wages rise, everything else seems to rise too.

"This appearance of prosperity seems to be caused by the return of a great number of Syrians who, a few years ago, emigrated to Brazil, the United States, and Australia. Having in various ways obtained large sums of money, they have returned with the intention of enjoying life so long as the money lasts. Of course, the old houses that their fathers lived in are not good enough for their descendants, who have been over half the world, and have seen so much. So the old houses must come down, new ones must be built, chairs and tables and all modern conveniences must be introduced, so that old manners and customs are being rapidly changed."

The new articles which the West introduced were most welcome for their utility as much as for their charm and novelty; they made the life of the Oriental more pleasant and more comfortable, altered his taste and raised his standard of living. But it must not be assumed that the commercial impact of the West made, at this time, any deep impression on the beliefs and the faith which lay treasured in his heart. The profounder issues remained untouched and unchallenged, even when Western education was introduced in the Arab lands of the Near East.

An important question remains to be asked: What role did Western education play in fostering anti-Turkish sentiment in the Muslim lands of the Near East? Almost every writer who has given an account of the "Arab Awakening" has emphasized the role of education in the "Awakening". These writers believe that the spread of Western political and democratic ideas in the

Asiatic provinces of the Ottoman Empire was the work of foreign schools. It is true, of course, that French, American, and Russian mission schools and other foreign missions such as the British Syrian Mission and the Prussian Mission of the Deaconess of Kaiserswerth, were actively engaged in educating the youth of the Near East. After 1831, the Jesuits opened schools in Beirut, Ghazir, Zahleh, Damascus, and Aleppo; the Lazarist Fathers reopened their College in 'Aintura, and the American Presbyterians who first came in 1820, had, it appears, established by 1860 no less than thirty-three schools. But the two biggest educational institutions were the Syrian Protestant College (now the American University of Beirut), founded in Beirut in 1866, and the Jesuit Université Saint-Joseph, established also in Beirut, in 1875.

It is however, the contention of the present writer that while education has been a potent factor[17] in the awakening of the Arab Near East, the role of *missionary education* in the *national-political* enlightenment of the Arab youth in the second half of the nineteenth century has been greatly exaggerated. The missionaries came to the Near East with the intention of spreading the Christian faith among the Muslims and, also, with the desire of converting some Christian denominations to their own brand of Christianity. Their schools were first and foremost Christian schools. The following words of Dr. Gregory Wortabet, one of the distinguished missionaries of the day, represent the true spirit of most of the missionaries and the true purpose of their educational institutions: "I have now spoken of two powerful mediums, viz., preaching the gospel and medical influence, as great agencies in spreading the knowledge of true Christianity. They are helpmates, and one is necessary to the other. . . . These, however, generally speaking, operate on adults. . . . But there is another powerful medium which is exclusively brought to bear on the young, and which, if rightly handled, might under the blessing of God, be the means of regene-

17. As early as 1843, the French Ambassador in Constantinople, M. Bourquency, writing to M. Guizot about the Jesuit educational activities said: "Le rôle des forces intellectuelles en Orient prend chaque jour une importance plus vraie, plus grande, et nous ne pouvons apporter trop de vigilance et de soin à organiser dès l'origine et à régulariser l'emploi et les tendances de ces forces—nous dont l'influence et l'honneur, dans ces contrées, semblent, aussi bien par la puissance des traditions que par la force même des choses intimement liés à leur développement et à leur progrès." France, Archives du Ministère des Affaires Étrangères, *Turquie, 1843-44*, Despatch No. 130/60, vol. 290, pp. 67-68.

rating Syria. I refer to the education of youths of this land. I do not mean the schools established by the various sects, where nothing but a corrupted liturgy is taught; but I mean Christian schools, where the Bible, 'the inheritance of the whole world, is a standard book, and where the youthful mind can drink deep of its pure waters. . . . Now, I argue, that if such schools were established all over Syria, especially now that the cry for them is like a hurricane blowing over the land, who can estimate the results from them to the rising generation — a generation growing up in the 'admonition and nurture of the Lord?' Or who will doubt the happy results on Syria, socially and morally?"[18]

The religious activities of most of the foreign missions not only aroused the suspicions and fears of the vast majority of the Muslim inhabitants of these lands but they often fanned the flames of denominational and sectarian rivalries and even animosity,[19] so much so that the intervention of the foreign consuls became necessary at times to avoid political complications.[20] It is also

18. Wortabet, *Syria and the Syrians*, 1: 205-6.

19. Ibid., pp. 47-49. The Muslims rarely sent their children to mission or foreign schools. They kept aloof from Christian institutions of learning. They wanted an education which was Arab and Muslim in form and in spirit. One of the Muslim schools which was founded in Beirut in 1895 by Shaikh Aḥmad 'Abbās al-Azharī was known as *Al-Kulliyah al-'Uthmāniyyah al-Islāmiyyah.* Many of the Arab Muslim political leaders and secret society organizers were graduates of that school.

20. The following document which the author found in the Public Record Office, in London, is most illuminating and worth quoting in full:

"Sir,

"I have received your despatch No. 36 of the 10th ultimo together with its several inclosures.

"With reference to one of those inclosures, namely your despatch No. 37 to Sir Stratford Canning on the subject of the protection which in consequence of the appeal made to you on the part of the part of the American Missionary, Mr. Smith, you had thought it right to afford to the Protestant converts from the Greek Faith in the Hasbeya and adjoining districts, I have to inform you that Her Majesty's Government perfectly approve of your affording general and efficient protection to all Christians in Turkey who may appeal to you against the oppression of the Mussulman Authorities of the Porte. But in admitting the propriety of acting upon this general principle, Her Majesty's Agents should observe the utmost discretion both with regard to carrying interference with the Mahomedan faith beyond due bounds, and to appearing to give official support to those efforts which American and other Missionaries are now making in the Ottoman territories to draw off the votaries of other Christian sects to Protestantism.

true that not all missionaries devoted their activities entirely to the religious field. Apparently with the exception of the American missions,[21] some missionaries of the Great Powers interested in the Near East considered it as part of their duty to enhance and foster the political prestige of their countries and for this purpose they were fully supported by their Governments.[22] With much zeal and enthusiasm they made every effort to inculcate the love of their countries in the hearts of their pupils.[23]

"Abstractedly, Her Majesty's Government would naturally desire to see the tenets of the Anglican Church embraced by persons of all faiths, whether Mahomedan, Greek or other. But it would be highly injudicious and improper and not a little hazardous for the peace of the world, were Her Majesty's Government to govern their own actions, or to permit British official Agents to govern theirs, by this principle. Such a mode of proceeding could scarcely fail to excite the active hostility of all other religions and sects.

"The attention of the Emperor of Russia, one of the most powerful heads of the Greek Church, has already been awakened to the conversions which Protestant missionaries in the East are actively endeavouring to effect, and have succeeded in effecting, from the Greek Church; and it is unnecessary to observe to you that the religious hostility or active interference of Russia in the East is not to be desired.

"You will therefore carefully abstain from any act which might be construed into giving support or countenance to the conversions from the Greek faith to Protestantism which foreign missionaries in Turkey are now labouring with injudicious zeal to effect; but you will at the same time not relax your exertions whenever they can be properly employed in protecting Christians from Mahomedan persecution." Great Britain, Foreign Office, 78/575, *Turkey* (Diplomatic), January to December 1844, The Earl of Aberdeen to Consul Rose (Beirut), Despatch No. 10, dated 19 September 1844.

21. According to the testimony of the French representative himself:

"J'ai longtemps cherché quel était le but poursuivi par les Américains en venant évangéliser ici. Je me suis convaincu à la longue que leur seul mobile était la propagande religieuse. Derrière-pensée politique je n'en vois réellement pas." France, Archives du Ministère des Affaires Étrangères, *Turquie, Beyrouth*, 1888, Viconte de Petiteville, French Consul General in Beirut, to the Ministry of Foreign Affairs, Paris, Despatch No. 13, Letter of 25 March 1888.

22. Rashid Riḍa in his editorial in *Al-Manār* of 28 December 1913 launched a violent attack against the evil influences of Western education in Muslim lands—an education which teaches the young Arabs to despise their ancestors and glorify everything foreign—in the name of civilization. These young men according to *Al-Manār* were the peaceful army used by the Westerners for the "peaceful penetration and conquest of Muslim lands." *Al-Manār* (Cairo), vol. 17, 28 December 1913, pp. 8-9.

23. Charmetant has quoted Gambetta's words to him: "Le Cardinal Lavigerie et ses missionnaires [in Syria] ont rendu à la France plus de services qu'un corps d'armée, plus qu'une escadre de notre flotte." And the Apostolic

But barring the patriotic interests of certain missionaries for their own countries, a glance at the curriculum of the mission schools will reveal that the subjects taught at that time had no bearing, whatsover, on politics or nationalism. The main emphasis was on language, literature and mathematics, i.e., the three Rs, and in addition, naturally, on religious education. For example, the list of subjects taught at the Syrian Protestant College (now the American University of Beirut), during its first year of existence, 1866-67, contained: Languages — Arabic, English, French, Turkish, and Latin; Arithmetic, Algebra, and Geometry, Ancient History of the Arabs, History of religions, and Bible study.[24] There was a "Faculty" of thirteen teachers and a total

Delegate himself wrote: "Il nous faut la Syrie toute entière, de Gaza à Adana et du Liban à Mossoul." Mgr. Charmetant, protonotaire apostolique, directeur général de l'Œuvre des Écoles d'Orient, Constantinople, Syrie et Palestine, *Lettre ouverte à nos hommes d'État*, pp. 13, 35.

On 14 October 1887, the French Minister of Foreign Affairs wrote to M. Petiteville, French Consul-General in Beirut—in connection with the eighty-two scholarships that France had offered for students in Syria to study in the Jesuit schools there: "Lorsque les bourses ont été instituées en Syrie, on s'est proposé deux buts principaux. Le premier a été de se créer des clients au sein des familles parmi lesquelles étaient choisis les boursiers. Le second but a été de stimuler l'ardeur et des chefs d'institution et des enfants vers l'étude de la langue française. Ces deux résultats ont été atteints en partie. Car nous nous sommes attachés un certain nombre de familles influentes dont les plus jeunes membres ont été élevés sinon dans l'amour de la France, au moins dans la connaissance de sa langue et de son histoire." France, Archives du Ministère des Affaires Étrangères, *Turquie*, vol. 30, Despatch No. 51.

"The British consuls of Syria believe that the imperial interests of England are bound up with the missionary interests of the several Bible Societies, whose agents are established in Syria. They imbibe the polemics of the missionaries, and they adapt their politics to them." Madden, *The Turkish Empire in its Relation with Christianity and Civilization*, p. 370.

24. The English examination questions of the Senior Class in 1871 included fifteen lines of simple English to be translated into Arabic and the following questions: "What is a Zone and where is the torrid Zone? What is the difference between principal and principle? State the difference between compare and contrast." The Senior History questions (in Arabic) for the year 1873 included the following: "Who were the Hyksos and when did they occupy Egypt? What evidence can you give that Babylon was the first among the inhabited countries of the world. What is the origin of the Kingdom of Assyria and how long did that Kingdom last?" (See Catalogues of the Syrian Protestant College, at the Registrar's Office of the American University of Beirut, Beirut, Lebanon.)

The program of the Presbyterian High School in Damascus embraced the following subjects: reading, Arabic grammar, Scriptures, history, geography, arithmetic, and the English language. "The school duties commenced by read-of sixteen students, only three of whom were from Beirut. Twelve years later, in 1878-79, the program of studies in the Collegiate Department offered the following courses : 1st year (Freshman) — Arabic Grammar, English Grammar and Literature, Algebra, Geometry, Holy Scriptures, Music, Composition, and Declamation; 4th year (Senior) — Astronomy, Mental Philosophy [sic], Ethics, History, Geology, Botany, or Zoology, Music, Composition, Declamation, and the Holy Scriptures. (I have omitted the second and third years in order not to prolong unduly this discussion.) There were at this time 48 regular and 45 special students in the College with only five students in the graduating class.

The great contribution of most of these schools was to teach a small proportion of the rising generation to read and write. After speaking of the establishment of Christian Missions, particularly the Jesuits and the Lazarists in Lebanon, Volney, writing towards the end of the eighteenth century, says: "The most important advantage that has arisen from these apostolical labours is that the art of writing is become more general among the Maronites, and rendered them, in this country, what the Copts are in Egypt; I mean they are in possession of all the posts of writers, intendants and Kiya among the Turks. . . ."[25] But, unfortunately, there wasn't much foreign literature to read in the Arab Near East, in those days[26] and the government imposed a rigid censorship on all foreign books and papers imported from abroad.[27] The truth is that most

ing a portion of the Scriptures, and prayer, and closed in like manner. This, in fact is the plan on which the Protestant schools are conducted. The principals are generally the missionaries who are assisted in teaching the higher branches by a graduate of the 'Abaih seminary." Wortabet, *Syria and the Syrians*, 1: 209-10.

25. Volney, *Travels in Syria and Egypt*, 1: 273.

26. "An estimate of the general want of instruction may be formed from the fact that the demand for books is so small in Syria that I could not find a bookseller in Damascus or Aleppo . . . . Some of the books printed by the Égyptian Government, at the Bulaq Press, are sent to Syria, and are sold there, but the demand is small; they, however, have made their way into some of the schools, and into a few private families." Great Britain, *Parliamentary Papers*, 1840, *Report on Commercial Statistics of Syria*, by John Bowring; quoted by Antonius, *The Arab Awakening*, p. 38, n. 2.

27. The following stories may be apocryphal but they do indicate the state of mind of some of the censors, and their ludicrous ignorance. It is said that one of the Turkish censors in Beirut refused, at first, to let a Physics textbook be received by the Syrian Protestant College because he had noticed several

of the foreign schools and institutions were "selling their own goods" and vying with one another to gain the love of the largest number of students for their own national ends. The one exception was the Syrian Protestant College where there was no attempt at any "Americanization," whatsoever.[28]

However, we have to wait for the reign of Sultan 'Abdul Ḥamīd II for the anti-Turkish sentiment in Arab lands to gather momentum and finally to break into open rebellion. But even at that time, the vast majority of the Muslim Arabs did not take part in any attempt to separate the Arab world from the Ottoman Empire. Only a small, enlightened, ambitious and, in most cases, non-Muslim, minority wanted to destroy Ottoman sovereignty. While due consideration and credit should be given to that minority, it must be emphasized that their opinion was in no way representative of the opinion of the vast majority of the Muslim Arabs who thought of the Ottoman Empire to be primarily a Muslim Empire.

times the word "revolution" in one of the chapters of that book! Another censor objected to a Chemistry textbook destined for the same College entering the country—except after much explanation—because he thought that the formula for water, H_2O stood for: Hamid ('Abdul) II is zero! See also Ernest E. Ramsaur, Jr., *The Young Turks: Prelude to the Revolution of* 1908 (Princeton: Princeton University Press, 1957), pp. 104-5.

28. The attitude of the Reverend Daniel Bliss, President of the Syrian Protestant College, was a rare exception. He was greatly respected and admired by the peoples of the Arab lands for the great understanding and deep sympathy which he had for them. On 7 December 1871, when the cornerstone of College Hall was laid by the Honourable William Earl Dodge, Sr., Dr. Bliss said: "This College is for all conditions and classes of men without regard to colour, nationality, race or religion. A man, white, black or yellow, Christian, Jew, Mohammedan or heathen, may enter and enjoy all the advantages of this institution for three, four or eight years; and go out believing in one God, in many Gods, or in no God. But, it will be impossible for anyone to continue with us long without knowing what we believe to be the truth and our reasons for that belief." Daniel Bliss, *The Reminiscences of Daniel Bliss*, ed. Frederick J. Bliss (New York, 1920), p. 198.

CHAPTER FOUR

ARAB REVOLUTIONARY ACTIVITIES AND THE YOUNG TURKS, 1865-1909

'ABDUL ḤAMĪD was born on 22 September 1842, in the Palace of Dolma-Baghcheh, on the European shore of the Bosphorus. " . . . On Thursday, 31 August 1876, 'Abdul Ḥamīd left the house of Perestu Hanum, the lady who had adopted him, accompanied by the Minister of War and a hundred and fifty soldiers on horseback, at half past eight in the morning arrived at the Imperial Palace at Stamboul, where the Ministers and high dignitaries were already assembled. At ten o'clock, the boom of a hundred guns announced the deposition of Sultan Murad and the appointment of his brother 'Abdul Ḥamīd. The new Sultan was then hailed as Padishah and embarked at Seraglio Point, followed by a great number of caiques belonging to the Court, and was conducted to the Palace of Dolma-Baghshe, which had been quitted a few hours earlier by Sultan Murad and his family. 'Abdul Ḥamīd had obtained his wish and was now undisputed Sultan of Turkey."[1]

The reign of Sultan 'Abdul Ḥamīd II saw one of the most disastrous phases of the Eastern Question; the Ottoman Empire suffered a greater dismemberment than ever before. Fear of the disintegrating effects of the external pressure exerted by the Great

1. Sir Edwin Pears, *Life of Abdul Hamid* (New York: Henry Holt, 1917), pp. 43, 44. For a balanced evaluation of 'Abdul Hamid and his foreign policy, see Ármin Vámbéry, "Personal Recollection of 'Abdul Hamid II and His Court," *The Nineteenth Century and After*, June-July 1909, pp. 69-88. The mother of Sultan 'Abdul Hamid was Tirimujgan (Kadin Efendi), who died when he was still a very young child.

See also the work of a distinguished Turkish historian, Enver Ziya Karal, *Osmanli Tarihi* [History of Turkey], 18 vols. (Ankara, 19-62), vol. 8, *Birinci Meşrutiyet ve Istibdat Devirleri, 1876-1907* [The first constitutional period and despotism, 1876-1907] (Ankara, 1956).

Powers and fear of internal rebellions made the Hamidian regime more tyrannical. 'Abdul Ḥamīd himself had an inordinate fear of assassination and an almost pathological suspicion of those who surrounded him. On one rare occasion — 30 November 1878 — he gave vent to his feelings by telling M. de Torey, the French military attaché at the French Embassy in Constantinople: "En ce pays d'intrigues... comment lutter toujours et contre tous?"[2]

Under 'Abdul Ḥamīd, suspicion between Arabs and Turks increased. He was greatly disturbed by the anti-Turkish agitation in the Lebanon and the appearance of revolutionary leaflets or placards in Beirut in the days when Midhat Pasha was the *Vali* of Syria. He was well aware of the growing feeling of discontent in his Asiatic possessions. Terrified of revolutionary activities and realizing that the administration of his provinces was greatly decentralized, he tightened up the controls from Constantinople and, more and more, laid an iron grip on the government of those provinces. Thanks to the new invention of telegraphy, his capital was now in close touch with the principal cities of his Empire. His fear of an Arab majority weakening the ruling Turkish element was heightened by his suspicion that the Arabs were working towards the establishment of an Arab Caliphate.[3] But at first, he made several attempts to win the Arabs,[4] either through expensive gifts, or through excessively generous hospitality according to Arab leaders visiting Constantinople, or by appointing Arabs to high administrative and military posts in the Government,[5] and finally, by posing as the champion of pan-Islamism.

2. France, Archives du Ministère des Affaires Étrangères, *Turquie*, vol. 423 (December 1878).

3. "In the early years of Abdul Hamid, the chief mosques in Stamboul contained extracts from the Sacred Books of the qualifications required in the Caliph. About 1890, by 'Abdul Hamid's command, these were ordered to be taken down, and a considerable amount of discontent was thus created amongst the Ulama. . . ." Pears, *Life of Abdul Hamid*, p. 149.

4. "Arabs and Circassians were always preferred by him as more faithful and more humble than the Turks; hence his predilection for Izzet Ebul-Huda and Emin Efendi." Vámbéry, "Personal Recollections of 'Abdul Hamid II and His Court," p. 989.

5. To mention only a few: 'Izzat Pasha al-Ābid, "contemptuously called by the Turks 'Arab Izzet,' " was the Second Secretary of 'Abdul Ḥamīd; Na'ūm Pasha, "The Syrian," was Under-Secretary for Foreign Affairs; Salīm Pasha Melhamah, a Maronite from Lebanon, was Minister of Mines, Forests, and Agriculture; Najib Pasha Melhamah (brother of the former) was entrusted

The dream of uniting the Muslim world and rebuilding the Muslim Empire has always been very close to the hearts of many Muslim leaders throughout the world. "The notion, however, that the religious headship of Islam might be politically utilized was adopted by 'Abdul Ḥamīd II.... The persons supposed to have impressed him with the idea are Si Muḥammad Zāfir, a Marabout of Tripoli who had foretold his accession, this Marabout's cousin, Sheikh Asad, and a certain 'Abdul Huda Effendi. They persuaded him that his predecessors had been mistaken in cultivating the friendship of European Christian Governments, and that his true course was to attempt to reunite Islam against Christendom."[6]

'Abdul Ḥamīd was led to believe that if he appeared as the champion of Islam and the protector of the Muslims living under Christian Governments, the Sunni Muslims, Arabs and non-Arabs, would rally round the Ottoman Caliphate and support it fully and unconditionally. It is believed that the railway line between Damascus and Medina — the Hejaz Railway — which was built with the monetary contributions of Muslims — had for one of its principal motives the winning of the friendship and support of Muslims throughout the world. Soon after the inauguration of the railway at Medina (September 1908), a leader in

with the safety of the Sultan (his official position was Under-Secretary at the Ministry of Public Works but he was actually the unofficial Head of the Secret Police and Special Political Envoy of the Sultan); Maḥmūd Shawkat Pasha (from a well-known family in Iraq) was Commander-in-Chief of the Third Army at Salonika. See Great Britain, Foreign Office, *British Documents on the Origins of the War*, 5: 7-20, and Aḥmad 'Izzat Al-A'zami, *Al-Qadiyyah al-'Arabiyyah* [The Arab question] (Baghdad, 1931), pp. 80-82.

6. Great Britain, Foreign Office, *Handbooks* ..., No. 96 a & b, *The Rise of Islam and the Caliphate; the Pan-Islamic Movement*, pp. 54-55.

"At his court there were a number of Arab divines, mostly associated with one or other of the orders of mystics, vying with each other to exalt his claims and so to win his favour. There was Shaykh Muḥammad Zafir of Mecca, a member of the Shadhili order; Shaykh Faḍl of the 'Alawi family from the Hadhramaut; and most influential of all, Shaykh Abu'l Huda al-Sayyadi of the Rifa'i order. An Arab from the province of Aleppo, he belonged to a family which for at least two generations had had a local reputation in the mystical orders. Gifted with great force of personality, he acquired a far wider fame; travelling first to Baghdad, then to Constantinople, he established a personal ascendancy over Abdulhamid, partly because of his reputation for supernatural powers, partly through his sagacity and political understanding...." See Albert H. Hourani, *Arabic Thought in the Liberal Age, 1798-1939* (London: Oxford University Press, 1962), p. 107.

the *Times*, discussing the motives of 'Abdul Ḥamīd, stated: "He saw from the outset that the making of the line would strengthen the position he claims for himself as the spiritual head of Islam; and he perceived, perhaps even more acutely that the railway will have a very great strategic value, when it is linked up with the Anatolian system. It lies very near the flank of Egypt, and it affords a rapid means for the transport of troops towards those provinces of Arabia which have never been properly subjugated by Turkey." [7]

'Abdul Ḥamīd need not have had any worries about his Arab subjects as far as the Caliphate was concerned. In his days, it was inconceivable to the vast majority of the Muslim Arabs not to support the Caliphate, because the support of the Caliphate was the support of Islam. Moreover, the thoughtful among them looked upon European designs on the Ottoman Empire with great alarm lest the Powers should eventually partition that Empire, which would mean the end of the Caliphate and of Arab existence in a Muslim Empire. But, if the Arabs as Muslims acquiesced in the excesses of 'Abdul Ḥamīd's regime, they were nevertheless alienated by his despotic measures and pleaded for reforms in the Arab provinces of the Empire. 'Abdul Ḥamīd, no doubt, realized that it was not possible to conduct the policy of his multi-national and theocratic Empire in accordance with nationalist principles and constitutional methods of government. Pressed at the beginning of his reign into accepting Midhat Pasha's constitution, 'Abdul Ḥamīd acted for a while as a constitutional monarch. The first Turkish Parliament met on 19 March 1877 in the great Reception Hall of Dolma-Baghcheh and heard the Sultan's speech from the throne. The debates which took place in that Parliament and which have been collected and published recently, seem to indicate that its subservience to 'Abdul Ḥamīd has been greatly exaggerated. [8]

7. Cited by *The Illustrated London News*, vol. 133, no. 3625 (10 October 1908): 498.

"Externally, he ('Abdul Hamid) was very popular among the Muslims of other countries. Very shrewdly, he saw that England and France, the two countries with the largest number of Moslem subjects, would naturally be affected by Pan-Islamism. The building of the Hejaz railway was a masterly demonstration of his Pan-Islamism." Halidé Edib Adivar, *Turkey Faces West: A Turkish View of Recent Changes and their Origin* (New Haven: Yale University Press, 1930), p. 93.

8. Rūḥī Khālidī al-Maqdisī, *Al-Inqilāb al-'Uthmānī wa Turkiyya al-Fatāt* [The Ottoman revolution and the Young Turks], cited in *Al-Hilāl* (Cairo), vol. 17, pt. 3 (1 December 1908): 139, and Hakki Tarik Us, *Meclis-i-Meb'usan*, A.H. 1293 [The Ottoman parliament, A.H. 1293 (1877 A.D.)], 2 vols. (Istanbul, 1954).

On 14 February 1878, by the Sultan's command, the Ottoman Parliament was dissolved *sine die*[9] and the Constitution suspended. As for the deputies, the more enlightened and the more outspoken in their criticism were ordered to leave Constantinople. Among them were a number of prominent Arab representatives. This humiliation of the representatives of the nation evoked no emotions of protest either among the Turkish public or in the Turkish press.

Nevertheless, Arab demands for reforms continued to be openly voiced after the suspension of the Constitution of 1876. The pages of one of the earliest Arabic papers in Beirut — the *Lisān-ul-Ḥāl*, published by Khalil Sarkis, contained in 1878 many articles on the needed reforms in Lebanon and in the Near East.[10] When 'Abdul Ḥamīd appointed Midḥat Pasha, the "Father of Reform," as the *Vali* of Syria (1878-1880), there was great rejoicing in the country and hopes ran high that such reforms would be instituted.[11] However, one of the consequences of 'Abdul Ḥamīd's repressive policy was that reforms and reform movements and all anti-Ḥamidian opposition were driven either underground or beyond the boundaries of the Empire, particularly to Paris, London, Geneva, and Cairo.[12] Hence, also, the rise of secret societies

9. Gallenga, the correspondent of the *Times* (London) in Constantinople, reported on 21 June 1876, that to create constitutional government in Turkey was "something like weaving ropes of sand." Cited in R. W. Seton-Watson, *Disraeli, Gladstone and the Eastern Question: A Study in Diplomacy and Party Politics* (London): Macmillan, 1935), p. 38.

10. See issues of *Lisān-ul-Ḥāl* (Beirut), no. 92 (14 September 1878), and no. 117 (11 December 1878). This newspaper is still published, daily, in Beirut.

11. See *Lisān-ul-Ḥāl* (Beirut), no. 109 (25 November 1878), and no. 112 (5 December 1878).

12. After the British occupation of Egypt in 1882, Arab and Turkish nationalists flocked to Cairo and Alexandria where they enjoyed great freedom for their political activities. Sometime, soon after 1897, the first political society founded by Arab leaders in Egypt appeared under the name of *Jam'iyyah al-Shawra al-'Uthmani* [The Ottoman Consultative Society]. Two of its founders were Muhammad Rashid Riḍa and Rafiq al-'Azim. But other nationals in the Ottoman Empire took part in its organization and its activities such as Turks, Armenians and Circassians. The purpose of the organization was to oppose 'Abdul Hamid's tyranny and unjust administration and to try to change the form of Government into a representative Parliamentary system. 'Abdul Hamid was, naturally, greatly perturbed by it. He himself confessed to one of his entourage that when he first heard about that Society, he could not sleep for three nights until he learned, through some of his spies in Egypt, who its founders were. He called it the "corrupting society."

with the object of working for the introduction of reforms in Arab countries and, in some extreme cases, for the entire liberation of the Arabs from Turkish or any other alien domination.[13]

We have already seen in the previous chapter that after Arabia, in the nineteenth century, it was in Egypt and in the *vilayet* of Syria (including the *sanjak* of Lebanon) that anti-Turkish agitation developed and gathered strength. During the second half of that century the strongest reaction to 'Abdul Ḥamīd's despotism and Turkish misgovernment came from the Syrian province of his Empire. Two assertions are, however, unsupported by any serious historical evidence, namely: (a) that a small group of 'enlightened élite,' through their secret society in Beirut, spread the seeds of *Arab nationalism*, and (b) that "the first organized effort in the Arab national movement" can be traced back to the activities of that group.[14] Unfortunately, the whole story has been exaggerated as far as the concept of "nationalism" is concerned. Perhaps it is worth recording here, briefly, the account which the author himself heard from the lips of the last surviving member of that small group of "enlightened élite," the late Dr. Faris

The *Jam'iyyah al-Shawra al-'Uthmani* had several branches throughout the Empire. Its propaganda material was printed in Arabic and Turkish. Some of it used to be sent with passengers and members of the crew of Russian ships to Turkish ports on the Black Sea. From there, secret messengers would take them and distribute them throughout Anatolia.

The society dissolved itself soon after the Young Turks came to power in 1908. See 'Uthman al-'Azim, ed., *Majmū'ah Athār Rafiq Bey al-Azim* [A collection of the writings of Rafiq Bey al-Azim] (Cairo, A.H. 1344 [A.D. 1925]), pt. 1.

Some years later, René Pinon wrote: L'Égypte devient . . . le centre d'une véritable renaissance de la vie et de la civilisation arabe, par la langue, par la littérature, par la religion. Il est donc naturel de supposer que la propagande nationale arabe et la publicité qui lui a été donnée dans l'Europe occidentale, loin d'être des phénomènes isolés, sont en connexion étroite avec le grand mouvement d'indépendance qui se manifeste dans l'Arabie péninsulaire et dont l'Angleterre a si ouvertement favorisé le succès." René Pinon, *L'Europe et l'Empire Ottoman* (Paris, 1908), p. 382.

13. Thanks to the existence of foreign Post Offices in the Asian possessions of the Ottoman Empire, the liberals and the anti-Turks could keep in touch with one another. Communications passing through these Post Offices were, generally, safe from 'Abdul Hamid's spies and censors—except in certain cases when some employee would be tempted with a large sum of money to "sell" to the Ottoman authorities certain important letters.

14. Antonius, *The Arab Awakening*, p. 79.

Nimr Pasha.[15] To begin with, Faris Nimr Pasha emphasized that the idea of "nationality" did not exist in the minds of the masses of the people in the Near East at that time. All the ties, relationships and loyalties were denominational and religious, primarily Muslim or Christian. The Muslim was principally either Sunni or Shīʿī and the Christian was chiefly either Maronite, Greek Orthodox, Catholic, or Protestant. National unity was impossible under the circumstances. A young "enlightened élite," most of whom were Christians,[16] and some of whom had studied at the Syrian Protestant College in Beirut, wanted first and foremost to emancipate the *Lebanon* from the Turkish yoke. They formed a "secret revolutionary society" sometime around 1876, which

15. Faris Nimr Pasha was born in Lebanon, in the village of Hasbaya, most probably in 1854. He left Beirut for Cairo in February 1885 where he, together with Yaʿqub Sarruf and Shahin Makarius, founded in 1886 the Arabic daily paper called *Al-Mukattam*, one of the most famous newspapers in the Arab world. Faris Nimr died in 1951.

16. The following were some of the prominent members: Ibrāhīm al-Ḥourānī, Yaʿqūb Sarrūf, Ibrahim al-Yāzijī, Faris Nimr Pasha, and Shahin Makarius.

According to Faris Nimr Pasha, the group consisted at first of about twelve members, increasing later to nearly seventy. He told the author about the great influence of Elias Habbalin who taught French at the Syrian Protestant College in Beirut from 1871-74. He was a Maronite, then he joined the Freemasons. He had read Voltaire and was very progressive and revolutionary in his ideas. After going briefly over the French lesson in his class, Habbalin would turn to politics and talk about getting rid of the Turks with all their injustices and corrupt Government. His students, all of whom were Christians, soon became his enthusiastic disciples. Every one of them wanted to become a Habbalin "and more than a Habbalin." They started to teach their ideas to others. Another young enthusiast was Salim ʿAmmun from Dair-al-Qamar. His uncle had been the Governor of Lebanon in the days of Ibrahim Pasha. He had read Dumas' *Three Musketeers*, and together with two other friends of his tried to become like the three musketeers and form a secret society to free Lebanon from the Turks. According to Faris Nimr Pasha, the first revolutionary ideas which he and a group of his friends got while at the Syrian Protestant College, were of French origin and came to them secretly through Elias Habbalin.

Elias Habbalin was born on 1 November 1839 in the village of Zuq in Lebanon and died on 8 October 1889 in Egypt. He studied at the Lazarist Fathers' College in ʿAintura and became well versed in French literature and language. He taught for a time in some of the best-known colleges and schools in Beirut, became, in 1866 the Editor of the official Lebanese gazette, "Lubnan" and was appointed by the French Government as the First Dragoman of the French Consulate in Beirut until 1875 when he left for Egypt. For a brief biographical note on Habbalin see Vicomte Philip de Tarrazi, *Taʾrīkh al-Ṣaḥafah al-ʿArabiyya* [History of the Arabic press] (Beirut, 1913), pp. 115-16.

used to meet during certain evenings, on the rocky seashore, near the Pigeon Rocks, south of Beirut, to exchange views and discuss ways and means of achieving their objective. What was uppermost in the minds of these young men was their being humiliated and made to feel "inferior" by the Turk. One of the sayings of the time was: "the Turk is 'riding over' the Muslim and the Muslim is 'riding over' the Christian!" The Arab Muslim, speaking of the Ottoman Empire, could say: "It is also *my* Empire," for it was a Muslim Empire and the Muslim felt at home in it. But the Christian was conscious most of the time that he was only one of the *ra'iyyah*. The Turkish Government could not be *his* Government.

It soon became evident to these young men that for the success of their goal, the cooperation and support of the Muslims was necessary. It was imperative that a common and united front be presented to the Turks. The only common denominator of the Muslim Arabs and the Christian Arabs was *Arabism* or *'Urūbah*. The battle-cry of *'Urūbah* would stir Arab national feelings and could rally around it both Muslim and Christian Arabs who were bitterly dissatisfied with the Turkish Government. Hence, the young Christian *élite* members of the secret revolutionary society reached the conclusion that the only way to get rid of Turkish domination in the Lebanon and to be treated on a footing of equality with the Arab Muslims was through a successful Arab movement directed against the Turks and based on Arabism. They also had recourse to a new strategem which was to try and enroll notable Muslims in the Masonic Lodge of Beirut.[17] The leading members of the secret society had already joined this Lodge. They hoped to induce their Muslim "brothers" as Masons to become members of the secret society. A few Muslims did join the Lodge and did learn about the existence of the secret society. Muslims and Christians agreed on combatting Turkish injustices and despotism, on asserting their Arabism and insisting on equal rights for the Arabs and the Turks; but they disagreed on the ultimate goal of the society. No understanding could be reached on the expulsion of the Turks from the *vilayet* of Syria which included the already

17. Several Masonic Lodges had already been established in Beirut and Damascus. The Grand Orient of France had issued a warrant in 1868 for a Lodge in Beirut to be called "Liban". This Lodge was constituted on 4 January 1869. There was also a Lodge organized under warrant from the Grand Lodge of Scotland. See Robert Morris, *Freemasonry in the Holy Land*, 5th ed. (New York, 1873), pp. 470-73, 557.

autonomous *sanjak* of Lebanon, and "a wonderful opportunity was lost," according to Faris Nimr Pasha. Sometime between 1882 and 1883, this particular secret revolutionary society, the existence of which was one of the best kept secrets of the time, suspended its activities, burned its records and dissolved itself. Other secret societies were formed a few years later.

In his book, *Sutūr min al-Risālah*,[18] 'Ādil al-Solḥ tells the story of the emergence of Arab political awakening in the province of Syria, as related to him by his father Munaḥ al-Solḥ. It was during the Russo-Turkish war of 1877-78: the insurrections in the Balkans, the chaotic internal situation in the Ottoman Empire and the advance of Russian armies towards Constantinople led a group of Arab leaders in the *vilayet* of Damascus to deliberate the question of the future of Syria in case the Empire collapsed. The instigator and the distinguished leader of this group was Aḥmad al-Solḥ, the grandfather of 'Ādil al-Solḥ.

After studying the matter carefully and discussing it with a number of notables in Beirut, Sidon, and Damascus, Aḥmad al-Solḥ decided to visit the famous and much respected Algerian leader, the Emir 'Abdu'l Qādir al-Jazā'irī, in Damascus, to discuss with him the future fate of the Arab provinces of the Ottoman Empire and the means of saving them from the destruction and ruin which threatened that Empire.

As a result of further consultation with some notables and leaders in northern Syria, i.e., in Hama, Homs, Aleppo, and Lattakia, a number of them accepted the invitation of Aḥmad al-Solḥ to accompany him to Beirut. Several secret meetings were held in this town, after which they decided to go to Damascus. There, they held a secret Congress in which it was agreed to work for the independence of the vilayet of Damascus and to proclaim the Emir 'Abdu'l Qādir as the ruler of Syria.[19] Meanwhile, the Russo-Turkish war ended with a Russian victory and a Russian army standing almost at the gates of Constantinople.

Long discussions and negotiations ensued with the Emir, but the latter insisted that the spiritual ties between Syria and the Ottoman Caliphate should not be severed. The Ottoman Caliph

18. Ādil al-Ṣolḥ, *Sutūr min al-Risālah* [A brief message] (Beirut, 1966), pp. 91-127.

19. See also Muḥammad Jābir al-Safa, *Ta'rīkh Jabal 'Amil* [History of Jabal 'Āmil] (Beirut, 1963), p. 208.

should remain the Caliph of all (Sunni) Muslims. The great majority of the Congress members agreed with the Emir concerning the Caliphate.

As to the question of independence, they all decided on the principle of trying to achieve independence for Syria, but to postpone consideration of its nature and extent until the final outcome of the Russo-Turkish war became known. At the same time, they were to watch carefully the developments at the Congress of Berlin. If it appeared that a foreign Power wanted to occupy Syria, the way Austria had occupied Bosnia and Herzegovina, then they were to demand the full independence of Syria; but if it transpired that there was no intention of a foreign occupation, then their demand would be for autonomy, similar to the autonomy of Egypt and some of the Balkan countries.

However, soon after, the work of the Arab Congress came to an end and its members — about thirty notables and leaders — disbanded. The authorities learned about their activities, with the result that some of the members were placed in forced residence, in remote regions of Syria; others were exiled outside this *vilayet*, and a ban was placed on any meeting between Aḥmad al-Solḥ and the Emir 'Abdu'l Qādir. Meanwhile, the Congress of Berlin saved the Ottoman Empire from imminent disintegration and ruin. Thus, under the circumstances, it became impossible to carry out the decisions of the Congress of Damascus.

A word must be said about the anonymous placards, in Arabic, which appeared in 1880 and which denounced the evils of Turkish misgovernment and exhorted the population to overthrow it. They appealed to the Arabs, to their patriotism (*waṭaniyyah*) and their "glorious past," to rise and expel the Turks from the Arab lands and, thus, emancipate themselves from the evils of Turkish despotism. These placards were stuck, after midnight, on walls specially near the Consulates of foreign Powers, in various towns of the *vilayet* of Syria, particularly in Beirut, Damascus, Tripoli, and Saida. Faris Nimr Pasha told the author that their secret society was responsible for issuing a number of these placards and that several of them were in his handwriting. (These "revolutionary papers" were small enough to be hidden in one's coat pocket.) They were among the first public expressions of Arab nationalist sentiment during the second half of the nineteenth century.

On 28 June 1880, the British Acting Consul-General John Dickson in Beirut, considered it important enough to inform, telegraphically, the British Ambassador G.T. Goschen in Constantinople, that "revolutionary placards" had appeared in Beirut.[20] The telegram was followed by his Despatch of 3 July 1880[21] in which he wrote that such placards had, recently, appeared several times in Beirut, "calling upon the people to revolt against the Turks," adding "there is no doubt that for the last five years a secret society has existed in Syria, having branches at Baghdad and Constantinople.... These placards may have emanated from this society." He enclosed one original, handwritten, placard, in Arabic and a copy of a second placard.[22] According to Dickson, "these revolutionary papers were posted up in the streets" of Beirut "for the third time." In his despatch from Beirut, dated 2 June 1880, the French Consul, Sienkiwicz, wiiting to Charles de Freycinet, Minister of Foreign Affairs, refers also to the recent appearance of placards in Beirut and Damascus, claiming autonomy for the *vilayet* of Syria.[23] He seems to think that the Russo-Turkish war of 1877-78 and the partial dismemberment of the Ottoman Empire had revived the hope and aspirations of the people of Syria for independence. In subsequent despatches, he refers to the appearance of the placards reported in the above-mentioned despatch of Consul-General Dickson.

More placards of "a revolutionary nature" continued to appear towards the end of 1880 in Syria where "a certain amount of discontent manifests itself amongst a class of persons connected

20. Great Britain, Foreign Office, 195/1308. *Turkey*, 1880, vol. 2.

21. Ibid., Despatch No. 47.

22. For photostatic copies of these placards, see Figs. 1 and 2, Appendixes G and H.

23. France, Ministère des Affaires Étrangères, *Turquie*, vol. 23, 1880. Less than a year earlier, on 9 October 1879, the French Consul in Beirut, Delaporte, having apparently got some knowledge about the existence of a secret society there, reported to Waddington, Minister of Foreign Affairs, about the possibility of the existence of an Arab conspiracy with ramifications in Aleppo, Mosul, Baghdad, Mecca, and Medina with the intention of forming an Arab Kingdom ("un royaume Arabe"). The name of the famous Algerian leader, 'Abd al-Qadir, living in Damascus is also mentioned as the future "Sultan" of this Arab Kingdom. All this, the Consul emphasizes, is only a rumor and he is not in a position to confirm it. However, he adds that there is such complete anarchy and disorganization in the Ottoman Empire that the realization of such a scheme is neither improbable nor impossible. France, Ministère des Affaires Étrangères, *Turquie*, vol. 22, 1879, Despatch No. 19.

probably with some secret society."[24] One appeared in Saida, and "on the 31st ultimo, during the night two were posted up in the streets of Beyrouth," wrote Dickson to F. R. St. John, Her Majesty's Chargé d'Affaires in Constantinople.[25]

A few days later, Dickson wrote again, enclosing "a copy and translation of one of the revolutionary placards which appeared in the streets of Beyrout in the night of the 31st ultimo."[26] But he is now more certain than before that these placards

> "are not the production of two or three disaffected individuals, as many supposed, but of a Secret Society, having branches in different parts of the country."

The rest of Dickson's despatch states:

> "The language, moreover, in which some of these placards are couched, would show that they are the composition of educated persons. Competent judges of Arabic declare the style to be of the purest kind, such as only those acquainted with the Koran and Arab poetry would use.... The Authorities have been endeavouring to discover the authors of these placards, but from what I can learn, their efforts have not met with success. Two persons, besides those already taken into custody at Sidon, have been arrested at Damascus by the secret police. They are both Christians, one being a Protestant and I am informed that the evidence against them is barely sufficient to convict them. They have, however, both been condemned to banishment from the country. It is stated that two or three days ago a Christian of Sidon wrote to the Governor General, and accused the 'Society of Good Intentions, ' referred to in my Despatch No. 61 of the 17th of November last, as being the originator of the revolutionary placards, but I am not yet aware as to whether the authorities have decided to take any steps against this Society. An address has been forwarded to the Wali, signed by most of the rich and influential inhabitants of Beyrout, expressing their loyalty to the Sultan, and deprecating any wish to sympathize with a revolutionary movement....
>
> "I would scarcely have deemed it necessary to trouble you, by forwarding a specimen of the placards in question, but there are

24. Great Britain, Foreign Office, 195/1368, *Turkey*, 1881, vol. 2, Despatch No. 1, Beyrout, 3 January 1881.

25. Ibid.

26. See Fig. 3, Appendix I.

certain expressions in the one of which copy is inclosed, to which I would respectfully venture to draw your attention. You will observe that mention is made of the Lebanon, and the desire set forth is that the condition of the Syrians should be assimilated to that of the people of the Mountain, who practically possess an autonomous government. The wish seems to be to get rid of oppression and injustice, and to procure the establishment of a government in which the people are to have a voice, and under which they are to enjoy liberty of person and of expressing their thoughts." [27]

Several of these placards were, undoubtedly, put out by the secret society, formed in Beirut [28], although other possibilities as to their origin have not been excluded in the despatches of John Dickson. On 3 July 1880, he wrote that "there appears to be a prevailing opinion with several persons, Moslems and Christians, that His Highness Midḥat Pasha is the author of these Placards." But he dismisses this opinion as "scarcely probable that His Highness is the prime mover in a revolutionary project...." About six months later, on 17 January 1881, he gave a new explanation for the placards, combining the three possible sources of authorship into one: "the Society of Good Intentions":

"The opinion at present prevailing amongst most persons, is that the revolutionary placards which have lately appeared in different parts of Syria, are the work of the 'Society of Good Intentions.' Although this society was formed under its present name about a year and a half ago, by Midḥat Pasha, yet I have been assured that a disaffected society, desiring a change in the government of the country, existed for a considerable time previously. It seems to have incorporated itself with the 'Society of Good Intentions,' when the latter was established. Under such a euphonius name it would have more scope to carry out its

27. Great Britain, Foreign Office, 195/1368, *Turkey*, 1881, vol. 2, Despatch No. 2, Beyrout, 14 January 1881.

28. A revolutionary leaflet in Arabic, apparently printed in London, found its way even to far away Baghdad of those days, entreating the Arabs and "the Christians of Syria" to unite and emancipate the "Arab Ummah" from the Turkish aggressors. It is entitled "Proclamation of the Arab Ummah"—from the Society for the Protection of the Rights of the Arab Millet (*Jam'iyyah Ḥifz Ḥuquq al-Millah al-'Arabiyyah*) and is dated "17 *Rabi' al-Thani*, A.H. 1298" [19 March 1881]. Great Britain, Foreign Office, 195/1370; Turkey, (Baghdad), 1881, vol. 1, Despatch No, 21 of 20 May 1881, from Political Agent and Consul General Chichele Plowden to the Earl of Granville.

designs without fear of detection. On the other hand, I have been informed that the revolutionary society was the cause of the formation of the 'Society of Good Intentions;' that His Highness Midḥat Pasha was secretly a member of it, and that he established the latter Society purposely for the promotion of the former. He is stated, moreover, to be still in communication with it, although now at Smyrna, and that it is partly at his instigation, through his secret agents, that the placards in question have appeared in Syria. I am, however, unable to verify these accusations against him....

"That the Syrians are capable of a combined insurrectionary movement, without Foreign aid, against the Turks, I do not consider at all likely. The great number of sects and races that exists in Syria would prevent this...; and the inhabitants of the Lebanon who live in comparative liberty and contentment, would be reluctant to join in an insurrection of the Syrians. The Placards therefore, that have lately appeared may be looked upon merely as an expression of disaffection without more dangerous forebodings...."[29]

The importance of these placards should not be exaggerated. "I am glad to inform your Excellencey," to quote again Dickson, writing from Beirut to the British Ambassador in Constantinople, G.T. Goschen, in his above-mentioned despatch on 3 July 1880, "that very little effect has been produced on the minds of the people of Beyrout, by the publication of the Placards in question. The feeling evinced is more one of curiosity as to their origin than anything else. However, they may be taken as an indication of the times and that the Moslem as well as the Christian has at last begun to raise his cry against Turkish misrule."[30]

29. Great Britain, Foreign Office, 195/1368, Despatch No. 3, Confidential, Beyrout, 17 January 1881.

30. It is of much interest to note that an earlier "cry against Turkish misrule" in the *vilayet* of Syria, perhaps the earliest recorded, was raised in 1858. It is found in a Report sent by J. H. Skene, British Consul at Aleppo to the British Embassy in Constantinople of 31 July 1858. "It would also appear," Skene wrote, "that the Mussulman population of Northern Syria harbours hopes of a separation from the Ottoman Empire and the formation of a new Arabian State under the sovereignty of the Shereefs of Mecca.... " Great Britain, Foreign Office, 78/1389, No. 20 of 31 July 1858, enclosure in No. 33 of 7 August 1858. These lines may seem startling at first sight but if Skene's Report is read carefully, it becomes clear that "a seditious spirit against the constituted authorities" in Aleppo had existed for some time leading to "some

Between 1882 and 1885 two new developments completely unconnected with the events in the *vilayet* of Syria stirred up, in an unexpected way, anti-Turkish sentiment in that province: the revolt of 'Urrābī Pasha in Egypt and the rebellion of the Mahdī in the Sudan. The despatches of British Consuls in Damascus and Jerusalem contain several references to the profound sympathy of the "Musulman population" for both 'Urrābī Pasha and the Mahdī — the former as "the champion of the Arab Musulman race, upon whose success they based possibilities affecting the future of their race other than the mere repelling of the invasion of Egypt;"[31] and the latter as "not only the champion of the Mohammedan religion but as an opponent of the Turkish Government...."[32]

About a year later, on 7 March 1885, the French Consul in Damascus, T. Gilbert, reported in a telegram to the Ministry of Foreign Affairs in Paris that according to confidential information he had received, an understanding ("entente") between the Mahdi and the Chiefs of the great tribes of the (Arabian) desert had been confirmed. The principal conditions of this "Entente" would be first the expulsion of the Turks from the Arab countries ("expulsion des Turcs des pays Arabes") and then the proclamation of (their) autonomy in the form of a federation....[33]

But these rumblings, complaints and clandestine expressions of rebelliousness against Turkish misgovernment should not be

excitement" and a number of "incidents". The anti-Turkish sentiment thus generated was caused partly by some of the leading inhabitants who, according to Skene, "considered themselves aggrieved in their private interests by its local government" and partly by the encouragement and support that Arab insurgents received from "the survivors of the Janissaries, who numbered no less than 25,000 affiliated in Aleppo when that corporation was suppressed in 1826." Moreover, the "hatred felt by the Arab population of this part of Syria (was) for Turkish troops and officials in general whom they regard as degenerate Mahometans," showing once more the importance of the religious factor in Arab-Turkish relations. Such Arab "revolutionary movements" against the Turkish authorities can in no way be construed as evidence of the existence of Arab nationalism but they must be regarded as an expression of intense disaffection of the population towards those authorities. I am grateful to Mr. Norman Lewis for calling my attention to the above-mentioned despatch.

31. Great Britain, Foreign Office, 195/1412, *Turkey*, Despatch No. 7, Jerusalem, 23 September 1882; British Consul N. Moore to the Earl of Dufferin.

32. Great Britain, Foreign Office, 195/1480, *Turkey*, Despatch No. 16, Damascus, 19 April 1884; Acting British Consul General John Dickson to the Earl of Dufferin.

33. Paris, Ministère des Affaires Étrangères, *Turquie*, Damas, vol. 14.

interpreted as widespread and organized attempts on the part of the Muslim Arabs to break away from the Ottoman Empire and establish an independent Arab State. The enlightened Muslim leaders, moreover, were not blind to the ambitions and interests of the Great Powers in the Ottoman Empire and feared lest any further weakening of that Empire should lead to the occupation of the Arab lands in the Near East by one or more than one of those Powers. It must be recalled, in this connection, that Western colonial expansion in Africa and Asia was in full tide between 1844 and 1900. Consequently, Turks and Muslim Arabs alike had no thought of either destroying Ottoman sovereignty which was Muslim sovereignty or seceding from the Ottoman Empire which was "the only powerful Islamic Empire that remained." All that they asked for were political, economic and social *reforms*. The "extremists," i.e., the "revolutionaries" among the Arabs asked for autonomy or independence *within* the Ottoman Empire.

Leading Muslims, as well as the vast majority of the inhabitants of the Arab Near East, remained loyal to the Ottoman Government. Thus, the over-worked phrase "Arab Awakening" was originally an awakening to the abuses, the corruption and the despotism of the Turkish regime and a desire to reform it, i.e., to put an end to misgovernment, to demand for the Arabs equal rights with the Turks and a greater measure of political freedom and civil liberty. The alternative of establishing an independent sovereign Arab State as a result of separation from or extinction of the Ottoman Empire did not occur to the vast majority of the Muslims either as desirable or as possible. Thus, while the Christians of Lebanon wanted political reforms and political independence, the Muslim Arab intellectuals in the rest of the Ottoman Empire sought to cleanse and to strengthen the Empire by advocating administrative reforms and a return to the purity of Islam and Muslim institutions. They were apostles of Pan-Islamism. The best known among them were Shaikh Muḥammad 'Abduh (1849-1905), 'Abd al-Raḥman al-Kawākibī (1849-1902), and Muḥammad Rashīd Riḍa (1865-1935), the founder of the periodical *Al-Manār*.[34]

34. Almost always the name of Jamal al-Din al-Afghani is associated with the above-mentioned Arab Muslim reformers. But Jamal al-Din was not an Arab and, in all probability, was not an Afghani but a Persian. He had a great personal ambition for religious leadership and political power. He acquired much fame in the Muslim world among Persians, Indians, Arabs, and Turks, particularly in religious and political circles, by preaching political freedom

Muḥammad 'Abduh, called by H. A. R. Gibb "the greatest of the real reformers of Islam," wanted to free the mind from the fetters of tradition. He believed that "the disease" of the Muslims was in the first place their ignorance of their own religion, and secondly, the despotism of their Muslim rulers.[35] His program included "the purification of Islam from corrupting influences and practices" and "the defense of Islam against European influences and Christian attacks."[36] Both Al-Afghānī and Muḥammad 'Abduh opposed European control of Muslim lands and "the pervasive influences of European culture and material civilization."

As to Al-Kawākibī, he has left us two remarkable books which describe his ideas and ideals for the revival of the Muslims in general and the Arab world in particular: the *Umm al-Qurā* and the *Ṭabā'i' al-Istibdād*. Although his teachings about the regeneration of Islam and the unification of the world of Islam do not differ basically from all the exponents of Pan-Islamism, he "drew a sharp distinction between the Arab and the non-Arab Moslem peoples" and laid particular emphasis on "the special place to which Arabs were entitled in the fortunes of Islam by their language and by their descent."[37]

Only the Arabs of Arabia were prepared to renew the glories of Islam, according to Al-Kawākibī, for they have been saved by Divine Providence from becoming morally corrupt as the Turks

and independence for all Muslims and by vehemently condeming Western imperialism. He maintained that unity among the Muslims was a natural and logical necessity for their protection and, indeed, their very existence. In 1884, joined by his friend and pupil, Muhammad 'Abduh, he began the publication (in Paris) of Al-'Urwah al-Wuthqa [The indissoluble bond] "with the object of arousing the Muslim peoples to the need of uniting forces against Western aggression and exploitation."

See Charles C. Adams, *Islam and Modernism in Egypt: A Study of the Modern Reform Movement Inaugurated by Muhammad 'Abduh* (London: Oxford University Press, 1933), pp. 1-13; *Al-Manār* (Cairo), vol. 8 (17 August 1905): 55. Hourani, *Arabic Thought in the Liberal Age*, pp. 108-29. For a most illuminating book of previously unpublished Persian and Arabic documents on the life and activities of Jamal al-Din al-Afghani, see Iraj Afshar and Asghar Mahdavi, eds., *Documents Inédits Concernant Seyyed Jamal al-Din Afghani* (Tehran: Tehran University Press, 1963).

35. *Al-Manār* (Cairo), vol. 8, pt. 12 (17 August 1905): 465, and vol. 8, 23 (26 January 1906): 893.

36. Hamilton A. R. Gibb, *Modern Trends in Islam* (Chicago, 1947), p. 33.

37. See Antonius, *The Arab Awakening*, pp. 95-98.

had become.[38] But his bitter attacks against the Turks does not make him an Arab nationalist. The Ottoman sultans, he believed, were not good Muslims because they put their political and imperial interests before the interests of Islam.[39] If he praises the Arabs and glorifies their superiority over the Turks, it is because the Arabs are better Muslims and they know how to protect Islam and defend it.[40]

The fundamental character of Rashīd Riḍa's reforms, which he preached through the pages of his influential *Al-Manār*, followed the general line of his two predecessors: it was religious. He tried "to prove the suitability of Islam as a religious system... and the practicability of the Divine Law as an instrument of government." But it was first necessary to have "a thorough reform of the religion of Islam." The nationalists and political reformers in Egypt and Turkey were, he believed, "atheists and infidels because religion is not fundamental to their ideas of nationality."[41]

Towards the end of the nineteenth century, the internal situation began to deteriorate rapidly. Discontent, corruption and anarchy spread with alarming speed.[42] The following two docu-

38. 'Abd al-Raḥman al-Kawakibi, *Umm al-Qura* [Mecca], pp. 238-40.

39. Ibid., pp. 228-31.

40. Ibid., pp. 217-22.

41. See Adams, *Islam and Modernism in Egypt*, pp. 181-87.

In recent years, Shaykh Rifā'a Rāfi' al-Ṭahṭawī (1801-1873) has been included in the above mentioned group of Arab reformers. Shaykh Rifa'a was a young Egyptian who became a great admirer of French ideas and the French Enlightenment, having spent five years in Paris (1826-1831). He expressed this admiration in a book which he wrote upon his return to Egypt, *Takhlis al-Ibriz fi Talkhis Bariz*. But Ṭahṭawi was neither a reformer nor a "liberal revolutionary." He was primarily interested to modernize Egypt and Egyptian society. French Enlightenment was not, however, a substitute for Muslim orthodoxy—and Ṭahṭawī was a good Muslim. There is no evidence of any change in his attitude or any transformation in his outlook concerning Islam. He marvels at the strange and mysterious things which he saw and learned in France, but still, France was to him a land of heresy and stubbornness ("*diyār Kufr wa 'inād*"). Indeed, he believed that most of the inhabitants of the Western countries were heretics; so were, also, for that matter, the inhabitants of the United States. Rifā'a Rāfi' al-Ṭahṭawī *Takhlis al-Ibriz fī Talkhis Barīz* [The quintessence of Paris] (Cairo, A.H. 1250 [A.D. 1872]), pp. 5, 7, 15-16. See also Jamal Mohammed Ahmed, *The Intellectual Origins of Egyptian Nationalism* (London: Oxford University Press, 1960), p. 11.

42. "The state of the law courts is worse than it ever was before, and complaints of want of justice are continually being made." Great Britain,

ments are significant. On 24 August 1888, the French Minister of Foreign Affairs wrote the following letter to M. Guillois, the French Consul in Damascus:

"Je vous remercie des indications que vous m'avez fait parvenir par votre rapport No. 21 au sujet de symptômes de mécontentement qui paraissent s'être manifestés depuis quelques temps parmi les officiers du Corps d'armée ottomane de la Syrie. Je n'ai pas lu sans inquiétude les passages de votre dépêche dans lesquels vous envisagez la possibilité d'un mouvement plus grave auquel prendrait part les populations arabes du Vilayet. Vous avez trop bien compris pour que j'ai besoin de vous le rappeler que le maintien de l'ordre dans cette partie de l'Empire ottoman est considéré par nous comme nécessaire à tous les points de vue. . . ."[43]

The second document refers to the situation in Beirut and Damascus as "L'anarchie la plus complète," the words being those of M. de Petiteville, the French Consul General in Beirut, to M. Flourens, the French Minister of Foreign Affairs. M. Petiteville wrote in his despatch of 11 January 1888, from Beirut:

". . . Il se trouve une foule de petits complots parmi les employés subalternes de l'ancien Vilayet. Le Mutéssarref de Beyrouth est destitué, d'autres sont menacés d'un sort analogue, et ne pensent plus qu'à mettre en sûreté le pécule amassé aux dépens des administrés. En un mot, c'est l'anarchie la plus complète qui règne ici et à Damas."

And again in his despatch of 9 February he stated:

"Ainsi que j'ai eu l'honneur de l'écrire précédemment à votre Excellence, l'anarchie règne ici — complète. Au sérail, le pouvoir est partagé entre trois hommes qui se le disputent; le Moutéssarref d'une part qui n'est pas sûr du lendemain, car il a été relevé de ses fonctions par la S. Porte; le cadi d'autre part — qui s'est arrogé un pouvoir discrétionnaire et enfin le Gouverneur militaire de la Place, Osman Pacha qui cherche à brimer

Foreign Office, 195/1365, "*State of Affairs of Syria*," Despatch No. 46, dated Beyrout, 5 October 1881. See also Great Britain, Foreign Office, 195/1306, Despatch dated Damascus, 10 February 1880, and Foreign Office, 195/1369, Despatch No. 60, dated Beyrout, 19 December 1881.

43. France, Archives du Ministère des Affaires Étrangères, *Turquie*, vol. 14, Damas. 1855-1888.

l'autorité civile et qui trouve l'occasion opportune de frapper sur l'élément Chrétien."[44]

At the beginning of February 1894, M. Paul Cambon, the French Ambassador in Constantinople, in his despatch to M. Casimir-Perrier, minister of Foreign Affairs, in connection with the Armenian Question, reported that the situation was not particular to Armenia, but that from one end of the Empire to the other, the Greeks, the Albanians, the Arabs complained of lack of justice, of the corruption of Government officials and of the insecurity of life.[45]

What is often omitted or ignored in a study of the situation in the Ottoman Empire towards the end of the nineteenth century is the fact that the bitterest and most vehement attacks on that Empire came from the Turks themselves and their leading reformers. It is not within the scope of this Essay to discuss here the activities of the Young Turks against the despotism and injustices of Sultan 'Abdul Ḥamīd and his government. As shall be seen presently, it was they who finally overthrew 'Abdul Ḥamīd in 1908-09 and restored the Constitution of 1876 — a Constitution which produced little impression amongst the Arabs, according to the despatch of the British Ambassador, Sir G. Lowther, to Sir Edward Grey on 17 February 1909,[46] for "they seemed sceptical of reform, tolerating Turkish rule as a Moslem rule, and harbouring some veneration for the Sultan as the religious head of the Ottoman Empire." After 1890 the young Turks intensified their attacks on 'Abdul Ḥamīd. There are two Reports, in French, among the Private Papers of Sir P. Currie, the British Ambassador in Constantinople.[47] The first is dated 27 January 1894 and says that two days earlier, new seditious placards had been stuck in the two great mosques of *Sulaymāniyeh* and *al-Fatiḥ*. The second was written on 9 November 1895 and reports that on 7 November, great placards were glued on the doors of the principal mosques of Istanbul as well as on the door of the Chamber of Ceremonies at the Palace of Yildiz, attacking in violent language Sultan 'Abdul Ḥamīd and

44. France, Archives du Ministère des Affaires Étrangères, *Turquie*, Beyrouth, 1888.

45. See Contenson, *Les réformes en Turquie d'Asie*, p. 3.

46. See Appendix E.

47. Great Britain, Foreign Office, 800/113, *Reports*, 1893-96 (in French).

his government.[48] It seems that one day before these placards were stuck up, the Sultan found in his work room ("cabinet de travail") an anonymous letter warning him that if he did not follow without delay the public announcement which would be given to him and to the population of the Capital (a reference to the placards which appeared a day later) his end would be near. The Report adds that general discontent was continuously increasing. In coffee-houses, in street-cars, on board ships and in other public places, people were not afraid to disparage, in a loud voice, the Sultan and his government. At the turn of the century, when 'Abdul Ḥamīd celebrated, on 31 August 1900, the twenty-fifth anniversary of his accession to the throne with great pomp and ceremony, Turkey's cup of iniquity was already overflowing. The die had been cast and the day of reckoning was approaching.

During the first years of the twentieth century, the existence of the "Arab Question" became known here and there in the Western world. *Le réveil de la nation arabe*, published in French, in Paris, by Négib Azoury, in 1905, contained the text of a strongly worded manifesto addressed to the Great Powers by the "Arabian National Committee." This manifesto stated with much exaggeration and a great flight of imagination: "A great pacific change is on the eve of occurring in Turkey. The Arabs, whom the Turks tyrannized over only by keeping them divided on insignificant questions of ritual and religion, have become conscious of their national, historic, and racial homogeneity, and wish to detach themselves from the worm-eaten Ottoman trunk in order to form themselves into an independent State. This new Arab Empire will extend to its natural frontiers, from the valleys of the Tigris and Euphrates to the Isthmus of Suez, and from the Mediterranean to the Sea of Oman. It will governed by the constitutional and liberal monarchy of an Arabian Sultan. The present Vilayet of the Hedjaz, together with the territory of Medina, will form an independent empire whose sovereign will be at the same time the religious

48. "Ces placards portent en susbtance ceci: "O toi Abdul Hamid, indigne de régner, tes actes infâmes, ta tyrannie, ta politique personnelle ont fait déborder la coupe. Ton gouvernement n'a plus ni dignité, ni influence, ni puissance. La nation est devenue le jouet du monde civilisé et l'Empire s'écroule, de jour en jour. Tes peuples te maudissent; le carnage désole nos villes et campagnes et a amené partout le désolation, la désespoir et la famine. Pendant qu'il en est temps encore et que tu as encore un peu de sagesse, hâte-toi de descendre du trône, si non tu ne tarderas pas à être mis en pièces." Ibid.

Khaliph of all the Mohammedans. Thus one great difficulty, the separation of the civil and the religious powers in Islam, will have been solved for the greater good of all."[49]

But it was the "Young Turks," successors to the "New Ottomans," who were stirred to action to save the Ottoman Empire from utter disintegration and ruin. Much has been written about the genesis of the Young Turk movement.[50] Their aim was to establish a Parliamentary government in the Empire by restoring Midhat Pasha's Constitution of 1876 and to put an end to the interference of European Powers in that Empire. The following brief account is worth quoting here:[51]

> "Driven underground by 'Abdul-Ḥamīd in the seventies, the movement sprang up again in the closing years of the century among the Turkish expatriates in Europe. In 1902 the first Young Turkish Congress met in Paris.[52] There and then the

49. English translation, in Lothrop Stoddard, *The New World of Islam* (London, 1921), pp. 143-44. For the original French text, see Négib Azoury, *Le réveil de la nation arabe dans l'Asie turque, en présence des intérêts et des rivalités des puissances étrangères, de la Curie romaine et du Patriarcat œcuménique* (Paris: Plon, 1905), pp. i-iv.

Négib Azoury was a Maronite Christian with a French education and with strong French sympathies. He could neither speak nor write on behalf of Muslim Arabs. He, of course, denounced the Turks and praised the Arabs. But his writings do indicate an awakening of political consciousness among certain Arab intellectuals. "In 1904 he founded a *Ligue de la Partie arabe*. . . . The activities of the League, if in need it ever really existed, were limited to issuing manifestos. Later, he published in Paris a short-lived monthly periodical, *L'Indépendance arabe* (1907-8)." Hourani, *Arabic Thought in the Liberal Age*, pp. 277-78.

50. See Great Britain, Foreign Office, *British Documents on the Origins of the War*, 5: 248-62, 272-307; Wade Dewood David, *European Diplomacy in the Near Eastern Question* (Urbana: University of Illinois Press, 1940), pp. 60-61; Eliot Grinnell Mears, *Modern Turkey: A Politico-Economic Interpretation, 1908-1923* (New York, 1924), pp. 476-90; E. F. Knight, *The Awakening of Turkey: A History of the Turkish Revolution* (London, 1909), pp. 70-94, and Jurji Zaidan in *Al-Hilāl* (Cairo), vol. 17 (1908): 3-31. See also Ahmet Bedevi Kuran, *Inkilap Tarihimiz ve Jon Türkler* [A history of the revolution and the Young Turks] (Istanbul, 1945) and *Inkilap Tarihimiz ve Ittihad ve Terakki* [A history of the revolution and the Union and Progress] (Istanbul 1948); Tarik Z. Tunaya, *Turkiyede Siyasi Partiler, 1859-1952* [The Political parties in Turkey, 1859-1952] (Istanbul, 1952), p. 91, and Ramsaur, *The Young Turks*.

51. See David, *European Diplomacy and the Near Eastern Question*, pp. 60-61.

52. "As the result of differences on the method to be pursued, the delegates to the Congress split into two factions. The Turkish delegates bolted and organized the 'League of Union and Progress' while the rest, composed of representatives of the disaffected minorities, organized themselves as the 'League of

fundamentally nationalistic spirit of the old movement reasserted itself with redoubled vigor among the Turkish delegates, who now styled themselves the 'League of Union and Progress.' (L.U.P.)[53] In the face of the steady political and economic encroachments of the European Powers upon the independence of their Fatherland and in the face of the increasing separatist tendencies among the minorities in the Empire,[54] the L.U.P. gradually and inevitably assumed the leadership of the movement. By 1907, it succeeded in galvanizing the ranks of all the Young Turks for action. For the eventful years of 1905-08 gave this revolutionary movement a tremendous impetus. The relentless Macedonian Crusades, the naval demonstrations, the recrudescence of Russian activity in the Near East, the Anglo-Russian rapprochements, and the recurring rumors of dismemberment had terrified the Turkish patriots, who now came to regard the despot on the Golden Horn as the virtual prisoner of the 'Intriguing Powers."

Consequently, in January 1907, the moderate wing of the Young Turks, the "Union Libérale" declared publicly for the principle of "The Ottoman Empire for the Ottomans" and demanded of Europe complete abstention from any further interference in

Private Initiative and Decentralization' (better known as the *Union Libérale*) under the leadership of Prince Sabahiddin, the exiled nephew of Abdulhamid. The former (L.U.P.) advocated the transformation of the whole State system into a compact unit in order to save the Empire from dismemberment; the latter (Union Libérale) proposed to achieve the same end through decentralization, a system of communal and religious particularism. See Ahmed Niyazi, *Khawāṭir Niyazi* p. 29; *Al-Manār*, p. 852 ff.; Ismail Kemal, *The Memoirs of Ismail Kemal Bey* (London, 1920), pp. 306-8; G. Hanotaux, *La Politique de l'Equilibre, 1907-1911*, pp. 135-6, 319; A. Hamilton, *Problems of the Middle East* (London, 1909), pp. 11-13; D. von Mikusch, *Gasi Mustafa Kemal*, pp. 43-45." Ibid., p. 60, n. 4.

53. "The term 'Young Turks' denotes the body of reformers within the Ottoman Empire, while the term 'League of Union and Progress' usually abbreviated into L.U.P., designates the organization of Turkish liberals that became the driving power behind the Revolution. Likewise, the term 'Central Committee of Union and Progress,' more frequently designated as C.U.P., refers to the inner circle of the L.U.P. Up to the autumn of 1908, there were several C.U.P.'s or 'Committees.' " Ibid., p. 60, n. 5.

54. "The L.U.P. published in Paris an official organ, *Mechveret*, through which it propagated revolutionary ideas. Its distinctly nationalistic and anti-European tone drew the admiration of Abdulhamid himself. Tahsin Pasha, *Abdulhamid ve Yildiz Hatiralari* (Istanbul, 1921), p. 295. Cf. Driault et l'Héritier, *Histoire diplomatique de la Grèce*, V, 2-3." Ibid., pp. 60-61, n. 6. See also Ramsaur, *The Young Turks*, pp. 23-37.

Turkish affairs. In December, the second Young Turks Congress met in Paris under the leadership of the L.U.P. and adopted a "Declaration of Principles" that was clearly nationalistic, anti-European, and revolutionary. It openly advocated rebellion against the Sultan to save the Empire "from the venomous clutches of the greedy Powers," and projected a military uprising for the spring of 1909.[55]

The Young Turk movement had branches in different parts of the Ottoman Empire.[56] Egypt was one of the important centres of the Young Turk activities. Its distance from Constantinople, and particularly because it was under British administration, made the country a refuge for men with enlightened political ideas fearing the iron hand of 'Abdul Ḥamīd. There is evidence that in 1899 a printing office was opened in Cairo by two members of the Young Turk party for the purpose of publishing a newspaper called "*El-Qānūn al-Asāsī*" in the interests of their propaganda.[57] The nerve centre of the movement was the secret society of the

55. In addition to the Young Turks Committee, there were other non-Muslim and non-Turkish revolutionary Committees: "En 1907, les groupes arméniens, macédoniens, bulgares, serbes, grecs, bosniaques et herzegoviniens se réunirent de nouveau à Genève et exprimèrent le vœu de voir proclamer l'autonomie de la Macédonie, de l'Arménie, de l'Albanie, de la Bosnie et de l'Herzegovine, formant ensemble une Confédération Balkanique avec une constitution unique pour tous, y compris les Turcs. Ces idées flottaient dans l'air, elles échauffaient l'âme de tous les chrétiens d'Orient." Traudafil G. Djuvara, *Cent projets de partage de la Turquie* (1281-1913) Paris: Alcan, 1914), p. 503, citing *Le Journal de Genève* of 15 February 1905, "le Prince Sabaheddine adressa aux Chancelleries un Mémoire qui finissait par ce cri patriotique: L'Empire Ottoman aux Ottomans. C'était la devise de la *Turquie Libérale*, qui devait assurer 'la paix universelle.' C'était vraiment trop beau; six ans après, nous eûmes la mêlée balkanique."

56. Of the centers outside Turkey, Paris and Geneva were the most important. In Geneva, the Young Turks published among other papers *The Osmanli*. In the first issue of its English Supplement, dated 15 July 1898, they wrote: "We desire that this publication should be as far as possible the organ of the legitimate claims of all Ottoman subjects irrespective of race and religion, and our demand is for those reforms needed not only in this or that part of the empire but in the empire as a whole . . . . At the end of this issue there is an article attacking 'Abdul Hamid in violent language: "Of all the Sultans who have reigned over Turkey, Abdu'l Hamid is the sole figure essentially abject."

57. Great Britain, Foreign Office, *Further Correspondence Respecting the Affairs of Egypt*, 1902, pt. 60, Document 44, p. 114, and Document 50, pp. 116-19: The Earl of Cromer to the Marquess of Lansdowne, dated Cairo, 11 and 14 April 1902.

Young Turks at Salonika, in Macedonia, where it "gained the allegiance of a considerable portion of that formidable Turkish army without whose co-operation, as the Christians in Macedonia knew well, no revolution had a chance of success." [58]

The July Revolution of 1908 put an end, temporarily, to the Ḥamidian regime.[59] 'Abdul Ḥamīd acquiesced and on 24 July restored the Constitution of 1876. There was great rejoicing among Arabs and Turks, marked with parties, receptions and daily fêtes. The words "Liberty, Equality and Fraternity" were inscribed on Turkish banners. The Arabic literature of the time in Syria, Lebanon, Iraq, and Egypt is full of panegyrics by the best poets about Sultan 'Abdul Ḥamīd for restoring the Constitution to the nation and inaugurating an era of liberty, justice, and equality.

The following eye-witness description of the reaction in Syria is worth recording here:

> "On Sunday, P. M. July 26 (1908) as we were leaving the little Aleih chapel after the English service, Consul-General Ravendal started us all with the telegraphic news that theMidḥat Constitution of 1876, which had been suppressed by Abdul Ḥamīd II for thirty two years, had now, July 23, been restored by a bloodless revolution effected by the Young Turkey Party....
>
> "The whole empire burst forth in universal rejoicing. The press spoke out. Public meetings were held, cities and towns decorated; Moslems were seen embracing Christians and Jews, and inviting one another to receptions and feasts.... The universal voice of the Moslems was... 'Now we are brethren and we can live in peace. We shall henceforth know each other only as Ottomans. Long live liberty! long live the army! Long live the Sultan!"
>
> "The pent-up feelings of the populace everywhere burst forth in loud hurrahs in the public streets. Syria has never seen such rejoicing. Can it be true? Will it last? were questions in all

58. Knight, *The Awakening of Turkey*, p. 93.

59. It may be of interest to state that one of the modern means of communication, the telegraph, which had recently been introduced in Turkey, played an important role in the success of the Revolution. The orders which the Sultan sent telegraphically from Yildiz against the C.U.P. became immediately known to the Committee because it had among its members "most of the telegraph and railway employees." Talaat, one of the principal leaders of the Revolution, was the secretary-general of the Telegraph Bureau at Monastir. 'Abdu'l Ḥamid himself was threatened telegraphically that if he did not restore the Constitution of 1876, the army of Salonika would march on Constantinople.

mouths. It was startling to those who had left Syria, early in July, under the old regime to be greeted in New York harbour with the news of free institutions in Turkey. It seemed too good to be true, and for weeks we here, foreigners and Syrians alike, seemed to be living in a dream. The Golden Age seemed to be dawning."[60]

The popularity of Abdul Ḥamīd suddenly soared to a great height.[61] *The Illustrated London News* of 22 August had a photograph of Abdul Ḥamīd in his carriage at the first "Selamlik" after the granting of the Constitution, with the caption: "Once Abdul the Damned, now Abdul the Blessed: The Sultan's New Popularity."[62]

The first meeting of the new Parliament took place on Thursday, 17 December, 1908 in the presence of the Sultan and the Ottoman princes.[63] There was a total of 260 members, 119 of whom

60. Henry Harris Jessup, *Fifty-three Years in Syria*, 2 vols. (New York: Fleming H. Revell, 1910), 2: 785-87.

The Official British Extract from the Annual Report for Turkey for the year 1908 says: "It would hardly be possible to find a more violent contrast than that between the Reports on Syria which reached this Embassy up to the end of July and those sent during the remainder of the year.

"For the first seven months one finds nothing but complaints of every kind of injustice, venality, and corruption, from the Vali (the chief offender of all) downwards. Public security hardly existed. Smuggling was rampant, carried on as it was under a well-organized system.

"Nazim Pasha, after only four months of office, has succeeded in keeping an effective control on the various Government Departments, and in improving the efficiency of the police and gendarmerie, with the result that the administration of the vilayet has been satisfactory, order has been maintained, and the flourishing business in contraband of arms, tobacco, and tombac stopped, and this without recourse having been had to the military authorities." Great Britain, Foreign Office, *British Documents on the Origins of the War*, 5: 303.

61. "At one time, the unpopularity of the Sultan was such that he ceased to attend the ordinary Friday prayers—the ceremony known as Selamlik at the Hamidie Mosque. Since the granting of the Constitution all that is changed, and the Sultan's guard have now to protect him from the enthusiasm of his people. . . ." *The Illustrated London News*, 22 August 1908, p. 264.

62. Ibid.

63. For an account of the Revolution of 1908, the meeting of the new Parliament and the speech of 'Abdul Hamid at the opening of Parliament, see George Stitt, *A Prince of Arabia: The Emir Shereef Ali Haidar* (London, 1948), pp. 95-101. "Hunched and haggard, he (Sultan 'Abdul Hamid) shuffled slowly to the Imperial Box and gazed down upon the House, looking pale and nervous. All rose and saluted. 'Abdul' Hamid replied, and then signed to his First Secretary to read the speech from the throne . . . ." Among other things, 'Abdul

were Turks and 72 Arabs. By religions, 214 were Muslims, 42 Christian and 4 Jews. The Decentralization Party was represented by 35 members, the great majority of whom were non-Turks. Aḥmad Riḍa Bey was elected President. The vice-presidents were a Greek, Aristidi Pasha, an Albanian, Nedchia Draga, and an Arab, Rūḥī 'Abd al-Hādī. But 'Abdul Ḥamīd, almost from the very first day, set about to get rid of the Young Turks, the Constitution and the New Parliament. On 13 April 1909, there was an attempt at a counter-revolution in Constantinople.

However, the army in Macedonia, under the command of Shawkat Pasha, was ready. It marched on the capital and laid siege to the Sultan's palace, Yildiz. The Parliament and the Senate met and voted the deposition of 'Abdul Ḥamīd in favor of his brother, Muḥammad Rashād, as Muḥammad V.[64] Immediately afterwards, on the evening of 27 April 1909, 'Abdul Ḥamīd accompanied by some members of his *harem* and by a small retinue was exiled to Salonika and interned in Villa Alatini on the outskirts of the city.[65] Thus passed into history the last absolutist Sultan of the Ottoman Empire, the last "Shadow of God" which fell upon a medieval and a legendary East — and with him ended the old destiny of the Turks which had been linked for nearly six hundred years with that of Asia and the peoples of Islam.

Hamid said: ". . . The intellectual progress of the people having reached the desired standard, we have acquired the conviction that Parliament should once more assemble as a guarantee of the present and future prosperity of our country. . . . Our resolution to govern the country in conformity with the Law of the Constitution is irrevocable (cheers). May it please the Almighty to grant that your endeavours shall be crowned with success and that our Fatherland shall enjoy every blessing. God aid us in our task." Ibid., pp. 99-101.

64. The Shaikh al-Islam supported the decision by a *fatwa* based on the *Shari'a*.

65. He requested to be allowed to spend the rest of his life in the Cheraghan Palace, on the European shore of the Bosphorus. But this request was refused. In 1912 he was transferred back to Constantinople to the Palace of Beylerbey on the Bosphorus, where he died on 10 February 1918.

For a personal narrative of 'Abdul Hamid and his last hours at Yildiz, see *Babam Abdülhamid* [My father, Abdul Hamid] (Istanbul, 1960) written by his daughter Ayşe Osmanoglu.

CHAPTER FIVE

THE EMERGENCE OF ARAB NATIONALISM

PART ONE — UNDER THE YOUNG TURKS, 1909-1914

WE HAVE SEEN in the previous two chapters that although the Arabs had many grievances against the Turkish Government, they entertained no idea of separation from the Ottoman Empire. Their main emphasis was on reforms; and even when they severely criticized the Sultanate, they remained loyal to the Caliphate. However, at the beginning of the twentieth century, between 1908 and 1918, when the Young Turks were in power, Arab-Turkish relations suffered a great strain and underwent a marked change. The Arabs continued to ask fo reforms but the main object of these reforms was Arab autonomy in their own Provinces and within the framework of the Ottoman Empire. The establishment of complete Arab independence and Arab national sovereignty was an afterthought.

"The Young Turk revolution of 1908," wrote Uriel Heyd, "promised equality to all Ottoman subjects without distinction of religion and race. These promises, however, were neve carried out."[1] This failure made the break between the Arabs and Turks inevitable.[2]

1. Uriel Heyd, *Foundations of Turkish Nationalism: The Life and Teachings of Ziya Gökalp* (London: Luzac and Harvill Press, 1950), p. 130.

The American Ambassador, Henry Morgenthau, says of the Young Turks that they "were not a government; they were really an irresponsible party, a kind of secret society, which, by intrigue, intimidation and assassination, had obtained most of the offices of state." For an elaboration of his views on the Young Turks, see Henry Morgenthau, *Ambassador Morgenthau's Story* (New York, 1918), pp. 11-19.

2. "Les Jeunes-Turcs ne surent même pas gagner la confiance des Arabes qui constituaient l'élément musulman le plus nombreux de l'Empire. Pendant toute cette période, les tribus de la Syrie et de la Mésopotamie étaient en effervescence continuelle, et le mouvement autonomiste grandissait parmi la jeunesse intellectuelle arabe." André Mandelstam, *Le sort de l'Empire ottoman* (Lausanne: Payot, 1917), p. 30.

Thus the years 1908 and, more especially, 1909 were decisive years in the destiny of the Ottoman Empire.[3]

3. "It was at Aleppo that I made acquaintance with the Turkey which had come into being on July 24, 1908. Even among those whose sympathies were deeply engaged on behalf of the new order, there were not many Europeans who, in January 1909, had any clue to public opinion outside Constantinople and Salonica. The events of the six stirring months that had just elapsed had yet to be heard and apprehended, and no sooner had I landed in Beyrout than I began to shed European formulas and to look for the Asiatic value of the great catchwords of revolution. In Aleppo, sitting at the feet of many masters, who ranged down all the social grades from the high official to the humblest labourer for hire, I learnt something of the hopes and fears, the satisfaction, the bewilderment, and the indifference of Asia. The populace had shared in the outburst of enthusiasm which had greeted the granting of the constitution—a moment of unbridled expectation when in the brief transport of universal benevolence, it seemed as if the age-long problems of the Turkish empire had been solved with a stroke of the pen; they had journeyed back from that Utopia to find that human nature remained much as it had been before. The public mind was unhinged; men were obsessed with a sense of change, perplexed because change was slow to come, and alarmed lest it should spring upon them unawares. The relaxation of the rule of fear had worked in certain directions with immediate effect, but not invariably to increase of security. True, there was a definite gain of personal liberty. The spies had disappeared from official quarters, and with them the exiles, who had been condemned by 'Abdu'l Hamid, on known or unknown pretexts, to languish helplessly in the provincial capitals. Everywhere a daily press had sprung into existence and foreign books and papers passed unhindered through the post. The childish and exasperating restrictions with which the Sultan had fettered his Christian subjects had fallen away. The Armenians were no longer tied to the spot whereon they dwelt; they could, and did, travel where they pleased. The namusiyeh, the identification certificate, had received the annual government stamp without delay, and without need of bribes. In every company, Christian and Moslem, tongues were unloosed in outspoken criticism of official dealings, but it was extremely rare to find in these freely vented opinions anything of a constructive nature. The government was still, to the bulk of the population, a higher power, disconnected from those upon whom it exercised its will. You might complain of its lack of understanding just as you cursed the hailstorm that destroyed your crops, but you were in no way answerable for it, nor would you attempt to control or advise it, any more than you would offer advice to the hail cloud. Many a time have I searched for some trace of the Anglo-Saxon acceptance of a common responsibility in the problems that beset the State, a sense the germs of which exist in the Turkish village community and in the tribal system of the Arab and the Kurd; it never went beyond an embryonic application to small local matters, and the answers I received resembled, mutatis mutandis, that of Fattuh when I questioned him as to the part he had played in the recent general election. 'Your Excellency knows that I am a carriage-driver, what have I to do with government? But I can tell you that the new government is no better than the old. Look now at Aleppo; have we a juster law? Wallah, no!" Gertrude Lowthian Bell, *Amurath to Amurath* (London: Heinemann, 1911), pp. 3-5.

There is no evidence however, that the Young Turks came to power with the avowed intention of ignoring Islam and the non-Turkish elements in the Ottoman Empire and of embarking on a policy of Turkification. An official and authoritative publication has given the following clear summary of the situation:

"The Committee of Union and Progress were not Nationalists to begin with, chiefly because they ignored the nationality problems of the Ottoman Empire. Their primary aim was to maintain the integrity of the Empire, especially in Europe; and in this they agreed with 'Abdul Ḥamīd and all previous rulers of Turkey. They only differed as to the means, for, while 'Abdul Ḥamīd believed in despotism at home and a balance of jealousy among the European Powers, the Committee of Union and Progress held that Turkey's best safeguard was internal strength, and the best source of strength, political liberty. Their ideas of liberty were drawn from the French Revolution. 'Liberty, Equality, and Fraternity' would be proclaimed; all inhabitants of the Empire would rally to the State as free Ottoman citizens, just as Picards and Marseillais and Alsatians rallied to the French Republic after 1789; and the question of Nationality would solve itself.

"This actually happened during the first six weeks after the proclamation of the Constitution in 1908. Men of all creeds and races embraced each other in the streets. But, then, they drew apart again and considered how they might turn the new regime to their own advantage. The Balkan nationalities rejected the offer of a liberal Turkey altogether, and determined to take the first opportunity of completing their own unity and independence at Turkey's expense. Others, like the Arabs, the Armenians and the Constantinopolitan and Anatolian Greeks, recognized that secession was impossible, but took measures to defend their own national individuality within the Ottoman State. The Arabs formed the main opposition in the new Parliament.... The Committee of Union and Progress found that the Turks were the only element in the Empire that was not opposed to centralization and had no political ideal incompatible with the Ottoman State idea. They, therefore, fell back upon their Turkish nationality, and came to think of Turkification as the natural means of achieving their ends...."[4]

4. Great Britain, Foreign Office, *Handbooks...*, No. 96 c & d, pp. 21-22.

It was not only towards the Arabs that they failed to pursue their cardinal policy of equal treatment for all races in their Empire, but the Young Turks showed equal, if not more, intransigence towards their Christian subjects in the Balkans. On 28 August 1910, Mr. A. Geary, the British Acting Consul at Monastir, wrote to Sir G. Lowther, the British Ambassador in Constantinople: "I have the honour to report to your Excellency that I have obtained from a confidential source the substance of the speech recently made at Salonica by Talaat Bey to the members of the local Committee of Union and Progress, assembled in secret conclave and am now informed that Djavid Bey's speech made in similar circumstances at Monastir substantially followed the same train of thought."

In this speech, Talaat Bey is reported to have said:

"You are aware that by the terms of the Constitution equality of Mussulman and Ghiaur was affirmed but you, one and all, know and feel that this is an unrealizable ideal. The Sheriat, our whole past history and the sentiments of hundreds of thousands of Mussulmans and even the sentiments of the Ghiaurs themselves, who stubbornly resist every attempt to Ottomanize them, present an impenetrable barrier to the establishment of real equality. We have made unsuccessful attempts to convert the Ghiaur into loyal Osmanli and all such efforts must inevitably fail, as long as the small independent States in the Balkan Peninsula remain in a position to propagate ideas of Separatism among the inhabitants of Macedonia. There can therefore be no question of equality, until we have succeeded in our task of Ottomanizing the Empire — a long and laborious task, in which I venture to predict that we shall, at length, succeed after we have at last put an end to the agitation and propaganda of the Balkan States." [5]

Nine days later, on 6 September, Sir G. Lowther wrote to Sir Edward Grey: "That the Committee have given up any idea of Ottomanizing all the non-Turkish elements by sympathetic and constitutional ways has long been manifest. To them 'Ottoman' evidently means 'Turk' and their present policy of 'Ottomanization' is one of pounding the non-Turkish elements in a Turkish mortar. It was hoped that perhaps as they became more firmly seated in

5. Great Britain, Foreign Office, *British Documents on the Origins of the War*, vol. 9, pt. 1, (No. 38) Confidential, enclosure in Great Britain, Foreign Office, 371/1014, pp. 208-9.

the saddle and effective opposition had disappeared under the pressure of the state of siege, the Committee would broaden rather than narrow their policy as regards internal administration but Talaat Bey's utterances seem to make the fulfilment of such hopes more remote." [6]

It seems that between 1909 and 1912, the leaders of the Young Turks had reached the conclusion that their Constitution could not do away with Pan-Islamism. They realized that the binding force of Pan-Islamism was much stronger than they had anticipated and it seems almost certain that "by the year 1911, the Committee of Union and Progress had definitely adopted the Pan-Islamic programme, in their foreign policy, at any rate." [7] On 27 December 1911, *The Times* (London) reported that the following decisions were among those arrived at by the Salonika Congress (1911) of the Committee of Union and Progress:

"A Congress of delegates, summoned from all the Moslem countries of the world, ought to meet annually in Constantinople, to discuss questions of interest to the Moslem world. Branches of the Committee should be formed in all Moslem countries, especially in Russia and in Persia. The Mohammedans of Russia ought to be persuaded, to make revolutionary propaganda among Russian soldiers...." [8] It has even been asserted that side by side with the Committee of Union and Progress, there was a great Pan-Islamic league, called "*Jam'iyyet Hairiyeh Hamiyeh*," the last meeting of which "was attended by five Indians." [9]

"Declarations that any real toleration by Islam of other religions and any progress of the Moslem world in the direction of European civilization were impossible are quoted by a collaborator of Sherif Pasha from the writings of a member of both these bodies, the Sheikh 'Abd al-Ḥaqq of Baghdad; and apparently the Comtist Aḥmad Riza, first President of the Ottoman Chamber of Deputies, came round to the view that the Moslem religion was the only force capable of uniting the different elements of the Ottoman Empire.... It was the duty (he held) of all Moslems to labour to maintain the integrity of the Ottoman Empire." [10] A Society

6. Ibid., 371/1014 (No. 635) Confidential, p. 207.
7. Great Britain, Foreign Office, *Handbooks...*, No. 96 a & b, p. 68.
8. Ibid., pp. 56-66.
9. Ibid., p. 68, citing *Mechroutiette* (Paris), December 1913, p. 58.
10. Ibid., pp. 68-69.

calling itself The Progress of Islam ("*Endjoman-i Terekki-Islam*") was founded in Geneva. It published (in French) its first Bulletin, in February 1913, in which it stated its purpose to be the strengthening of the ties between the divers Muslim nations and to help in their intellectual and economic progress. It made it clear that it championed the cause of Islam, defended the regime in Turkey and was at the same time violently anti-British and anti-French. A sheet in Arabic enclosed in that Bulletin speaks in glowing terms of the glories of Islam, glories which had now departed and concludes that it is now the duty of every Muslim to rise to the assistance of "the country of the Caliphate" (Turkey) which was "the last refuge of Islam." [11]

But the Arab Muslim leaders doubted the sincerity of the Committee of Union and Progress, mainly for two reasons: "In the first place, the leaders of that Committee [were] without exception, Freemasons; and such religious fanaticism conflicts with the principles of the Masonic Society" [12] and, secondly, "the Salonika Jews [were] inseparable from the Committee of Union and Progress." [13] Seton-Watson wrote: "The main fact about the Committee of Union and Progress is its essentially un-Turkish and un-Moslem character. From the very first, hardly one among its true leaders has been a pure-blooded Turk. Enver is the son of a renegade Pole. Djavid belongs to the Jewish sect of Dumehs. Carosso is a Sephardim Jew from Salonica. Talaat is an Islamised Bulgarian gypsy. Achmet Riza, one of the group's temporary figureheads, is half Circassian and half Magyar, and a Positivist of the school of Comte."[14]

11. Paris, Bibliothèque Nationale, under Library index no. 8o²g/779.

12. Great Britain, Foreign Office, *Handbooks...*, No. 96 a & b, p. 67.

13. Great Britain, Foreign Office, *Handbooks...*, No. 96 c & d, p. 18.

14. R. W. Seton-Watson, *The Rise of Nationality in the Balkans* (London, 1917), pp. 135-36.

Seton-Watson adds: "The real brains of the movement were Jewish or Judaeo-Moslem. Their financial aid came from the wealthy Dunmehs and Jews of Salonica, and from the capitalists—international or semi-international—of Vienna, Budapest, Berlin and perhaps also of Paris and London. . . ." Ibid., pp. 134-35.

"The Jews of Salonika, generally known as Dunmehs (converts) were the real parents of the Turkish revolution. They are a definite people—Hebrews, but indefinable as to creed. The popular verdict was that they were only nominal Moslem and were true followers of the Pentateuch. . . . At that time, only the most industrious students of the Near East knew of their existence. There

Soon Arab doubts were substantiated and the newly born Turkish nationalism of a most chauvinistic type asserted itself and clashed with the Arabs' pride in their race, religion and language. One can rightly say that the seeds of an Arab separatist movement began to sprout from the soil of Turkish nationalism from 1909 onwards. This expression of Turkish nationalism has been called "Pan-Turanianism — a supernational propaganda for a rapprochement between all the Turkish-speaking peoples, on the same lines as Pan-Slavism."[15] Perhaps the best exposition of this doctrine is found in *Turkismus und Panturkismus* of Tekin Alp,[16] published in Weimar in 1915, in the writings of Yusuf Bey Akçuraoglu[17] and Ziya Bey Gökalp[18] and in two Turkish books: *Qawm Jadīd* [A New Nation][19] containing the sermons delivered by 'Ubaidullah, a Shaikh of Afghanī origin, in the mosque of Aya Sofia, and *Ta'rīkh al-Mustaqbal* [A History of the Future] by the well-known Turkish writer Jalal Nuri Bey. All these works stirred the Turks for a national regeneration on "pure Turkish" lines based on the natural affinities of all Turkish-speaking peoples. "The moral drawn by the Young Turks was that return to their pre-Islamic institutions would bring national rejuvenation and at the same time would provide

was no man to prophesy that the Dunmehs were to be the chief authors of a revolution whose results were to shake the world." Aubrey Herbert, *Ben Kendim: A Record of Eastern Travel* (London, 1924), pp. 15-16.

15. It is believed that the idea was taken from the book of a French savant, Léon Cahun, *Introduction à l'histoire de l'Asie: Turcs et Mongols, des origines à 1405* (Paris: Colin, 1896), in which Cahun's theme was that the "Turanians" were originally a brilliant race which later degenerated when they abandoned the law of the steppes and adopted Muslim culture. Dr. Nazim, a prominent member of the Committee of Union and Progress, is said to have been converted to Pan-Turanianism by a copy of this book which was lent to him by the French Consul-General at Salonika. See Great Britain, Foreign Office, *Handbooks*, No. 96 c & d, p. 23, n. 1. See also Ahmet Emin Yalman, *Turkey in the World War* (New Haven, 1930), pp. 187-99.

16. "A pseudonym which is believed to cover the name of Albert Cohen, a Salonika Jew." See Foreign Office, *Handbooks*, No. 96 c & d, p. 18.

17. In addition to many articles in the Turkish press, Yusuf Akçuraoglu, published *Uç Terzi Siyaset* [Three types of policy] (Cairo, 1903; Istanbul, A.H. 1327 [A.D. 1909]).

18. Consult Heyd, *Foundations of Turkish Nationalism*. See also Charles W. Hostler, *Turkism and the Soviets: The Turks of the World and their Politico Objectives* (London, 1957), pp. 155-46.

19. For extracts from *Qawm Jadid*, see *Al-Manār* (Cairo), vol. 17, pt. 7, June 1914, pp. 539-44.

a basis for cooperation with other Turkish-speaking peoples outside the Ottoman frontiers."[20]

At first, the Committee of Union and Progress seems to have decided to exploit both Pan-Islamism and Pan-Turanism, at the same time, the former, principally in their Muslim territories outside Anatolia proper and the latter, at home. But there is little doubt that at heart the Committee made Pan-Turanism their main objective.

The following excellent summary of the anti-Islamic policy of the Young Turks will be recorded here in full in order to understand clearly, by contrast, the anti-Turkish reaction which that policy created among the Arabs, a reaction which had a disastrous result for the Ottoman Empire:

" (a) Ziya Bey's group first came into conflict with Islam over the language question. They probably thought of translating the Koran, etc., into Turkish because they knew that the translation of the Bible and Christian liturgy into English and German at the Protestant Reformation had been the foundation of the modern English and German national literature. The idea is not intrinsically contrary to the Muhammedan religion but it is distinctly contrary to Islamic prejudice, and has therefore not been taken up by the Committee of Union and Progress.

" (b) The opposition of the Moslem ecclesiastics to the translation of the Koran into Turkish led the Turkish Nationalists into an attack on Islam as an ecclesiastical institution. This secularist movement, too, is partly an imitation of Europe, as 'Takin Alp's' use of the word 'clericals' shows; but it also embodies sound and necessary reforms like the secularization of Education and the Law, and steps in this direction have been taken by the Committee of Union and Progress themselves. The chief difference on this head between the Committee of Union and Progress is try to carry secularization through with as little friction as possible, and without ever admitting that their measures are anti-Islamic.

20. Toynbee and Kirkwood add: "The practical bearing of this propaganda lay in the fact that two-thirds of the Turkish-speaking peoples of the world were to be found within the frontiers, not of Turkey but of Russia, so that Pan-Turanianism offered a lever for breaking up the Russian Empire." Toynbee and Kirkwood, *Turkey*, p. 57.

" (c) The Nationalists have also started a 'pre-Islamic' movement which is only paralleled in Europe by the 'Ur-Deutschtum' of the Hindenburg wooden idols. They are making a sentimental cult of the pagan Turanian conquerors, like Jenghis Khan and Hulaku (both of whom, incidentally, were Mongols and not Turks). Members of the 'Turk Kuji' ('Turkish Power') Society — an association for the promotion of Physical culture, probably modelled on the Slavonic 'Sokols' — have to take 'Turanian' club-names in place of Moslem (e.g., 'Oghus' for 'Muhammad'); and a corps of Turkish Boy-scouts has been instituted, who likewise take 'Turanian' scout-names, cheer for the 'Khakan of the Turks' instead of the 'Padishah,' and carry flags with the Turkish wolf on them though the representation of living creatures in art is tabu to good Moslems.

'Enver was said to be the patron of these boy-scouts; a Turkish army order came into the hands of the British War Office directing the troops to include the 'Grey Wolf' in their prayers; and the Turanian idea seems to have made a certain progress among individual Turks of distinction, even in this fantastic form. For instance, King Hussein's troops captured, on the corpse of a brother of the Turkish Commandant at Medina, a circular issued by the principal Pan-Turanian Society in Turkey, the 'Turk Ojagi' ('The Turkish Hearth'), in which the following passage occurs:

" 'That monstrous figment of imagination which is known as the Community of Islam, and which has for long past stood in the way of present progress generally, and of the realization of the principles of Turanian Unity in particular, has now entered on a phase of decline and ruin. We need not apprehend from it any further danger to the execution of our hopes and principles. This is abundantly shown by the state of affairs among the Moslems in India. . . .'

"This circular derives a certain importance from its source and ownership, but there is no evidence that the 'Back to Paganism' movement has any influence over the policy of the Committee of Union and Progress." [21]

21. Great Britain, Foreign Office, *Handbooks...*, No. 96 c & d, pp. 45-47.
For an account in Arabic and Turkish of the anti-Arab and anti-Muslim policy of the Committee of Union and Progress, see *Thawrah al-'Arab* [The Arab revolution] (Cairo, 1916), pp. 138-61.

As a result of the Young Turks' Turkifying program, the Arab leaders' objective of gaining full national independence received a great stimulus which consolidated it. As far as Arab political nationalism is concerned, it can safely be asserted that it was the national and racial policies of the Young Turks which fanned its flames. Nationalist sentiments are dangerous to play with in a multi-racial and multi-national empire. A nationalist revival is bound to generate so much rivalry and antagonism as to lead inevitably to the break up of such an empire. Hence, when the Young Turks made the nationalist ideal and their racial superiority the basis of a new Turkey, culturally and politically united and strong, the Arab leaders' reaction was to think precisely in the same terms about the future of the Arab lands. As a result, a number of Arab societies and political parties were formed by enlightened and educated young Arabs to defend the Arab cause and protect the Arab rights,[22] among which were the following, established after 1908: (1) *Jam'iyyah al-Ikhā' al-'Arabī al-'Uthmānī* [The Society of Arab Ottoman Brotherhood]; (2) *Al-Muntada al-Adabī* [The Literary Club]; (3) *Al-Jam'iyyah al-Qaḥṭāniyyah* [The *Qaḥṭanī* Society];[23] (4) *Al-'Alam al-Akhdar* [The Green Flag]; (5) *Al-'Ahd* [The Covenant], all of which were founded in Constantinople, and (6) *Jam'iyyat Beirut al-Iṣlāḥiyyah* [The Reform Society of Beirut]; (7) *Jam'iyyat Baṣrah al-Iṣlāḥiyyah* [The Reform Society of Basra]; (8) *Al-Nādī al-Waṭanī al-'Ilmī* [The National Literary Club] founded in Baghdad and finally the two most important organizations: (9) *Jam'iyyat al-'Arabiyyat al-Fatāt*, better known simply as *al-Fatāt* [The Young Arab Society] and (10) *Ḥizb al-Lāmarkaziyyah al-Idāriyyah al-'Uthmānī* [The Ottoman Administrative Decentralization Party].[24] It is not, however, within the scope of this chapter to give an account of all these societies but two of them will be briefly dealt with: *Al-Fatāt* and the *Ḥizb al-Lāmarkaziyyah*.

22. See *Al-Hilāl* (Cairo), vol. 17, pt. 7, April 1909, p. 415.

23. Broadly speaking, the Arab tribes of Arabia have been divided into two main divisions: the northern and the southern. The northern tribes are called 'Adnanites and the southern ones Yamanites. According to Arab genealogists, Qahtan was the ancestor of all Yamanites.

24. For a detailed account of these societies, their founders, their purpose and their activities, see Amin Sa'id, *Al-Thawrah al-'Arabiyyah al-Kubra* [Secrets of the great Arab revolt] 3 vols. (Cairo, 1934), 1: 6-50, and Antonius, *The Arab Awakening*, pp. 107-21. See also 'Arif al-'Arif, "Nushu' al-Ḥarakah al-Qawmiyyah bayn al-Shabab al-'Arab fi Istanbul," *Afkar* (Amman), no. 6 (November 1966): 4-12.

Al-Fatāt was an ultra-secret Arab society of which it has been written: "No other society had played as determining a part in the history of the national movement,"[25] while the Decentralization Party was, on the other hand, a public political party which became "the best organized and most authoritative spokesman of Arab aspirations."[26]

The *Al-Fatāt* society was founded in Paris on 14 November 1909 by a group of Arab students who were then pursuing their higher studies in that city, most active among whom was Tawfīq al-Nāṭūr.[27] It is significant that this society was an entirely Muslim Arab organization. It was first called *Jam'iyyah al-Nāṭiqīn bi'l-Ḍād*[28] which was later, in 1911, changed to *al-Jam'iyyah al-'Arabiyyah 'al-Fatāt*. The purpose of the society was, politically, to obtain Arab independence within the framework of a bi-racial Ottoman Empire, Arab and Turk, on lines similar to the Austro-Hungarian Empire. In addition, the society's aim was to raise the Arab '*Ummah*' to the level of the social and educational advance made by the Western nations. But all this was to be done without breaking down the unity or destroying the existence of the Ottoman Empire itself.[29] Halidé Edib herself, in her criticism of the Young Turks' policy, admits that "the reduced empire" could not be strong enough "to resist the overwhelming forces arrayed against it" except through "a close understanding between the Turks and the Arabs." She says further: "It is true that the Arabs were already seized with the nationalist fever, but there was an idea ascribed to Mahmoud Shevket Pasha, himself of Arab origin, which was worth a trial. It was the creation of a dual monarchy, Arabo-

25. Antonius, *The Arab Awakening*, p. 111.

26. Ibid., p. 109.

27. George Antonius has reported (*The Arab Awakening*, p. 111, n. 2) that Tawfiq al-Natur was "hanged by the Turks during the war . . . . " The truth is that he was condemned to be hanged by the Turkish military court in 'Aley. But while in prison, he was shot and severely wounded by one of the guards. When the time for his hanging came, he was still in the military hospital in Beirut. Consequently, he was exiled, for the rest of the war, to a remote village in Anatolia. The author is indebted to Tawfiq al-Natur himself for most valuable information on the *Fatat* society.

28. Literally, "the Society of those who use the letter *Ḍād*." *Ḍād* is the fifteenth letter of the Arabic alphabet. The Arabs claim that this letter is found only in their alphabet and that its correct pronunciation is the test of a true Arab.

29. See Al-'Azim, *Majmu'ah Athār Rafiq Bey al-'Azim*, pp. 136-44.

Turkish, with the seat of government at Aleppo. Whether it could have prevented Moslem disintegration or not, one cannot be certain but the experiment should have been made."[30] Ziya Gökalp who is "regarded by many as the spiritual father of Turkish nationalism and as one of the outstanding Turkish thinkers in modern times" hoped, at one time, that the non-Turkish nationalities in the Ottoman Empire could live side by side in cooperation and agreement with the Turks. "Shortly before the outbreak of the First World War, he suggested the establishment of a bi-national State (to be called the Turco-Arab State) under the Ottoman Caliph. In 1918, he proposed a federation or confederation of two independent States, Turkish Anatolia and 'Arabistan.' This union, he said, was natural for geographical as well as religious reasons and vital for the defense of both nations. It would be beneficial especially for the Arabs who, lacking civil and military organization, would be conquered by European powers as soon as they separated themselves from their Turkish brothers."[31] However, the defeat of the Ottoman Empire and the loss of all the Arab provinces put an end to all such possibilities.

"The idea of Arab nationalism — or 'Arabism' — was not yet strong in us," the late Tawfīq al-Nāṭūr told the author. "All that we, as Arabs, wanted was to have the same rights and obligations in the Ottoman Empire as the Turks themselves and to have the Empire composed of two great nationalities: Turk and Arab."[32] This same desire of unity in diversity was brought out in the political program of the Turkish party of *Ḥurriyyet wa E'telaf* [Freedom and Unity]. This party was based on one of the two currents of thought prevalent in the new Turkish Parliament of 1908: administrative decentralization of the Ottoman Empire as against the highly centralized policy of the Party of Union and Progress. Apparently, it was Prince Ṣabaḥ al-Dīn, the son of Dāmād Maḥmūd Pasha and nephew of Sultan 'Abdul Ḥamīd who first supported and promoted the idea of political decentralization: *'adem-i-Merkeziyet*. He, his brother Lutfallah and their father had escaped to France during the height of the Ḥamidian despotism, in 1899. He was very popular with the Turkish Liberals, the

30. Halidé Edib Adivar, *Conflict of East and West in Turkey* (Lahore: M. Ashraf, [1935?]), p. 98.

31. Heyd, *Foundations of Turkish Nationalism*, p. 131.

32. See also *Al-Manār* (Cairo), vol. 16, pt. 7, 4 July 1913, p. 547.

Aḥrār, whom he encouraged and directed, and with all non-Turkish elements in the Empire. He gathered together in Paris about forty-seven Ottoman liberals composed of all races and religions in the Empire — including Arabs — and encouraged them to remain united under the name of Ottoman.[33] Returning to Constantinople, immediately after the Young Turks' Revolution of 1908, he founded "La Ligue de l'initiative privée et de la décentralisation," his basic political platform being the internal autonomy of the Provinces while remaining united under the protection of the Ottoman flag and the Ottoman army in matters affecting the general policy and security of the Empire. But the chauvinistic policy of the Young Turks led them to dissolve Ṣabāḥ al-Dīn's Decentralization League in November 1908.[34] Later, sometime in 1912, a number of leading Palestinian emigrés in Cairo, formed a political party, with the knowledge of the Turkish Government, which they called the *Ḥizb al-Lāmarkazīyyah al-Idāriyyah al-'Uthmānī*. This political party was open to any Ottoman, Arab or non-Arab, who sympathized and supported its aims and its program.[35]

This Ottoman Administrative Decentralization Party published a statement explaining the advantages of decentralization in a multi-national, multi-racial Empire such as the Ottoman and gave for the purpose of its founding, the safeguarding of the Empire from external pressure and internal conflicts and the rallying of its peoples round the focal centre of the Empire's unity, "the Ottoman throne." This explanation was followed by the Program of the Party containing sixteen articles, the following four of which convey a clear idea of its aim:

Article 1 — "The Ottoman State (*Dawlat*) is a Constitutional State with a representative parliamentary Government. Every one of its *vilayets* is an inseparable part of the Sultanate which is itself indivisible under all circumstances. But the local administration of every *vilayet* will be on the basis of decentralization, it being

33. See *Al-Hilāl* (Cairo), vol. 17, pp. 17-26. Consult also Tarik Z. Tunaya, *Turkiyede Siyasi Partiler, 1859-1952* [The political parties in Turkey, 1859-1952] (Istanbul, 1952), pp. 315-44.

34. Mandelstam, *Le sort de l'empire ottoman*, pp. 14-16.

35. Its President was Rafiq Bey al-'Azim, a member of a well known Muslim family in Damascus. He died in 1925. For the history, Constitution, and program of the party see *Al-Manār* (Cairo), vols. 16 (1913) and 17 (1914), articles by Muhammad Rashid Rida and others; also Sa'id, *Al-Thawrah al-'Arabiyyah al-Kubrā*, 1: 14-18, and Antonius, *The Arab Awakening*, pp. 109-10.

understood that the Sultan will appoint the *Vali* and the Chief Judge."

Article 4 — "In the capital of every *vilayet*, there will be organized a 'General Assembly,' an 'Administrative Council,' a Council on Education and a Council on *Awqāf*."

Article 14 — "Every *vilayet* will have two official languages. Turkish and the 'local' language of its inhabitants."

Article 15 — "Education in every *vilayet* will be in the language of the inhabitants of that *vilayet*."[36]

After the coming of the Young Turks to power, Arab rejoicing following the proclamation of the Constitution ended in great disappointment. The Arab leaders believed that the Ottoman Empire, being composed of diverse races and nationalities with their different tongues, habits and traditions, could not be ruled effectively under a centralized system of Government. They wanted a constitutional and representative Government which was truly constitutional and truly representative of the nation. Their Government was only in name constitutional and representative. The different elements which composed the Empire did not have equal rights and equal opportunities. The governing body was restricted primarily to one element: the Turkish. This element was in a commanding and privileged position. Moreover, it pursued the policy of dissolving in its own Turkish matrix the Arab element. As a result of this policy, the Committee of Union and Progress insisted that Turkish should be the official and the only language of the Empire. This "Turkification" process became another great cause of Arab dissatisfaction with the Young Turks.

Sir Edwin Pears wrote that the Committee "would have no language but Turkish" — and wished to make of their heterogeneous subjects "a nation which should be one in language." The study of Turkish became compulsory in every school. Orders were given to change the name of the streets into Turkish, although it may fairly be said that in most cities in Turkey not one-twentieth part of the population can read Turkish."[37] Dr. 'Abdal-Raḥman Shahbandar has related two experiences which he had in 1910.[38]

36. See *Al-Manār* (Cairo), vol. 16, pt. 3 (8 March 1913), pp. 229-31.

37. Sir Edwin Pears, *Forty Years in Constantinople, 1873-1915* (New York, 1916), p. 271.

38. See the memoirs of Dr. Shahbandar, published under the title *Al-Thawrah al-Waṭaniyyah* [The national revolution] (Damascus, 1933), pp. 2-3.

First, Kāmil Bey al-Solḥ told Dr. Shahbandar. "When I was on my way from Monastir to Damascus to take charge of the Court of Cassation, I converged on Constantinople at the request of the Minister of Justice Najm-al-Dīn Munla Bey. The latter warned me that the language of my Court had to be henceforth Turkish, because, he said: 'We shall abandon the Arabs.' " Secondly, "When we were in the Central Committee of Union and Progress in Syria," wrote Dr. Shahbandar, "we received oral instructions from the Central Office of the Committee though Dr. Muḥarram Bey asking us to make Turkish the language of all our communications with the said Committee." There was a deliberate attempt, adds Dr. Shahbandar, to make the Turkish language supersede the Arabic in Arab lands.

The policy of substituting the Turkish for the Arabic language was doomed to failure right from the beginning. It was impossible to impose the Turkish tongue upon the Arabs. Indeed, the Turkish language itself had, probably by cultural and religious necessity become greatly enriched by both the Persian and Arabic vocabularies. It must be remembered that Arabic was the language in which the Qur'an had been revealed. The Muslims believe that as a medium of divine revelation in the days of the Prophet, God chose the Arabic tongue in its purest form which was the dialect of the tribe of Quraysh to which the Prophet Muḥammad himself belonged. Consequently, the Muslims consider the language of the Qur'an sacred and therefore as eternal and unchangeable as the Holy Book itself. The following passages from the Qur'an emphasize the fact that God's revelation to the Prophet was made, specifically, in Arabic: "An Arabic Qur'an have we sent it down, that ye might understand it."[39] "Verily, from the Lord of the Worlds hath this Book come down... in the clear Arabic tongue."[40] "Had we made it a Qur'an in a foreign tongue, they had surely said, 'Unless its signs be made clear....' What! In a foreign tongue and the people Arabian?"[41] No one who is not acquainted with the cascading beauty of the Arabic language of the Qur'an, now mighty and thunderous in expression, now gentle and soothing in its poetical charm, can begin to comprehend its almost hypnotic effect on Arab Muslims throughout the world.

39. Sura 12, *Yusuf* ["Joseph"] (The *Koran*, trans. J. M. Rodwell [London, 1909]), v. 2.

40. Sura 26, *Al-Shu'arā'* ["The poets"], v. 194.

41. Sura 41, *Fussilat* ["The made plain"], v. 43.

Indeed, the Muslims consider the language of the Qur'an a great miracle of Islam. They believe in the *i'jāz* of the Qur'an, i.e., in the impossibility of imitating it, for it is "the most perfect example of style and language."[42]

The Turks, as Muslims, had a great veneration for the Arabic tongue and had Arabicized the Turkish language to an extraordinary extent. But as a conquering race they were conscious of being the master nation among the mosaic of races and nationalities which they governed. The young Turks would not sacrifice their nationality and their race for the benefit of Islam, particularly at a time when the number of Arabs in the Ottoman Empire was probably greater than that of the Turks. They were more anxious than ever to keep the Empire Turkish and to preserve their privileged and dominating position; hence the attempt, though evidently too late in the day, of Turkifying the non-Turkish elements by trying to impose upon them the Turkish language.[43]

The Arabs, meanwhile, continued to press for reforms.[44] Indeed the keynote of the year 1913 whether in Constantinople itself or in the Arab Provinces of the Ottoman Empire was the word *Iṣlāḥ*,

42. The Prophet himself had challenged not only men, but even the "spirits"—the "Djinn"—to produce anything like it: "Say verily, were men and Djinn assembled to produce the like of Qur'an, they could not produce its like, though the one should help the other." Sura 17, *Al-Isra'* ["The night journey"], v. 90.

43. It was in vain that a few years earlier, Jamal al-Din al-Afghānī had recommended to Sultan 'Abdul Ḥamid, just the opposite process of substituting the Arabic language—"the language of that pure religion" (i.e., Islam)—as Sultan Selim had once proposed, for the Turkish. In so doing, he told the Sultan, Turkey as a Muslim Power and the Sultan as the Caliph of Islam would acquire far greater prestige and power in the Arab and Muslim world. Jamal al-Din thought the Turks were committing a grievous error by trying to Turkify the Arabs. Muḥammad al-Makhzūmī, *Khāṭirāt Jamāl al-Dīn al-Afghānī al-Ḥusainī* [Memoirs of Jamal al-Din al-Afghani al-Husaini] pp. 236-37.

All Arab reformers and Arab Reform Societies included in their program the necessity of having the Arabic language as the official language of the Arab provinces of the Ottoman Empire. See *Al-Hilāl* (Cairo), vol. 18, pt. 3 (1 December 1909): 161-63, and *Al-Muqtabas* (Damascus), vol. 4, pt. 2 (1909): 109-12.

44. "Au mois de décembre, 1912, le gouverneur de Beyrouth télégraphiait à son gouvernement: Le pays est travaillé par différentes influences. Pour améliorer sa situation devenue intolérable, une partie de la population se tourne déjà, ou vers l'Angleterre ou vers la France. Si nous ne prenons l'initiative des réformes, le pays nous échappe." K. T. Khairallah, *Les régions arabes libérées* (Paris, 1919), p. 39.

i.e., reform. The opening article in *Al-Moka*ṭṭ*am* (Cairo), No. 7227, 4 January 1913, is entitled "The Reform Movement in Syria." It was written by its Correspondent in Beirut. The Correspondent states that the people of Beirut want reforms and the *Vali*, Edhem Bey having consulted the central government in Constantinople has been instructed to ask the Beirutis for a Memorandum containing their proposed reforms. Consequently, on 21 December 1912 a group of reformers drew up a statement containing fourteen items of reform which included the appointment of foreign advisers and experts in various government departments, chosen from European countries with no political interests in the Ottoman Empire. The official language of every Province was to be the local language spoken in that Province. The Correspondent adds that the Government understands *iṣlāḥ* in one way, while the enlightened Arab youth and the Arab thinkers understand it in another. The latter believe that misgovernment in the Capital as well as in the *vilayets* is the root of all evil, while the former think of *iṣlāḥ* in terms of such "physical improvements" as drying marshy lands, building roads, and making rivers navigable.

The Beirut reformers formed a society which was called "The General Reform Society for the *vilayet* of Beirut." It was composed of eighty-six members[45] and elected by all the "*Millet Councils*" representing every religious denomination in that town. It held its first meeting on 12 January 1913 and elected an Executive Committee of 24 members.[46] They published a paper called *Le Réveil* with its head office in Khan Antun Bey and founded a Reformist Club where they met frequently to discuss all questions of public interest. At the third meeting of this Club, on 31 January, the assembled delegates drew up a program of reforms composed of fifteen articles. In its preamble, the Ottoman Government was defined as "a constitutional representative Government." The first article stated that the external affairs of the *Vilayet* of Beirut, the army, customs, postal and telegraph communications, legislation in Constantinople, and taxes were to be in the hands of the

45. There were "42 Moslems, 16 Greek Orthodox, 10 (12 ?) Maronites, 6 Greek Catholics, 2 Protestants, 2 Syrian Catholics, 2 Armenian Catholics, 2 Latins and 2 Israelites." Great Britain, Foreign Office, 195/2451, Despatch No. 8 of British Consul-General Cumberbatch to the British Ambassador Sir Gerard A. Lowther, dated Beirut, 24 January 1913.

46. See *Al-Mukattam* (Cairo), no. 7238, 18 January 1913, p. 1.

central administration while the internal affairs were to be placed under a General Council of the *Vilayet.* (This Council would have the authority to depose the *Vali* by a two-thirds majority vote.) According to the fourteenth article the Arabic language was to be recognized as the official language of the *Vilayet* and as an official language, like Turkish, in the Chamber of Deputies and in the Senate.[47] The British Consul-General Cumberbatch wrote on 12 March 1913, that the main reforms were "towards administrative decentralization," adding : 'and the main interesting proposal is the appointment of foreign advisers and inspectors."[48]

The answer of the authorities was to issue an Order declaring the Beirut Reform Society illegal and closing its Club. According to Cumberbatch, "they [the reformers] have been showing extraordinary activity, and for the country, unusual boldness in the reform campaign."[49] There was great agitation in Beirut against the Governors' arbitrary action. On 10 April 1913, the British Consul-General reported: "Yesterday, all the Beirut newspapers with one exception appeared with a copy of the Order in a black border as the sole contents of the paper, the three other pages being left blank...."[50] Three days later, many shops in Beirut closed

47. See *Al-Manār* (Cairo), vol. 16, pt. 4, 7 April, 1913, pp. 275-280.

48. Great Britain, Foreign Office, 195/2451, Despatch No. 26.

49. Great Britain, Foreign Office, 195/2451, Despatch No. 28 of 27 March 1913.

The Beirut Correspondent of the French paper *Temps* had written to his paper on 18 March: " . . . Chekri Asly Bey, ex-député de Damas au Parlement et promoteur du mouvement réformiste dans cet important centre, est appelé à Beyrouth où le gouverneur lui propose un poste de sous-gouverneur à Lattaquié.—'Ce ne sont pas des postes lucratifs,' lui répond Asly Bey, 'que nous, *Arabes*, nous réclamons, ce sont des réformes sérieuses, garanties dans leur application par les puissances de l'Empire. . . . '

"Et c'est actuellement cette même parole que répètent tous les Syriens ainsi que les populations des rives de l'Euphrate et des bords de la mer Rouge." Khairallah, *Les régions arabes libérées*, p. 40.

50. Great Britain, Foreign Office, 195/2451. Despatch No. 31. See also *Al-Mukattam* (Cairo), no. 7308, of Friday, 11 April 1913, p. 5. The new *Vali*, Hazim Bey, stated in his Order that the establishment of the Reform Society was contrary to the Law of Assemblies which clearly forbade it and that some of its demands were against the Constitution. For example of a Beirut paper which appeared with only the Order of the *Vali* on the front page, see *Lisan ul-Ḥāl*, no. 7207, 9 April 1913, a reproduction of which will be found in Appendix J (Fig. 10).

in protest.[51] The Decentralization Party in Egypt supported the Beirut Reform Society and sent two strongly worded telegrams of protest, the first to the Grand Vizier in Constantinople and the second to the *Vali* of Beirut himself.[52] But the Government considered the demands of the Society to be unconstitutional. Replying to a telegram sent by 1,300 notables of Beirut to the *Vali* of their city, the Grand Vizier Sa'īd Pasha wrote that if the inhabitants wanted any reforms, they had to ask, through their deputies, the Ottoman Parliament to enact them.[53]

The Arab leaders did not cease to assert their demands.[54] An important Arab Congress — the first of its king — was organized by the "Arab Community" ("*al-Jāliyah al-'Arabiyyah*") in Paris and with the support of the Decentralization Party of Cairo.[55] It

51. When the *Vali* closed the Club of the Reform Society of Beirut, some of its members went, first, to the British, then to the French Consul-General complaining and protesting against the action of the authorities. At the British Consulate, they were offered the hall of the American College (now the American University of Beirut) for their meetings, as they would be, then, on foreign soil and would, therefore, have full freedom to hold the meetings of their Society. The French Consul-General agreed with his suggestion and advised them to follow it. Consequently, the Society held a meeting on the American campus and after a long discussion, it was decided to go on strike and close all shops and stores in Beirut. *Al-Mukattam* (Cairo), no. 7312, 16 April 1913, p. 2.

52. *Al-Mukattam* (Cairo), no. 7310, 14 April 1913, p. 35.

53. "Telle est la réponse du grand vizir Said Pacha au télégramme des 1,300 notables Beyrouthains, adressée au Vali de Beyrouth: 'Nous avons reçu un télégramme de Beyrouth signé de plusieurs personnes, demandant l'autorisation pour le comité de réformes de se réunir de nouveau. Si les habitants veulent des réformes, ils doivent les demander au Parlement; et si, la majorité du Parlement les accepte, le Gouvernement les exécutera. Comme les habitants veulent fonder des comités et faire des demandes contraires à la loi, le Gouvernement ne peut pas prendre ces demandes en considération . . .' " Benoît Aboussouan, *Le problème politique syrien* (Paris, 1925), p. 61. See also *Al-Mukattam* (Cairo), no. 7309 of Saturday, 12 April 1913, and no. 7314 of Friday, 18 April 1913; and Khairallah, *Les régions arabes libérées*, p. 40.

54. See *Lisān ul-Ḥāl* (Beirut), no. 7275, 28 June 1913, p. 2.

55. The organizing Committee was composed of the following members elected from the Syrian and Lebanese community ("*al-Jaliyah al-'Arabiyyah*") in Paris: Shukri Ghanem, 'Abd al-Ghani al-'Araisi, Nadrah Mutran, 'Awni 'Abd al-Hadi, Jamil Mardam, Charles Debbas, Muḥammad Maḥmassani and Jamil Ma'luf. The representatives of the Decentralization Party were 'Abd al-Ḥamid Zahrawi and Iskandar 'Ammun. The delegates of the Beirut Reform Society were: Salim 'Ali Salam, Aḥmad Mukhtar Baihum, Khalil Zainiyyah, al-Shaikh Aḥmad Ḥasan Tabbarah, Dr. Ayyub Thabit and Albert Sursock.

was held in Paris, 18-23 June 1913, in the Hall of the Geographic Society at Boulevard St. Germain. The two most important items on the agenda for discussion were: the rights of the Arabs in the Ottoman Empire and the necessity for reforms on the basis of decentralization.[56]

The speeches delivered by the delegates at the Arab Congress and their deliberations during the six days of its sittings all emphasized the need of reforms on the basis of decentralization. There was no discussion on and no demand for separation from the Ottoman Empire.[57] Indeed, Iskandar ʻAmmūn, the Vice-President of the Party, summed up the aims and the political purpose of Decentralization in the following words when he delivered his address:

> "The Arab *Ummah* (nation) does not want to separate itself from the Ottoman Empire.... All that it desires is to replace the present form of government by one more compatible with the needs of all the diverse elements which compose that Empire, in such wise that the inhabitants of any Province (*vilayet*) will have the final word in the internal administration of their own affairs....
>
> "We desire an *Ottoman* government, neither Turkish nor Arab, a government in which all the Ottomans have equal rights and equal obligations so that no party or group may deprive any other party or group from any of its rights or usurp them, for reasons of either race or religion, be it Arab, Turk, Armenian, Kurd, Muslim, Christian, Jew or Druze."[58]

The Committee of Union and Progress, having failed to prevent the meeting of the Arab Congress in Paris, sent Midḥat Shukrī, the Secretary of their Committee, to the French capital to negotiate with the members of the Congress and reach some agreement

Two notables of Baalbek were also invited to join the Congress: Muhammad and Ibrahim Haidar. Tawfiq al-Suwaidi and Sulaiman ʻAnbar (both living in Paris) represented Iraq. There were also four representatives of the Lebanese and Syrian emigrants in the United States and in Mexico. See Al-Lujnah al-ʻUlya li-Ḥizb al-Lamarkaziyyah [The higher committee of the Decentralization Party], *Al-Mu'tamar al-ʻArabi al-Awwal* [The first Arab congress] (Cairo), 1913), pp. 3-8, 14-16.

56. Ibid., p. 10.

57. For the Resolutions passed at the Congress, see Appendix C. See also Khairallah, *Les régions arabes libérées*, pp. 48-54.

58. Al-Lujnah al-ʻUlya li-Ḥizb al-Lamarkaziyyah, *Al-Mu'tamar al-ʻArabi al-Awwal*, pp. 104-4.

with them on the proposed reforms in the Arab *vilayets*.[59] Towards the middle of July, the Turkish Government announced that an agreement had been reached with the Arabs to grant all their demands. On 15 July 1913, *Al-Mukattam* published the text of the agreement which was sent to it by Rafīq Bey Al-'Azim, President of the Decentralization Party in Cairo. In a covering letter to the Editor, Rafīq Bey stated that the Agreement had been signed in Paris by the representative of the Committee of Union and Progress, recognizing the rights of the Arabs in the Ottoman State and the need for reforms in the Arab Provinces, on the basis of administrative decentralization. The Agreement contained thirteen articles. Education in elementary and secondary schools was to be in the Arabic language. Arab soldiers were to give their services, when needed, in areas near their homelands. At least three Cabinet ministers were to be chosen among "the sons of the Arabs." There should, also, be Arab advisers and assistants in various ministries. At least five Arab *valis* and ten Arab *Muteṣarrifs* should be appointed. Foreign specialists and experts were to be employed in every *vilayet*. Official transactions in the Arab Provinces should be in Arabic.[60]

During the month of August, there were several outward expressions of warm friendship and fraternity between Arab delegations in Istanbul and the highest authorities of the Turkish Government, starting with Sultan Muḥammad Rashād and his heir to the throne. There were sumptuous banquets given by both sides at which eloquent and polished speeches were made on Arab-Turkish unity and brotherhood. On 5 August, an Arab delegation[61] headed by Sharīf 'Ali Ḥaidar was received by the Grand Vizier at the Sublime Porte. The Prime Minister expressed his pleasure at the removal of misunderstandings between Arabs and Turks.

59. Sharif 'Ali Ḥaidar who was highly respected by the Turks and was loyal to them, and who at the same time understood and sympathized with the Arabs and their grievances tried to reconcile the two parties. He advised the leaders of C.U.P. to agree on some reforms favorable to the Arabs. See, *Al-Manār* (Cairo), vol. 16, pt. 8, 2 August 1913, pp. 636-39, and Djemal Pasha, *Memories of a Turkish Statesman, 1913-1919*, pp. 58-59. For Sharif 'Ali Ḥaidar see George Stitt, *A Prince of Arabia: The Emir Shereef Ali Haider* (London: Allen & Unwin, 1948).

60. *Al-Mukattam* (Cairo), no. 7388, 15 Juy 1913, p. 5. See also Al-Lujnah al-'Ulya li-Ḥizb al-Lamarkaziyyah, *Al-Mu'tamar al-'Arabi al-Awwal.*

61. *Al-Mukattam* (Cairo), no. 7412, 12 August 1913, p. 1. See also As'ad Daghir, *Mudhakkarati* [My memoirs] (Cairo, n.d.), pp. 61-62.

It was his Cabinet's aim to bring prosperity and happiness to the Arabs in the Ottoman Empire — the most sincere of all Ottomans to the Caliphate. 'Abdul Karīm al-Khalīl speaking on behalf of the Arab youth (*al-shabībah al-'arabiyyah*), thanked the Grand Vizier for the reforms which he had promised and begged for the execution of those reforms at the earliest possible time. On that same evening, the Arab notables gave a banquet at Tokatlian Hotel in Constantinople to a distinguished group of fifty Turks and Arabs, including Ṭalaat Pasha, Jamal Pasha and Enver Pasha.[62]

Meanwhile, the Arab Congress of Paris had sent three of its members[63] to Istanbul to make a close study of the situation on the spot. On 23 August, they were received by Sultan Muḥammad Rashād to whom they expressed the attachment of the Arabs to the Ottoman throne.[64] Four days later, on 27 August, they had a cordial audience with the Heir to the Ottoman throne, who promised to do his best to improve conditions in the Arab regions. In the evening, the C.U.P. (Committee of Union and Progress) was host at an impressive banquet to leading Arabs and Turks, including the Arab Reform delegation and all the Cabinet Ministers. The Arab speakers were 'Abdul Karīm al-Khalīl and al-Shaikh Aḥmad Ṭabbārah. They declared their attachment to the "Ottoman Crescent," the need for Arab-Turkish brotherhood and the urgency of translating words into actions and, thus, executing the promised reforms.[65]

While it seemed to all appearances, that the "Syrian Arabs" were enjoying apolitical honeymoon in Constantinople, in far away Basra of those days, another Reform Committee had been formed which was violently anti-Turk and anti-C.U.P. For sometime past, reformers in Basra and Baghdad had been actively engaged in discussions on the necessity for reforms. In Baghdad, in particular, the movement was on a larger scale, thanks to the activities of the National Science Club, the honorary President of which was Ṭālib al-Naqīb.[66] On 28 August, the British Consul in Basra, Mr.

62. Ibid., pp. 62-63.

63. They were Salim 'Ali Salam, Al-Shaikh Aḥmad Ḥasan Tabbarah, and Aḥmad Mukhtar Baihum.

64. Daghir, *Mudhakkarati*, p. 63.

65. Ibid., pp. 63-65.

66. *Al-Mokattam* (Cairo), no. 7302, 5 April 1913, p. 1.

Crow, enclosed in his despatch the Program, in Arabic, together with an English translation, of "the so-called Baṣra Reform Committee headed by Sayyid Ṭālib Bey."[67] The Program contained twenty-seven articles, the most important of which seemed to be the following:

13 — The Central Government may appoint the *Vali* directly. He must be a native of Irak, fully acquainted with conditions and habits of local tribes....

18 — Arabic to be the official language in all departments and courts.

24 — All arts and sciences to be taught in Arabic in the schools, with due regard to the Turkish language and religious instruction.

Two days later, Mr. Crow's despatch contained a proclamation in Arabic (together with its translation in English) "issued by Sayyid Ṭālib of Basra." "The proclamation," Crow wrote, "has been distributed among the troops and Arab tribes of Mesopotamia.... It incites the army and the Arabs against the present Cabinet, accusing the latter of threatening to dethrone the Sultan.... It concludes by exhorting the Arabs and the troops to rebel if the demand is not conceded, and to declare the present Government *hors la loi* and unworthy of obedience."[68] There is also at the end of this manifesto a demand for independence: "They [the Arabs] demand an independent government in Mesopotamia (Jaziret-el 'Arab) according to the programme already published...."

"The proclamation," wrote Mr. Marling from Constantinople to Sir Edward Grey on 25 September 1913, "is meant to be a sort of indictment of the Committee of Union and Progress, with which organization Sayyid Ṭālib at one time cooperated.... He is now one of its bitterest opponents.... The recent attempt to assassinate

67. Great Britain, Foreign Office, 424/240, Part XII, *Further Correspondence Respecting the Affairs of Asiatic Turkey and Arabia*, Enclosures 1 and 2 in No. 13 of Mr. Charles M. Marling's despatch to Sir Edward Grey from Constantinople, on 25 September 1913.

68. Ibid., enclosure in No. 14. The Proclamation also accused the Committee of Union and Progress of being pro-Zionist, anti-Muslim, and anti-Arab. It said: " . . . It was they the (C.U.P.) who had encouraged the Zionist movement and who proposed to sell Palestine to the Jews in order to create an independent people there . . . These men are not Mohammedans, God forbid; they are rather unbelievers who have tricked Islam to destruction and torn it up by the roots. . . . These are the men who want to make Turks of us and suppress our language. . . . "

him was locally believed to be the work of the Central Committee of Union and Progress."[69] In another despatch of the same date,[70] Mr. Marling concludes: "Indeed, it may be noticed that the underlying tendency in the Basra programme is one of aversion from the rule of the Committee of Union and Progress, *rather than that of separation from the Ottoman or 'Turkish' Government.*[71]

Meanwhile, differences had arisen among the Arab leaders and in September the situation had deteriorated in Constantinople. Various reasons have been advanced for these differences, some personal and others concerning the future of Arab-Turkish relations and the execution of reforms. It has, actually, been strongly suspected that the C.U.P. itself had fomented, and engineered the conflict between themselves and the Arabs, specially when a second delegation from Syria appeared in Constantinople towards the end of August and accused the first delegation of being unpatriotic, of wanting to surrender the country to the foreigner and to "destroy the Caliphate, Islam and the Muslims."[72] The following excerpts are worth quoting from the above-mentioned despatch[73] concerning the relations between the Young Turks and the "Young Arabs:"

> "It ('The Basra Arab Reforms Committee's Programme') tallies in essentials with the reforms advocated by the Syrian Arabs, who recently held a Congress at Paris. The Committee of Union

69. Great Britain, Foreign office, 424/240, No. 14.

70. Ibid., No. 13.

71. Emphasis supplied. Indeed, Articles 1 and 3 of the Baṣra Program make this point clear. Article 1 says: "Our dear Fatherland ('*watan*') shall be an Ottoman monarchy under the banner of the Crescent." And Article 3 states, "The Ottoman State ('*Al-Dawlah al-'Aliyyah*') is a Muslim State under the sovereignty of the supreme Caliph of the Muslims." For the Arabic text of the Baṣra Reform Society's Program ('*Barnāmaj Jam'iyyah al-Islāḥ al-Baṣriyyah*') see Great Britain, Foreign Office, 195/2451, Despatch No. 51 of 28 August 1913.

72. For details, see *Al-Mokattam* (Cairo), no. 7430, 4 September, 1913, p. 1, and Daghir, *Mudhakkirati*, pp. 67-71. Daghir himself was present at a secret meeting which was held in Istanbul on 7 January 1914 to remove misunderstandings between the two actions and to bring about a general reconciliation. It is important to note his assertion that the Arabs, all that time, were not thinking in terms of breaking away from the Ottoman Sultanate. On the contrary, they wanted to strengthen it, by strengthening the position of the Arab elements in it and by introducing the necessary reforms to protect it from the dangers threatening the Empire.

73. Great Britain, Foreign Office, 424/240, No. 13.

and Progress sent emissaries to Paris, and as the result of the negotiations, succeeded in winning over the Younger Arab delegates. A sort of pact was come to between the Young Turks and Young Arabs on the basis of the concession of some of the Arab demands, and this Young Turco-Arabian alliance was consecrated at a banquet recently given here by the prominent members of the Committee of Union and Progress to the Young Arab delegates. The concessions made to the Arabs and sanctioned by Imperial *Iradé* came under four heads, viz:

"1. The revenues of local vakoufs are to be handed over not to the Constantinople Ministry of Vakoufs, but to local Moslem Councils which can utilise these funds for the foundation and upkeep of Moslem schools on the lines of similar institutions maintained by the Christians and Jews.

"2. In time of peace the recruits are to do their military service in their own locality....

"3. In regions where the majority of the population speak Arabic, that language is to be the medium of instruction in all schools....

"4. All officials in Arab provinces must be acquainted with Arabic as well as Turkish....

"Shortly after the Young Turko-Arab pact had been concluded on the above basis, the Arabs of Syria and other places declared that the Young Arabs who had been won over by the Young Turks were not representative of Arab feeling and wishes in this matter, and deputations of Arabs of the type of Seyyid Ṭālib of Basra arrived in Constantinople to insist on a wider basis of agreement. Talaat Bey and other Young Turks proceed to play off the fresh arrivals against the earlier delegates, and then split both on a Moslem *versus* Christian basis. Thereupon, the second deputation left in disgust and with the determination of insisting on the wider programme (the 'Baṣra Programme')...."

In connection with the differences which arose among the Arab leaders concerning their relations with the C.U.P. and their reaction to the Congress of Paris, the French Chargé d'Affaires in Constantinople, A. Bopp, wrote as early as 10 June 1913, to the French Consul-General in Damascus, M. Ottawi, that the Turkish newspapers continue to publish with the liveliest satisfaction the telegrams which are sent to them from Aleppo, Damascus, Beirut, and the principal cities of Arab countries to protest against the meeting of the Congress of Paris. But he adds that this manifestation of Arab loyalty seems to be due to "un mot d'ordre" given by the Committee of Union and Progress, owing to the almost identical composition of the telegrams. At the same time the Chargé d'Affaires quotes the text of a telegram sent from Medina and published that morning in the Turkish newpaper *Tesvir-i-Efkar* (Constantinople) under the title of "Faithfulness and attachment to the Fatherland." The Ulema and the notables of Medina refer to the Party of *Al-Lāmarkaziyyah* in that telegram as a group of traitors whose aim is to assure the influence of the foreigner in Syria and in other Arab countries. These boys ("ces enfants") do not and cannot represent the Arab nation or speak on its behalf.[74]

It must not be forgotten that while the Arabs were pressing the Ottoman Government for reforms, the Young Turks were engaged in a calamitous war in the Balkans. The defeat and humiliation suffered as a result of the Tripolitan War and the loss of Libya to Italy in 1912 were followed immediately by the first Balkan War on 18 October 1912. Bulgaria, Greece, Serbia and Montenegro joined hands against the Ottoman Empire. John A.R. Marriott quotes M. Gueshoff, the Minister of Bulgaria, as having written:

> "A miracle took place.... Within the brief space of one month the Balkan Alliance demolished the Ottoman Empire, four tiny

74. The following is the text of the telegramme:

"Nous soussignés, Ulemas et notables de Medina, nous venons dire que nous avons appris qu'un groupe de traîtres à leur religion s'est réuni en Égypte et forme une association appelée 'La Merkezié' et que quelques jeunes gens ignorants, d'accord avec quelques étudiants, ont entrepris de tenir un Congrès à Paris. En réalité ces deux groupements n'ont d'autre but que d'assurer l'influence de l'étranger dans la Syrie et d'autres contrées arabes. Ce sont des traîtres qui trahissent leur religion et leur Patrie.

"Que Dieu fasse échouer toutes leurs entreprises et les punisse de la punition qu'ils ont méritée. Nous sommes, nous qui vous envoyons ce télégramme, les proches du Prophète et les Chefs les plus autorisés des Arabes, et nous déclarons que ces enfants n'ont et ne peuvent avoir aucune qualité pour représenter la Nation Arabe et pour parler en son nom. Nous n'aimons donc aucun lien avec ces personnes et leurs partisans et nous ne demandons rien en dehors de ce que notre Gouvernement — qui est Éternel — nous voudra bien donner dans sa sollicitude envers nous. C'est l'État qui aprrécie les besoins de ses sujets mieux qu'un autre. Les Arabes constituent la race la plus fidèle au Sultanat et au Khalifat. Cette race n'a d'autre idéal que de sauvegarder et de défendre la religion musulmane que la glorieuse dynastie d'Osman a su défendre et protéger depuis plus de six siècles."

See *La vérité sur 'La Question Syrienne'* (published anonymously by Djemal Pasha at Constantinople in 1916), pp. 87-89: Fascimile No. 19.

countries with a population of some 10,000,000 souls defeating a great Power whose inhabitants numbered 25,000,000." [75] The First Balkan War ended with the Treaty of London on 30 May 1913. But the victors disagreed as to their share of the spoils of war. The result was the Second Balkan War which began on 29 June 1913. Greece, Serbia and Rumania attacked and defeated Bulgaria. The Turks took the opportunity to reconquer Adrianople on 20 July. This very short war came to an end when a treaty of peace was signed at Bucharest on 10 August. Although the Turks returned to stay in Adrianople, the two Balkan Wars had ended disastrously for the Young Turks. Almost all of European Turkey was lost. Whatever doubts the C.U.P. still had as to which policy should be the basis of the building up of a new Turkey, were settled by those wars, for "the shock of this disaster penetrated to wider circles than had been affected by the academic movement of the previous years, and seems to have kindled a genuine desire for national regeneration among all educated Turks." [76]

The anti-Arab and anti-Muslim spirit of this new Turkish nationalism expressed itself openly and violently on the eve of the First World War.[77] Of the many societies which were formed with Government inspiration and support, in order to promote Pan-Turanianism, the most famous was the *Turk Ojagi* ("The Turkish Hearth") with is headquarters in Constantinople and many branches in the towns and villages of Anatolia. The Pan-Turanian

75. Marriott, *The Eastern Question*, p. 452.

76. Great Britain, Foreign Office, *Handbooks...*, No. 96 c & d, p. 19. It should be remembered that after the coup d'état of 28 January 1913 when Nazim Pasha, the Minister of War, was shot dead and Kamil Pasha, the Grand Vizier, was forced to resign, the Young Turks obtained supreme power over the destiny of Turkey.

77. After the publication of the book *Qawm Jadid* [A new nation] a very strongly worded article expressing anti-Arab sentiments and anti-Arab criticism appeared in the well-known Turkish newspaper *Eqdam*. It caused a furore among the Arab youth, mainly students, who were living in Constantinople. They organized a demonstration and marched to the editorial office of *Eqdam* which they attacked with stones breaking the glass of its windows. Then a delegation of them went to the Prime Minister and protested against the publication of that humiliating article.

This article had also great repercussions in the Arab Provinces of Turkey, Syrian and Iraqi newspapers rose in defence of the Arabs and were bitterly indignant towards the Turks. See Aḥmad 'Izzat al-A'zamī, *Al-Qadiyyah al-'Arabiyyah* [The Arab question], pp. 102-9. See also Tunaya, *Turkiyede Siyasi Partiler*, pp. 375-86.

ideas penetrated into the Turkish army and created deep antipathy between the Arab and Turkish officers.[78]

Early in 1914, Ludovic de Contenson referred to the existence of an "Arab question" and to the awakening of the national conscience among the Arabs. He wrote:

"D'ailleurs, depuis que l'Europe a reconnu aux Albanais, musulmans et chrétiens, le droit de se gouverner eux-mêmes en tant que nationalité, sans que les Turcs conservent le droit de s'immiscer dans leur administration, on aurait mauvaise grâce à refuser aux Syriens ce que les Albanais ont eux-mêmes obtenus. La logique est du côté Syrien, si l'on s'en tient aux principes posés par la politique européenne. Nous ne blâmons pas l'Europe d'avoir ainsi reconnu le principe des nationalités, même musulmanes, dans l'Empire Ottoman. Mais nous sommes convaincus que ces principes de décentralisation sont destinés à prendre de l'extension et à porter de nouvelles conséquences dans l'avenir. Ce qu'il importe, c'est de concilier la politique de décentralisation, au point de vue syrien, avec le respect de l'intégrité ottomane en Turquie d'Asie."[79]

78. Professor Bernard Lewis does not judge the Young Turks harshly. While admitting that 'they have been blamed for many things" and that "the record of the ten years from 1908 is indeed at first sight a black one," he writes: "The Young Turks Revolution was a patriotic movement of Muslim Turks, mostly soldiers, whose prime objective was to remove a fumbling and incompetent ruler and replace him by a government better able to maintain and defend the Empire against the dangers that threatened it. Ottoman non-Muslims played a small and diminishing role in the movement and the regimes that grew out of it; foreigners hardly any at all. The young officers were little interested in ideologies and social panaceas as such. The fundamental question that concerned them was survival, the survival of the Ottoman state which they and their fathers had for generations served, and both their actions and their discussions revolved around this central problem. *Bu devlet nasil kurtarilabilir*? — How can this state be saved?

"It is, perhaps, through the different solutions that were sketched and attempted for this problem, that the Young Turk Revolution, despite its disappointments and its failures, was so profoundly important in the development of modern Turkey. In the years of freedom that followed the ending of Abdulhamid's autocracy, there was an opportunity for discussion and experiment such as the country had never known before. In a spate of periodicals and books, the basic problems of religion and nationality, of freedom and loyalty in the modern state, were discussed and examined; in the new parliamentary and administrative apparatus that followed the Revolution, new methods of government were devised and put to the test. And even though the discussion ended in silence and the experiments in dictatorship, new hopes and new appetites had been created which could not be indefinitely denied." Bernard Lewis, *The Emergence of Modern Turkey*, pp. 208-9.

79. Contenson, *Les réformes en Turquie d'Asie*, pp. 3, 68.

CHAPTER SIX

THE EMERGENCE OF ARAB NATIONALISM

PART TWO — THE WAR YEARS, 1914-1918

AS WE APPROACH the eve of the World War, a word must be said about the tentative Franco-British understanding about "Syria." Raymond Poincaré writes in his memoirs that in 1912 there were rumors of a British move in Syria "where most of the inhabitants looked to France for protection." But on 5 December of that year, Sir Edward Grey told the French Ambassador, Paul Cambon: "We have no intention of doing anything whatever in Syria, where we have neither aspirations nor designs;" a phrase, adds Poincaré, which "the Secretary of State willingly allowed me to quote to Parliament." "But is is needless to tell the Senate," continues Poincaré, quoting his own address to the Senate, "that in Lebanon and in Syria we have special and long-seated interests which we must see respected. The British Government, in the most friendly manner, had declared that in that part of the world it has no political aspirations and no wish or intention to do anything."[1]

On 13 January 1913, Sir Edward Grey wrote to Sir Rennell of Rodd, the British Ambassador in Rome, about his conversation with the Italian Ambassador in London: "I said that we ourselves had no designs in Asia Minor. All that we desired was the maintenance of a satisfactory *status quo* which would secure the Persian Gulf and its littoral against disturbance. But Russia had special interests in Asia Minor owing to her strategic frontier; Germany had vested interests in the Anatolian and Baghdad Railways; and France had

1. *The Memoirs of Raymond Poincaré*, trans. and adapted by Sir George Arthur (London, 1926) 1: 336, 338. The French text of these memoirs is entitled *Au service de la France*, 10 vols. (Paris, 1926-32).

the Syrian Railways. I thought that all or any one of them might raise objections to a self-denying ordinance as to Asia Minor."[2]

But the German documents contain a different story. Prince Lichnowsky, the German Ambassador in London from 1912-1914, wrote: "When I came to London in November 1912, ... Sir Edward Grey... had not given up the idea of reaching an agreement with us.... With Herr von Kuhlmann, the capable and business-like Envoy, as intermediary, an exchange of views was in progress concerning a renewal of the Portuguese Colonial Agreement and concerning Mesopotamia (The Baghdad Railway), the unavowed object of which was to divide the colonies in question, as well as Asia Minor, into spheres of interest."[3]

During the nineteenth century the British Government helped to maintain the independence of the Ottoman Empire which, of course, included the Arab Provinces in the Near East. On the eve of the First World War, Britain still refused to join with the other Powers in partitioning the Turkish possessions in Asia. On 27 June 1913, Sir Edward Grey wrote to Sir G. Goschen, British Ambassador in Berlin: "Respecting Asiatic Turkey, I had observed that there were two possible courses. One was to consolidate the remaining Turkish dominions and to put Turkey on her feet.... The other course was a division of Asiatic Turkey into spheres of interest. This would lead to partition and to the complete disappearance of the Turkish Empire." The German Ambassador, this despatch continues, told Sir Edward Grey that "the Arabs seemed to be rather restless, and an Arab Chief from Nejd had already made advances to the Germans, apparently on the assumption that Turkish rule was being broken up; but the Germans had declined to entertain his advances...." And Sir Edward Grey replied that "we also had advances of the same sort made to us from Chiefs, I thought more in the region of Basra and the Persian Gulf; but we had not encouraged them because they presupposed a break-up of Turkish authority. Amongst other things, it would give great offence to Moslem opinion in British territory if we took part in a policy of destroying the Turkish Government and dividing

2. Great Britain, Foreign Office, *British Documents on the Origins of the War*, vol. 9, *The Balkan Wars*, p. 404.

3. *The Times Documentary History of War* (London, 1919), vol. 9, pt. 3, pp. 3-4.

its territory."[4] In a telegram to Sir G. Buchanan, British Ambassador in Constantinople, dated 4 July 1913, Sir Edward Grey wrote: "A grave question of policy is involved and *the only policy to which we can become a party is one directed to avoid collapse and partition of Asiatic Turkey.* The effect of the opposite course upon our own Musulmans in India would be disastrous to say nothing of the complications that would be produced between European Powers."[5]

On 30 October 1914, the British Ambassador at Constantinople demanded his passport and the next day, at 5:05 p.m. G.M.T. the following fateful message was sent out by wireless from London: "Admiralty to all Ships. Commence hostilities at once against Turkey. Acknowledge."[6] In the eleven words of that cable lay the final collapse of the Ottoman Empire and the beginning of unforeseen events and incalculable forces which gave birth to the present Arab states in the Near East.

No sooner had hostilities begun on 5 November than the British press made it clear what fate awaited Turkey. On 3 November, *The Times* (London) wrote: "Turkey has betrayed the interests of Islam by making wanton war on the Allies, and has thereby pronounced her own death sentence." Among other papers which predicted the same fate for Turkey was the *Daily Mail* (London) which wrote on 23 November: "That the Ottoman Empire in Europe, won by the sword, is now about to perish by the sword we have no doubt whatever," and the *Daily News* (London) of November 31 which said: "If Germany is defeated, the punishment of Turkey for partnership with Germany will be practical annihilation as a Power."

No evidence has come to light yet to show whether the British Cabinet itself had any clear plan for her own share of the spoils in the Near East. Nearly five months after the opening of hostilities, Sir Edward Grey told the French Ambassador, M. Cambon:[7] "The Cabinet here had not yet had time to consider our desiderata" (concerning the Turkish possessions in Asia).... The Cabinet,

4. Great Britain, Foreign Office, *British Documents on the Origins of the War*, vol. 10, pt. 1, pp. 456-66.

5. Ibid., p. 481. Emphasis supplied.

6. Winston Churchill, *The World Crisis, 1911-1918* (London, 1939), 1:495.

7. Viscount Grey of Fallodon, *Twenty-Five Years, 1892-1916* (New York, 1925), 2: 236: Despatch of Sir Edward Grey to Sir Francis Bertie, dated "Foreign Office, March 23, 1915."

however, seems to have reached one conclusion: "I said that we had already stipulated that, when Turkey disappeared from Constantinople and the Straits, there must, in the interests of Islam, be an independent Moslem political unit somewhere else. Its centre would naturally be the Moslem Holy Places and it would include Arabia. *But we must settle what else should be included.* We ourselves had not yet come to a definite opinion whether Mesopotamia should be included in this independent Moslem state, *or whether we should put forward a claim for ourselves in that region.*" [8]

The India Office, on the other hand, was very definite about the necessity of bringing Mesopotamia directly or indirectly under British rule for the protection of India and British security in the Persian Gulf. Writing a Minute, on 26 September 1914, on "The role of India in a Turkish War," Sir Edmund Barron, military secretary of the India Office, was strongly in favor of an expedition being sent to occupy Baṣra and he concluded his Minute in the following words:

"This seems the psychological moment to take action. So unexpected a stroke at this moment would have a startling effect:

1) It would checkmate Turkish intrigues and demonstrate our ability to strike.

2) It would encourage the Arabs to rally to us, and confirm the Sheikhs of Muhammara and Koweit in their allegiance.

3) It would safeguard Egypt, and without Arab support a Turkish invasion is impossible.

4) It would effectually protect the oil-installation at Abadan. Such results seem to justify fully the proposed action." [9]

When Turkey joined the Central Powers in 1914, British policy towards the Asiatic provinces of the Ottoman Empire was determined by the fact that these provinces occupied an area which was of tremendous strategic importance to the prosecution of the War. As these provinces were inhabited mainly by Arabs and as the Arabs had already shown various degrees of dissatisfaction towards Ottoman rule, it was natural and logical that the British

8. Emphasis supplied.

9. See Great Britain, Mesopotamia Commission, *Report of the Commission Appointed by Act of Parliament to Enquire into the Operation of War in Mesopotamia* (London, H.M.S.O., 1917), p. 12.

should "attack the Turkish Empire through its Arab subjects."[10] Hence, all the efforts made by the British and all the promises and pledges given by them to the Arabs to win them to their side. "As a feature of the general strategy of the war," wrote Lloyd George, "the elimination of Turkey from the ranks of our enemies would have given us that access to Russia and Rumania which was so disastrously lacking, and without which they were driven out of the war.... The course of the war would have been altered and shortened.... The Turkish Empire lay across the track by land or water to our great possessions in the East.... It was vital for our communications, as it was essential for our prestige in the East, that once the Turks declared war against us, we should defeat and discredit them without loss of time. The importance of a speedy victory over the security of the British Empire was undeniable...."[11] Hence, the British turned towards the "disaffected population" of the Turkish Empire — the Arabs. The ground had already been prepared and the soil was fertile.

When the Ottoman Empire entered the World War on 5 November, she sealed her own doom. The Sick Man, at last, committed suicide.[12] In that hour of destiny the Empire was ruled by a triumvirate of three brave and ruthless men: Enver, Talaat, and Jamal. They were ably supported by "the skilful and incorruptible Finance Minister, Djavid."[13] These Turkish leaders were apparently convinced that Germany would win the war on land.[14] Tewfik

10. Harold W. V. Temperley, *The History of the Peace Conference of Paris* (London, 1924), 6: 178.

11. David Lloyd George, *War Memoirs* (London, 1933-36), 4: 1802-3.

12. It is interesting to note that before the opening of hostilities, Sharif Husain of Mecca wrote a personal letter to Sultan Muhammad Rashad, pleading with him not to enter the war on the side of Germany against Russia, Britain, and France. King 'Abdallah, *Mudhakkarati* [My Memoirs] (Jerusalem, 1945), pp. 98-99.

13. Actually, a Turkish Parliament was, theoretically at least, ruling the country. It was the third Parliament after the restoration of the Constitution in 1908 and was elected on the eve of the World War. It held its first session on 14 May 1914 in the presence of the Sultan. Out of a total of 245 members in that Parliament, only 69 were Arabs while 142 were Turks, the rest being Armenians, Greeks, and Jews; also 209 were Muslims and 36 Christians. *Al-Hilal* (Cairo), vol. 22, pt. 9, 1 June 1914, p. 708.

14. When the Young Turks came to power, they tried to abrogate the Capitulations but the pressure of the Foreign Powers and the Balkan Wars prevented them from doing so. However, when the World War began, the Porte informed the Ambassadors of the Powers on 9 September 1914, of her decision

Pasha, the Turkish Ambassador in London, told Sir Wyndham Deedes: "We firmly believe that if the Entente wins, Turkey will be divided up — Syria to France, Armenia to Russia, Persian Gulf hinterland to England. On the other hand, Germany will probably, if her group win, leave us what we have. Our obvious duty is to throw what weight we can into the scale against the Allies and with Germany."[15] Every effort made by Britain, France, and even Russia to keep Turkey out of the war had proved in vain: especially as the Turks saw in the Anglo-Russian Convention of 1907 "a definite alliance between the Power who had been Turkey's strongest and most disinterested supporter and friend with the Power who was her ancient and inexorable enemy."[16] "Nothing could supplant in the Turkish mind the fear of Russia... the sense of peril from the North still outweighed all else in Turkish thoughts."[17]

Meanwhile, the Arabs found their lands pluged in a war they had not wanted. A small minority secretly rejoiced that the collapse of the Ottoman Empire was imminent and thus the hour of retribution and restoration was at hand." The vast majority of the Arabs remained loyal supporters of the Caliphate and the Sultanate, but some of the Arab leaders found it imperative for the Arabs to leave the sinking Ottoman ship and establish their independence even if it were necessary to seek "foreign" help. Nor was this "foreign" help lacking. Both France and Britain had been waiting for this moment. They were aware of the grievances of the Arabs against the Turks and particularly of the dissatisfactions of Sharif Ḥusain, Emīr of Mecca. Nearly seven months before the war, Britain had actually been approached for help but at that time the help had naturally been declined as she could "never entertain

to abolish the Capitulations beginning 1 October. The Powers refused to accept that decision but the abrogation went into force on that date. The Capitulations were officially abolished by Article 28 of the Treaty of Lausanne, on 24 July 1923.

15. Mrs. Gladys Skelton [John Presland], *Deedes Bey: A Study of Sir Wyndham Deedes, 1883-1923* (London, 1942), pp. 139-140.

16. Churchill, *The World Crisis*, 1: 435.

17. Ibid., pp. 433-4.

Talaat Pasha to Aubrey Herbert: "Rightly or wrongly, you made friends with Russia: that was your policy at home and that was your policy at the Embassy in Constantinople. . . . If the leaders liked you (when we made our revolution) the people adored you; they took the horses out of your Ambassador's carriage and they pulled it up to the Embassy. . . . We Young Turks practically offered Turkey to you, and you refused us." Herbert, *Ben Kindim*, pp. 310, 312-13.

the idea of supplying arms to be used against a Friendly Power." The approach had come from Emīr 'Abdullah, second son of Sharīf Ḥusain, both to Lord Kitchener and to (Sir) Ronald Storrs to whom he had "unlocked his heart during his visit to Cairo."[18] Now, however, the situation had radically changed. Hence, the following two historic cables from Lord Kitchener, Secretary of State for War, cables which were the official starting point of the British invitation to the Arabs to revolt:[19]

"Sept. 24, 1914. Following from Lord Kitchener. Tell Storrs to send secret and carefully chosen messenger from me to Sharif Abdullah to ascertain whether 'should present armed German influence in Constantinople coerce Khalif against his will, and Sublime Porte to acts of aggression and war against Great Britain, he and his father and Arabs of the Hejaz would be with us or against us.' "[20]

On 31 October, Lord Kitchener cabled again:

"Salaams to Sharif 'Abdullah. Germany has now bought the

18. "In April 1914 occurred a visit to Cairo the ultimate impact of which upon the War and the destinies of the Near and Middle East is not even yet fully calculable. The Amir Abdallah, second son of Husain, Grant Sharif of Mecca, arrived from Constantinople as the guest of the Khedive and was received by Lord Kitchener. . . . Meanwhile, we were advised from Constantinople that such audiences were displeasing to the Sublime Porte, always suspicious of Arab intrigue in the Hejaz and in Syria. . . . Travelling by a series of delicately inclined planes. . . . I found myself . . . being categorically asked whether Great Britain would present the Grand Sharif with a dozen, or half a dozen machine guns . . . 'for defense' . . . against attack from the Turks. I needed no special instructions to inform him that we could never entertain the idea of supplying arms to be used against a Friendly Power. Abdallah can have expected no other reply, and we parted on the best of terms." Ronald Storrs, *Orientations* (London, 1945), pp. 122-23. Storrs quotes a private letter from Lord Kitchener to Sir W. Tyrell dated British Agency, Cairo, 26 April 1914, which contains the following excerpt.

"Sharif Abdallah. . . . He sent for Storrs who under my instructions told him the Arabs of the Hejaz could expect no encouragement from us and that our only interest in Arabia was the safety and comfort of Indian pilgrims. . . ."

See also Great Britain, Foreign Office, *British Documents on the Origins of the War*, 10: 826-29.

19. Wavell says: "The idea of binding the Arabs of the Hejaz to the British cause was suggested by Sir John Maxwell, as early as October, 1914." Major-General Sir John Maxwell was in command of the British forces in Egypt in September 1914. See Archibald P. Wavell, The *Palestine Compaigns* (London, 1928), n. on p. 52

20. Great Britain, Foreign Office, 371/2139, Cypher telegram to Mr. Cheetham (Cairo), Nº 219. Secret.

Turkish Government with gold, notwithstanding that England, France and Russia guaranteed integrity of Ottoman Empire if Turkey remained neutral in the War. Turkish Government have against the wish of Sultan... committed acts of war by invading the frontiers of Egypt with armed bands.... If Arab nation assists England in this war... England will guarantee that no internal intervention takes place in Arabia and will give Arabs every assistance against external foreign aggression." [21]

It is not the purpose of this chapter to describe or discuss the protracted negotiations which followed. However, some of their salient points may be worth repeating here. Upon receipt of the above cable, Storrs sent a letter to Emīr ʻAbdullah with a secret messenger. The latter returned with "a long and favourable reply" from ʻAbdullah. On 10 December, the same messenger returned from a second visit to Sharīf Ḥusain who "was friendly but unable to break with the Turks immediately." "The first definite proposals from the Sharif reached Sir Henry McMahon [22] in July 1915 (with a personal letter from ʻAbdullah to myself,

21. Ibid., N° 303. It may be of interest to note that Kitchener's invitation to the Arabs of Hejaz to "assist England in this war" was not the only one of its kind. Lawrence writes, " ʻAziz el-Masri, Enver's rival, who was living, much indebted to Egypt, was an idol of the Arab officers. He was approached by Lord Kitchener in the first days of the war, with the hope of winning the Turkish Mesopotamian forces on our side." T. E. Lawrence, *Seven Pillars of Wisdom: A Triumph* (London, 1935), p. 59.

Concerning ʻAziz ʻAli al-Misri, see Great Britain, Foreign Office, *British Documents on the Origins of the War*, vol. 10, pt. 2, pp. 832-38. He died on 16 June 1965. See also Majid Khadduri, "Aziz ʻAli Misri and the Arab Nationalist Movement," in St. Antony's Papers, no. 17, *Middle Eastern Affairs*, no. 4, ed. Albert Hourani (London, 1965), pp. 140-65.

Moreover, the Mesopotamian leader Talib al-Naqib himself, as early as 1911, and a group of Arab deputies had appealed to Sharif Husain to "shake the yoke which weighed on the Arabs and to deliver them from tryanny and slavery." K. T. Khairallah, *Les régions arabes libérées* (Paris, 1919), pp. 32-33.

The appeal was repeated in 1915. "In January 1915, Yasin, head of the Mesopotamian officers, Ali Riza, head of the Damascus officers, and Abd el-Ghani el-Areisi, for the civilians, sent down to him (Sharif Husain) a concrete proposal for a military mutiny in Syria against the Turks. The oppressed people of Mesopotamia and Syria, the Committees of the Ahad and the Fetah, were calling out to him as the Father of the Arabs, the Moslem of Moslems, their greatest prince, their oldest notable, to save them from the sinister designs of Talaat and Jemal." Lawrence, *Seven Pillars of Wisdom*, p. 50.

22. Sir Henry McMahon was appointed in December 1914 as High Commissioner for Egypt. "He is slight, fair, very young for 52, quiet, friendly, agree able, considerate and cautious." Storrs, *Orientations*, p. 191.

unsigned and undated) when he solicited the support of His Majesty's Government for the cause of Arab independence, and proposed certain boundaries for the independent Arab area."[23]

We must now turn to the events in Syria. Jamal Pasha says in his *Memories of a Turkish Statesman* that about ten days after Turkey's entry to the war, Enver Pasha, the Minister of War invited him to his house and told him, among other things, that "the news from Syria points to general disturbance in the country and great activity on the part of the revolutionary Arabs. In these circumstances, I have wondered whether Your Excellency would not give a further proof of your patriotism by taking over the command of the 4th Army."[24] The result of this interview was that Jamal Pasha arrived in Syria in December 1914 as Commander-in-Chief of the Fourth Army "to start an offensive against the Suez Canal to keep the English tied up in Egypt... and also to maintain peace and internal order in Syria."[25] He tried at first to win the Arabs by what he called "a policy of clemency and tolerance."[26] In a speech which he delivered in Damascus early in January 1915, he said: "Gentlemen, the programme for the welfare of the Arabs which our party means to carry out in its entirety is more comprehensive

23. Ibid., p. 152.

The exchange of letters which took place between the Sharif and McMahon from 14 July 1915 to 30 January 1916, belongs to a complicated phase of secret negotiations and secret promises in which the Allies indulged, under the strain and stress of war, for the purpose of winning that war. The story of this Correspondence has already appeared in numerous publications. See Lawrence, *Seven Pillars of Wisdom*, chaps. 4-6; Antonius, *The Arab Awakening*, pp. 164-83, and Appendix A, pp. 413-27; Storrs, *Orientations*, chap. 8, Cmd. 5957 (Miscellaneous No. 3): Correspondence between Sir Henry McMahon, His Majesty's High Commissioner at Cairo and the Sherif Hussein of Mecca, July 1915-March 1916 [London, 1939], and Cmd. 5974, *Report of a Committee set up to Consider Certain Correspondence between Sir Henry McMahon (His Majesty's High Commissioner in Egypt) and the Sherif of Mecca in 1915 and 1916* (London, 1939). See also Harry N. Howard, *The Partition of Turkey: A Diplomatic History, 1913-1923* (Norman: University of Oklahoma Press, 1931), pp. 187-93.

For these and other negotiations with Ibn Sa'ud and the Shaikh of Kuwait and in general for the relations of Great Britain and the Arab peoples during the war, see Temperley, *The History of the Peace Conference of Paris*, 6: 118-33.

24. Djemal Pasha, *Memories of a Turkish Statesman*, pp. 137-38.

25. Ibid., "... Djemal himself, just before his train started made this public declaration: "I shall not return to Constantinople until I have conquered Egypt." Morgenthau, *Ambassador Morgenthau's Story*, p. 171.

26. Djemal Pasha, *Memories of a Turkish Statesman*, p. 201.

than anything you can imagine. I, myself, am not one of those who think it a harmful or dangerous thing that the two races, Arab and Turkish, should secure their unity while remaining separate nations, subject to the same Khalife.... Today, I am in a position to assure you that the Turkish and Arab ideals do not conflict. They are brothers in their national strivings, and perhaps their efforts are complementary...."[27] He also emphasized that the war was essentially a *Jihād* in defense of Islam and a great Muslim Power — the Ottoman Empire.

Although it is very difficult to pass a fair and balanced judgement on any man who has been placed in authority, under abnormal and highly critical circumstances, there is much evidence to warrant the statement that Jamal Pasha seems to have been, essentially, a very ambitious and despotic man. Soon after his arrival in Syria, he instituted a reign of terror, through executions and deportations. After the failure of his expedition against the Suez Canal in February 1915, he returned to Syria and carried out a ruthless policy towards many Arab leaders by condemning them to death as "traitors" who wanted, through Decentralization, to dismember the Ottoman Empire and "sell their countries to the foreigner." On 21 August 1915, eleven Arab notables (ten Muslims and one Christian) were hanged at *al-Burj*, the principal square of Beirut, and on 6 May 1916 another group of twenty-one most prominent Muslim and Christian leaders (seventeen Muslims and four Christians), were executed at dawn; fourteen went to the gallows in Beirut and seven in *al-Marjeh* square in Damascus.

There were also from time to time, other executions of single individuals both in Syria and the Lebanon. No less than seventy-one notables were condemned to death *in absentia*. Many families were exiled to remote regions in Anatolia and much property was confiscated. The following American document of May 1916 is of much interest: "Turkish authorities appear to be pursuing policy of Turkifying Syria and adjacent Arabic-speaking provinces. Many notables both Christian and Moslem are stated to have been arrested, imprisoned and executed.... I understand that Turks put forward as ostensible reason for this action that Syrians and other Arabs subjected to this treatment were disloyal to the Turkish Government, that they held meetings in Egypt and elsewhere to

27. Ibid., pp. 199-201.

consider and decide steps to be taken for the separation of Syria from the Ottoman Empire. . . ."[28]

Moreover, because of the blockade of the Allies and the fact that Jamal Pasha was collecting the produce of the country for the Turkish and German armies, and also because of the greed of certain wheat merchants and their callous disregard of human suffering, thousands among the inhabitants became paupers and many thousands perished from starvation and disease.[29] To make the scarcity of food worse, clouds of locusts descended on Syria, Lebanon, and Palestine in 1915 ravaging the crops and eating up every green leaf.[30] Jamal Pasha took up his own defense in his *Memories* and in the *Red Book* which was published in Constantinople in 1916[31] containing photostatic documents of correspondence between some of the Arab leaders and the French Government.[32]

28. U.S., Department of State, Telegram (1821) from the Chargé d'Affaires in Turkey (Philip) to the Secretary of State (Lansing). See U.S., Department of State, *Papers Relating to the Foreign Relations of the United States, Supplement: The World War, 1914-1918* (Washington, 1928-33), 1916 Suppl., p. 851.

29. Yusuf al-Ḥakīm, *Beirut wa Lubnān fi 'ahd al-'Uthmān* [Beirut and Lebanon during the Ottoman period], (Beirut, 1964), pp. 250-52; Jirjus al-Khuri al-Maqdisi, *A'zam Ḥarb fi'l-Ta'rikh* [The greatest war in history] (Beirut, 1928), pp. 64-65.

30. Al-Ḥakīm, *Beirut wa Lubnān fi 'ahd al-'Uthmān*, p. 249; al-Maqdisi, *A'zam Ḥarb fi'l-Ta'rikh*, p. 48.

31. *La vérité sur la Question Syrienne*. Also published simultaneously in Turkish and Arabic.

32. "On the day of my arrival in Damascus, Hulussi Bey, the Governor General of Syria, told me he wanted to confer with me on extremely important matters. We met the same night at Government House. He handed me some very important documents which had been seized at the French Consulate, and told me that most of the documents implicated the most highly-placed and influential Mussulmans of Damascus, Beirut and other cities . . .

"Judging by these documents, there was not the slightest doubt that the Arab revolutionaries were working under French protection and, indeed, under the guidance and for the benefit of the French Government." Djemal Pasha, *Memories of a Turkish Statesman*, p. 197.

"Telegramme secret du Ministre à Berne.

"No. 338; 2/15 Juin 1916

"Je me refère à mon 329.

"Mandelstam demande de transmettre: "A propos des événements de Syrie. J'apprends complémentairement que Djemal Pacha a adressé à la population de Syrie une proclamation dans laquelle il accuse les puissances de l'Entente de viser au partage entre elles, de l'Empire turc et explique l'exécution des Syriens par la découverte d'un complot fomenté encore avant la guerre et ayant pour but l'annexion de la Syrie à la France. Les Turcs auraient soi-

He tried to prove that those leaders, were traitors to Turkey by being in secret communication with the enemy, particulary with France, and that Syria was on the verge of rebellion against the Turkish rule. It must be remembered, of course, that at the time of the execution of the Arab leaders, the British attack on the Dardanelles had already begun and British troops had landed at Gallipoli. A large number of Arab and Turkish troops had been despatched from Syria to the scene of those decisive battles on which hung the fate of Turkey and Russia. Jamal Pasha was naturally worried lest the Allies should make landings on the coast of Lebanon and be helped by "fifth-columnists" in the country — who, he knew for certain, had been in communication with Foreign Powers.

But many of the documents in the *Red Book*, when read carefully, do not justify his wholesale accusations against theArab leaders and some of his statements in his *Memories* are untrue. A number of these documents are contradictory and others clearly demonstrate that their authors did not want separation from the Ottoman Empire, alhough they worked for local independence. Might it not be that one of Jamal Pasha's real motives for these condemnations was the fear of losing his life should his own "secret negotiations with the enemy" become known in Constantinople, as a result of the indiscretions of one of the Arab leaders,[33] to whom he had confided his secret designs? There seems to be little doubt that he

disant saisi au consulat français de Damas une correspondance établissant les rapports secrets des Syriens avec la France. S'il en est ainsi, ces papiers se trouvaient entre les mains du gouvernement turc depuis le début de la guerre et cependant ce dernier n'avait pas fait usage jusqu'à présent. C'est pourquoi on peut supposer qu'au cours des derniers temps de nouveaux événements se sont produits qui ont décidé les Turcs à prononcer l'ostracisme contre les Syriens. En tout cas, les exécutions et les bannissements in-interrompus des Syriens vont provoquer fatalement de l'agitation dans tout le monde musulman et augmenteront la haine contre les Jeunes Turcs. Un fait également digne de remarquer est que le rôle principal dans ces persécutions est joué par Djemal Pacha qui a apparemment abondonné toute idée de rapprochement avec les puissances de l'Entente." René Marchand, *Un libre noir, diplomatie d'avant-guerre et de guerre d'après les documents des archives Russes (1910-1917)*, vol. 3, *Avril à Septembre 1916* (Paris, 1922-34), p. 67. See Djemal Pasha's statement published in the newspapers of Syria on 7 May 1916 (cited in *Thawrat al-'Arab*, pp. 164-67).

33. It is reported that 'Abd al-Karim al-Khalil who was the first to be executed, while standing at the foot of the gallows said: "I know the real reason for which Djemal Pasha is hanging me and it will be known to history, one day." Sa'id, *Al-Thawrah al-'Arabiyyah al-Kubra*, 1: 85.

was in communication with Russia and with France with the intention of getting out of the war on condition that he would be allowed to build up for himself an independent state from the Arab provinces of the Ottoman Empire.[34] The secret documents in the Russian Tsarist archives throw much light on this matter.[35]

34. "The Turkish world seemed to be disintegrating in Djemal's time, just as the Roman Republic was dissolving in the days of Antony; Djemal believed that he might become the heir of one or more of its provinces and possibly establish a dynasty. He expected that the military expedition on which he was now starting would make him not only the conqueror of Turkey's fairest province, but also one of the powerful figures of the world." Morgenthau, *Ambassador Morgenthau's Story*, p. 172.

35. These negotiations are of such great interest to the history of the period and might have had such an incalculable effect on the course of the war and on the destiny of the Arab countries that it may not be out of place to give here a brief summary of them. The first document is dated 26 October 1915. It is a letter from Sazanoff to Russian Embassies in Paris and Rome referring to news he had received from "American circles" in Istanbul expressing Djemal Pasha's desire to undertake "a hostile act' towards the Porte—if his conditions were granted. . . . Djemal Pasha's primary condition was that he—and after him his children and grandchildren—should become "The Sultan of an independent federated state composed of Syria, Palestine, Iraq, Arabia, Cilicia, Armenia and Kurdistan"—under the guarantee of the Allies. In December 1915, news of this nature kept coming to St. Petersburg and later to Paris from Russian representatives abroad. But France was not sympathetic with Djemal's project because while it satisfied Russia by giving her Constantinople and the Straits, it deprived the French of fulfilling their ambition of having Syria, Palestine and a part of Cilicia. In another document dated 17 January, Edward Grey is mentioned by Sazanoff, as believing that the French should directly negotiate with Djemal Pasha. On 27 January 1916, Britain made the Russian Ambassador, Benkendorff, understand that she was not interested to take part in the negotiations with Djemal. She was dealing directly with the Arabs for what was both to her and to the Arab's satisfaction. She was relying first and foremost on the Arabs alone, taking advantage of the hostile feelings towards the Turks and towards Djemal who had hanged their leaders. The last published communication in the Russian Archives, dated 13 March 1916, indicates the failure of the negotiations because of Anglo-French opposition. See Amin Sa'id, *Al-Thawrah al-'Arabiyyah al-Kubra*, 1: 168-75, and J. Polonsky, *Documents diplomatiques secrets russes, 1914-1917* (Paris, 1928), Section 6, pp. 249-331, and particularly Document No. 1999 of 30 December 1915.

Firuz Kazemzadeh has also written: "In December 1915, Zavriev informed the Russians that Jemal Pasha, one of the three most important political personages in Turkey, was dissatisfied with the government and would probably like to overthrow it. . . . The Russian Foreign Minister, Sazonov, then telegraphed Izvolskii, the Russian Ambassador in London (Count Benkendorf), and the Russian Ambassador in Rome (Giers), that Jamal Pasha would rebel against his Government and against the Germans provided the Allies agree to the following: 1) A free and independent Asiatic Turkey, consisting of autonomous

However, whatever the motives were, the consequences of Jamal Pasha's anti-Arab policy were to widen still further the gulf between Arabs and Turks and thus to intensify the Arab struggle to obtain their independence. Indeed, it may not be an exaggeration to say that Jamal Pasha's rule in Syria was one of the determining factors which helped most of the Muslim Arab leaders to make up their minds once for all to break away completely from the Ottoman Empire.[36] After the executions of 6 May 1916, Arab nationalism in Syria gathered momentum and strength. Arab political independence and Arab national sovereignty became an absolute necessity for sheer survival if for no other reason.[37]

provinces under the rule of a Sultan, including Syria, Mesopotamia, Armenia, Cilicia, and Kurdistan. 2) Jemal Pasha shall be the Sultan. 3) He shall march on Constantinople and declare the present Sultan and Government deposed as the prisoners of the Germans. 4) During his march on Constantinople Jemal shall receive military aid from the Allies. 5) After the war Jemal shall be given financial support. 6) Jemal shall acquiesce in the loss of Constantinople and the Straits. 7) Jemal shall take immediate measures to save and feed the Turkish Armenians until the end of the war. Sazonov added that even if Jemal Pasha should prove unable to overthrow the Government, the attempt would be worth while since it would create confusion in the ranks of the enemy." See Firuz Kazemzadeh, *The Struggle for Transcaucasia, 1917-1921* (New York and Oxford, 1951), pp. 28-29, citing Evgenii A. Adamov, ed. *Razdel Aziatskoi Turtsii* (Moscow, 1924).

See also Albert Pingaud, *Histoire Diplomatique de la France pendant la Grande Guerre* (Paris, 1940), vol. 3, *Les Neutralités et les Tentatives de Paix*, p. 228 where he writes that during the negotiations which preceded the Sykes-Picot Agreement, Djemal Pasha was trying secretly to pass into the Allied camp, "si on lui offrait de constituer pour lui, à la paix, une principauté dans le centre de l'Asie Mineure."

36. General Liman von Sanders, in a report to General Ludendorff, dated Constantinople, 25 October 1916, wrote: "En Syrie, les mesures de rigueur exagérées prises par Djemal Pacha ont détourné les Arabes de la cause turque. A Damas ont eu lieu ce mois-ci des troubles assez graves, qui ont nécessité l'intervention de la force armée." And speaking of Faisal, Liman von Sanders adds: "La déplorable politique arabe du gouvernment turc en avait fait un adversaire acharné." Liman von Sanders, *Cinq Ans de Turquie* (Paris, 1923), pp. 166, 240. The effect of Ahmed Djemal Pasha's 'reign of terror' was not only to deprive Syria of almost all possible leaders of revolt, but to increase in the people the spirit of revolt. It crowned seven years of Ottomanising efforts by making Ottomanism impossible for Arabs." Great Britain, Foreign Office, *Handbooks...*, No. 88, *Turkey in Asia* (London, March 1919), p. 16.

37. However, there were still Arab leaders in the Near East, in 1916, who had great misgivings when it came to their breaking away completely from the Ottoman Empire. Sulaiman Faidi, an Iraqi deputy in the Ottoman Parliament became a bitter enemy of the Young Turks and joined Talib al-Naqib against

If Jamal Pasha's oppressive rule in Syria was the second decisive factor[38] in the consolidation of Arab nationalism, the third equally decisive factor was the Allied encouragement and support of the Arabs to rebel against the Turks and gain their freedom and independence. Lloyd George wrote in his *War Memoirs*: "Our agents among them [the Arabs], who included men long skilled in the arts of Oriental diplomacy, encouraged this attitude of rebellion, and promised them arms and ammunition...."[39] It is significant that the *Jihād* or Holy War which was proclaimed by Turkey against the Allies at the beginning of the War failed to produce any effect in the Arab provinces. Liman von Sanders remarks in his *Cinq ans de Turquie* that this Holy War bore an appearance of unreality because Turkey was allied with Christian States, and German and Austrian officers and men were serving in the Turkish army.[40] Speaking of this *Jihād*, Halidé Edib says: "But such was the irony of fate that not only were there Moslems fighting in the French, and even Russian armies, but Turkey's own Moslem subjects, chiefly Arabs, were in league with the enemy camps."[41]

We have already noted how Kitchener got in touch with Sharīf 'Abdullah through Storrs and how, as a result, an exchange of letters took place between Sharīf Ḥusain and Sir Henry McMahon. The final outcome of these negotiations was the Arab Revolt which started in Mecca on 10 June 1916, under the leadership of Sharīf

the *Vali* of Basra. Nevertheless, at a meeting which took place between him and T.E. Lawrence in Basra on 7 April 1916, in the office of Capt. C. C. More, General Staff Intelligence, he refused, to the great surprise of Lawrence, to lead a revolt against the Turks. "Our struggle against the Ottoman Government," Faidi told Lawrence, "either in secret or in public, was in the sphere of internal affairs, for the purpose of obtaining certain legitimate rights which the Government had denied the Arabs, and certain internal reforms. . . . If the Turks had granted these demands, the disagreement between us and them would have ceased to exist. . . ." *Fi Ghamrat al-Niḍāl: Mudhakkarāt Sulaimān Faidī* [In the throes of the struggle: memoirs of Sulaiman Faidi] (Baghdad, 1952), pp. 218-19.

38. The first being the chauvinistic policy of the Young Turks discussed in Chap. 5 above.

39. Lloyd, George, *War Memoirs*, 4: 1910.

40. Liman von Sanders, *Cinq ans de Turquie*, pp. 44-45.

41. Adivar, *Turkey Faces West*, p. 141.

Ḥusain,[42] and with the military and financial support of Great Britain.[43]

Although a detailed study of the Revolt does not fall within the scope of this book, a brief summary of some of the events which preceded it will give the reader the immediate background of this historic step in the development of Arab nationalism.

The Sharīf, in his correspondence with Sir Henry McMahon, supported the cause of Arab independence and insisted on certain boundaries for an independent Arab State which, he thought, was going to emerge after the fall of the Ottoman Empire. Meanwhile, the Arab nationalists, particularly the influential members of the secret society *Al-Fatāt*, encouraged the Sharīf to rebel against the Turks and promised him their support, sometime during the months of March, April, and May 1915, part of which time Faisal spent in Damascus while on his way to and from Istanbul where he had gone to discuss the conditions in the Hejaz and to enlighten himself on the war situation. Several prominant Syrians and members of secret societies visited Faisal when he was a guest at the residence of the Bakrī family in Damascus — among them

42. 'Abdullah, *Mudhakkarati*, pp. 108-52. See also Sa'id, *Al-Thawrah al-'Arabiyyah al-Kubra*, 1: 145-65.

For the full text of Sharif Husain's proclamation of 26 June addressed to "All his Muslim Brethren," see Sa'id, *Al-Thawrah al-'Arabiyyah al-Kubra*, pp. 149-57. It is significant that after giving the reasons for the revolt, the Sharif states its purpose to be "complete separation and independence" of "the Arab countries" from the Government of the C.U.P., and its goal: "the defense of the Muslim religion and the raising of the station of Muslims" based on the foundation of the Shari'a Law, "the sole source of guidance and support."

43. Sir Ronald Storrs states that the total cost of the Arab Revolt to the British taxpayer was £ 11,000,000. He writes: "In addition to the initial sum I took, Husain received from August 8th, 1916, £ 125,000 a month; in all, less than one million sterling. The remaining ten million represent military operations and supplies from Great Britain." Storrs, *Orientations*, p. 153, n. 2.

It should be added that the French Government, too, contributed its help which, though limited, nevertheless, in the words of Sir Reginald Wingate "assisted largely in the success of the joint operations in which they took a very gallant and conspicuous part." A French Military Mission, headed by Lieutenant-Colonel Brémond and composed of notable Muslim representatives of Algeria, Tunisia, Morocco, and French West Africa, arrived at Jeddah on 20 September 1916, bringing with it for Sharif Husain a subsidy of 1,250,000 gold francs. It was followed shortly by a small contingent of French forces and a small number of French machine guns, field artillery, and rifles. The Mission was warmly welcomed by Sharif Husain. See Edouard Brémond, *Le Hedjaz dans la guerre mondiale* (Paris, 1931), pp. 48-53, 64-67, 348-49.

were Ali Rida Pasha al-Rikabi on behalf of *Al-Fatāt*, Yasīn al-Hāshimī representing *Al-ʻAhd* society, Shaykh Badr al-Dīn al-Ḥusaynī, the most prominent of the Syrian ʻulema, Nasīb Bey al-Atrash, one of the great Druze leaders of Syria, Shaykh Nawāf al-Shaʻlān, son of Nūrī al-Shaʻlān, the Shaykh of the powerful Ruwalah tribes of the Syrian desert.

After his departure from Damascus for Mecca in June, Faisal reported to his father and brothers the results of his preliminary studies of the Arab leaders' opinion on starting an Arab revolt under the leadership of the Sharīf. An important family meeting was held in Ta'if and it appears that at this meeting it was secretly decided to proclaim a revolt against the Government of the Young Turks, sometime after the following winter.[44] Faisal returned to Damascus in January 1916, "with the settled purpose of fomenting a revolt of the Arab divisions in the Turkish army and a mass rising of the population, on a signal from his father."[45] But because of Jamal Pasha's iron grip everywhere and on everything, the situation had now completely changed to the great disadvantage of the Arab nationalists. It was, therefore, necessary for Faisal to return to Mecca.

Meanwhile, on 16 April 1916, Sir Reginald Wingate, Sirdar of the Egyptian Army and Governor-General of the Sudan, wrote to the High Commissioner in Cairo:

"I have the honour to confirm my telegraphic summary of the contents of the latest communication from the Sherif of Mecca and to transmit originals and copies of the Arabic letters received. I also attach a copy of a further telegram giving information obtained in course of conversation with the Sherif's emissary.

"I have little doubt that the Sherif now feels himself definitely committed to the movement for Arabian independence and is merely awaiting the first favourable opportunity to declare himself openly.

"He has secured promises of recognition and support by a great number of chiefs throughout the Arabian Peninsula and, provided that the necessary monies and arms are forthcoming, there appear to be strong grounds for believing that the rising will

44. ʻAbdullah, *Mudhakkarāti*, p. 104.

45. George Antonius, *The Arab Awakening*, p. 188.

be successful in overthrowing the last shreds of Turkish authority in Arabia...."[46]

Faisal was back in the Hejaz towards the end of May and learned that the revolt was imminent. There was little time to lose, specially as a new and special Turkish force under Khairy Bey had arrived in Medina, accompanied by a German expedition headed by Baron von Stotzingen with the purpose of strengthening Turkish domination in the Peninsula and opening a new sphere of operations against the Allies."

It is worth noting that in the brief but threatening note which the Emir Faisal sent to Jamal Pasha on 9 June 1916, twenty-four hours before the revolt there are three references to the *Arab nature* of the struggle against the Turks. First, the note speaks of moderate "Arab demands" which have been rejected. Secondly, it says that the (Arab) troops who have prepared themselves to engage in a Holy War, on the side of the Turks, do not see why they should sacrifice themselves for a cause which is neither Arab nor that of Islam. Thirdly, it warns the Ottoman Government that there will not be any relations, henceforth, between the "Arab Ummah" (*al-Ummah al-'Arabiyyah*) and the "Turkish Ummah", but there will be a "state of war between the two Ummahs."

A few hours after the above note was sent to Jamal Pasha, the railway line between Damascus and Medina was cut, and the next day, Saturday, 10 June, at sunrise, the Arab Revolt began.[47]

The story of the Arab Revolt has been told in numerous publications; but, in particular, it has been related in a literary masterpiece: T. E. Lawrence's *Seven Pillars of Wisdom*, in the Introduction of which Lawrence wrote:

"Some Englishmen of whom Kitchener was chief, believed that a rebellion of Arabs against Turks would enable England, while fighting Germany, simultaneously to defeat her ally Turkey. Their knowledge of the nature and power and country of the Arabic-speaking peoples made them think that the issue of

46. Sir Ronald Wingate, *Wingate of the Sudan* (London, 1955), p. 182.

47. See 'Abdullah, *Mudhakkarāti*, p. 107. See also Sa'id, *Al-Thawrah al-'Arabiyyah al-Kubra*, pp. 106-8, for the Arabic text of Sharif Husain's Proclamation of 26 June, addressed to the Arabs and Muslims throughout the world explaining his reasons for revolting against the Ottoman Government. The Proclamation quotes an Islamic tradition (*ḥadīth*) to the effect that the Prophet said, one day: "If the Arabs are humiliated, Islam will be humiliated."

such a rebellion would be happy and indicateed its character and method. So they allowed it to begin, having obtained formal assurances of help for it from the British government. Yet none the less the rebellion of the Sherif of Mecca came to most as a surprise, and found the Allies unready. It aroused mixed feelings and made strong friends and enemies, amid whose clashing jealousies its affairs began to miscarry."[48]

It must be recorded in all historical fairness that by no means all the Arabs and Arab leaders in the Arab provinces of the Ottoman Empire were in favor of being ruled by Sharīf Ḥusain of Mecca. Nor were they all united as to their understanding of Arab independence or the ultimate form of Government in Arab lands. The following is an excellent summary of the conflicting Arab interests as recorded by Sir Wyndham Deedes, who was in the Egyptian branch of the British Intelligence Service and of whom it has been said that he had "the most exhaustive knowledge... of the play and counter-play of forces in the Turkish Empire...." Under the date of 21-29 February 1916, Deedes writes:

"But into the network of conflicting interests was woven an even more tangled thread: the Arab question. In addition to the Turkish parties we have some three Arab parties here:

"1. Those representing the Syrians, who are mainly concerned with the future of Syria, and their general concern in the matter is that the French should not be allowed to go to Syria, that they should have no more at the very outside than economic and financial concessions. So great is their dislike of the French that it is very questionable that if the French were to reign today in Syria they would not drive the Moslems straight away into the hands of the Turks.... It is difficult to account for this extraordinary dislike and, if asked, they quote Tunis and other places where the French have colonies of Moslems. The Christians too are by no means yearning for the French, in fact, with the exception of the Maronites, the Christians of Syria are as opposed to the French going there, by which I mean territorial concessions, as are the Moslems. How difficult this makes our position at the present moment is quite obvious, because we ourselves know that our F.O. have made some sort of arrangement with the French by which we believe they are to have some territorial aggran-

48. Lawrence, *Seven Pillars of Wisdom*, p. 28.

disement.... News of this is only [now] reaching our friends who are continually coming to us and asking whether it is true we have sold them to the French.

"2. We have the party of the Shereef. With this party we really are negotiating on the lines of a spiritual and temporal Arab Kingdom. That at all events is what the Shereef wants. Personally, and I think it is the view of most of us, and is the view of many of the Arabs and all of the Turks themselves, this idea is not a practical one. For... it will never be possible to get all the Arabs of Syria, Iraq, Yemen and the others to acknowledge one temporal chief, even if they acknowledge one spiritual chief. And if they were prepared to acknowledge one man the question is who that man is to be. The Shereef of Mecca's influence is accepted over a certain part of the countries named but not over others.... The Shereef's [party] is much the most moderated and sensible of all... they are very loyal to us for their own ends; secrecy being vital they are very anxious that none other than their own party should have wind of what is going on....

"3. Finally, we have the party of Iraq. They want an independent Government for those parts and they are very anxious to get out of us now what zone we mean to allot and, if they can, what form of Government. Now our *great difficulty* is the Indian Government, who view all our flirtations with these parties with the greatest suspicion and particularly any arrangements made about Iraq, Basra and the Persian Gulf.

"What with the French and the Indian Governments our difficulties sometimes appear insuperable. It should be noted, too, that the Turkish parties, especially those that incline most to the present form of government, or who are anxious to see some form of government of the Rahmi-Prince Sabahattin type set up again in Turkey, view this Arab movement with the greatest misgiving...." [49]

Meanwhile, the three Great Powers, Great Britain, France, and Russia, were defining "their own respective claims in Turkey-in-Asia." "The resulting secret agreement between the three Powers about the disposal of Asiatic Turkey, known as the Sykes-Picot Agreement, was signed in May 1916, and its terms were afterwards

49. Skelton, *Deedes Bey*, pp. 244-5.

published by the Bolsheviks when the Petrograd archives fell into their hands."[50]

For an understanding of what the future had in store for the Arab Near East, as far as Britain was concerned, it is of great interest to be acquainted with following two significant documents, both of which were written in 1917. The first is a British "Statement on Foreign Policy made to the Imperial War Council." It was communicated to the American Secretary of State, Mr. Lansing, in Washington on 18 May 1917, by Mr. Balfour, Chief of the British Special Mission which was then visiting the United States. The policy concerning Turkey was a follows:

> "The practical destruction of the Turkish Empire is undoubtedly one of the objects which we desire to attain. The Turks may well be left — I hope they will be left — in a more or less independent position in Asia Minor. If we are successful, unquestionably Turkey will be deprived of all that in the larger sense may be called Arabia; she will be deprived of the most important portions of the Valley of the Euphrates and the Tigris; she will lose Constantinople; and Syria, Armenia and the southern parts of Asia Minor will, if not annexed by the Entente Powers, probably fall more or less under their domination."[51]

The second document discusses "The Asiatic Provinces of Turkey" and reads, in part:

> "If I were to set myself to make a brief for the Turk I should not be without arguments. No one who knows him and his history can accuse him of having been the sole agent of destruction in

50. Arnold J. Toynbee, *The Western Question in Greece and Turkey* (London, 1922), p. 48. Toynbee adds in explanation the following footnote: "The final text of the agreement was drafted by Sir Mark Sykes and M. Georges Picot on behalf of the British and French Governments, respectively, but these gentlemen only settled details of phraseology. The flundamental points in the agreement had already been worked out in conferences of leading statesmen and officials on both sides, before it was handed over to them for completion. The unofficial name, used for brevity, gives a wrong impression of the part they played, and now that the agreement is discredited and Sir Mark Sykes unable to defend himself, owing to his lamentable death from influenza during the Peace Conference at Paris, it is important that no injustice should be done to his memory. The responsibility on the British side for this agreement lies with the British Government." For an official and authoritative account of the Sykes-Picot Agreement, see E. L. Woodward, and Rohan Butler, *Documents on British Foreign Policy 1919-1939*, 1st ser. (London, 1952), vol. 4, 1919, pp. 241-51.

51. U.S., Department of State, *Papers Relating to the Foreign Relations of the United States: The Lansing Papers, 1914-1920* (Washington, 1940), 2: 23.

the lands he governed. A heavy burden of blame lies upon the nations of Europe, for whom Turkey has been a pawn in an age-long and shameful game of jealous cupidity. But the time for such pleas is past. It has been blotted out by the blood and tears of the subject races. Venit summa dies et ineluctabile tempus — let us consider what the new day should bring.

"I take it for granted that the Arab provinces cannot be allowed to remain under Turkish rule.... We are dealing with one of the most important agricultural areas in the world. The Iraq alone is not second in productiveness to Egypt, while in acreage, it is more than twice as large; the Syrian granaries, without modern facilities to transport, helped to feed Rome, and the commerce of the ancient as well as of the medieval world flowed of necessity to eastern industrial centres.... The rehabilitation of the Near East may once more alter the balance, or let us say establish a just balance, by recreating a market which has been for centuries in abeyance. It will add immeasurably to the wealth of a universe wasted by war and provide new fields for the reviving industries of Europe.... East and West will once more be linked together by common advantage."[52]

The story of the Arab rebellion, the roles of Lawrence and Faisal in carrying out the "Revolt in the Desert" and triumphantly terminating it in Damascus on 1 October 1918, the Anglo-French promises of "independence" to the Arabs, on the one hand, and on the other, the secret negotiations and treaties among the Allies themselves concerning their own spheres of direct and indirect rule in Arab lands, based on thier own interpretation of the word "independence," have been the subject of bitter controversy for

52. Great Britain, Foreign Office, *Iraq*, Memo. No. 20, dated 25 July 1917, and written by "the Chief Political Officer in charge Iraq Section, Arab Bureau, Baghdad" to "the Officer in Charge, Arab Bureau, c/o Director, Military Intelligence, Cairo."

This Memo was addressed to:

1. Secretary of State for Foreign Affairs, London, S.W.
2. Foreign Secretary to the Government of India in the Foreign and Political Department, Simla.
3. Political Secretary, India Office, London, S.W.
4. Chief of the General Staff, I.E.F. "D", G.H.Q.
5. Secretary to the Government of India, Army Department, Simla.

nearly half a century.[53] They do not fall within the scope of this Essay for they do not belong to the history of Arab-Turkish relations but are part of a broader and more complicated phase in the history of the relations between the Near East and the West.

The last year of the war saw the final collapse of the Ottoman Empire and the occupation of the Near East by the Allied armies. Early in January 1917, British forces (the Egyptian Expeditionary Force) invaded southern Palestine and on 9 December occupied Jerusalem. Nine months later, in one big onrushing wave, Allenby's army swept though the rest of Syria and Lebanon defeating the Turkish Fourth Army. Haifa was occupied on 23 September 1918, Damascus on 1 October and Beirut on 8 October. By one of those striking ironies of fate, the final surrender of the Turkish army came on the very plain of Marj Dābiq where almost exactly four hundred years earlier, the troops of Sultan Selim I had won a decisive victory — the victory which made the Ottomans masters of this very Syria which they had now lost to the Allies. Aleppo was captured on 25 October and, the next day, the last engagement of the war against Turkey in the East took place some eight miles northwest of the city. Five days later, came the news of the armistice,[54] which Turkey signed on board a British battleship, the H.M.S. *Agamemnon*, in the harbor of Mudros at Lemnos, in the Aegean Sea, on 30 October.[55] The 55th and last article of the Armistice read: "Hostilities between the Allies and Turkey shall cease from noon, local time, on Thursday, 31st October 1918."[56] Article 16 stipulated "the surrender of all garrisons in Hejaz, Assir, Yemen, Syria and Mesopotamia to the nearest Allied Commander."[57]

53. The issues were further complicated by the Balfour Declaration of 2 November 1917 concerning "the establisment of a Jewish national home in Palestine."

54. "In less than six weeks Allenby's army had captured 75,000 prisoners and 360 guns, and had moved its front forward 350 miles." Archibald P. Wavell, *Allenby, Soldier and Statesman* (London, 1946), p. 245.

55. The four signatories were Vice-Admiral Sir S. A. Cough Calthorpe, British Commander-in-Chief in the Mediterranean; Ra'uf Bey, Turkish Minister of Marine; Rashad Hikmat Bey, Under-Secretary for Foreign Affairs, Lieutenant-Colonel Sa'dallah Bey, Turkish General Staff. See Captain Cyrill Bentham Falls, *Military Operations: Egypt and Palestine, from June 1917 to the End of the War* (London: H.M.S.O., 1930), pt. 2, p. 625.

56. Ibid., p. 627.

57. Ibid., p. 626.

With the signing of the Armistice, Arab-Turkish relations as they had existed for four hundred years came to an end. The subsequent developments in Arab lands belong to a new phase in the history of the Arab Near East.

CHAPTER SEVEN

CONCLUSION AND POSTSCRIPT

THE ARAB NEAR EAST, bent under the weight of a long history and an old civilization, has been shaken out of its lethargy and thrown into a state of flux and confusion during the last five decades. The changes that have overtaken it have been bewilderingly rapid and, in some cases, profoundly disturbing because they have not been the result of slow and natural growth from the soil of its own history but have been thrust upon it, suddenly and forcibly from without. The time for adjusting to these changes and assimilating them has been exceedingly short. Hence, one must be extremely cautious to draw any final "conclusions" from the kaleidoscope of events which have succeeded one another in these lands. In this chapter, the author will try to sum up certain fundamental issues and problems in the background history of the Arabs, which he has described in the previous chapters. In that background, four factors stand out: Islam, the Turks, the impact of the West, and Arab nationalism.

If the Turkish rule lasted for four hundred years in Arab lands and if the Arabs acquiesced in that rule most of that time, it is essentially because the Turks were Muslims. The Ottoman Sultans as Ghāzis continued the expansion of Islam, after its fortunes had reached their lowest ebb with the destruction of Baghdad in A.D. 1258, at the hand of Hulagu and his horde of Mongolian conquerors. The Turks invaded Europe, the heart of Christendom, and carried the banner of Islam to the very gates of Vienna. Since the occupation of Spain by the Arabs and the battle of Poitiers in A.D. 732, the Christian nations had neither felt nor been shaken by the power of a Muslim nation as they were for nearly three hundred years by the might of the Ottoman Sultans. The Arabs as

Muslims were proud of Turkish power and prestige. The Ottoman Empire was their Empire as much as it was the Turks'. These facts should be remembered and taken into consideration in any study of Arab-Turkish relations and for any understanding of the Arab attitude towards the West. But, unfortunately, many students of contemporary Arab history are either uninformed or, looking through the colored glasses of modern political, and secular nationalism, deliberately ignore and, therefore, fail to comprehend the religious background of the forces which for centuries influenced and moulded the Arab Near East—Islam.

Hence, for a correct understanding and appraisal of the Arab Near East, today, a study of Islam, Muslim institutions, and Muslim psychology is imperative. Lacking this basic inquiry, other studies will touch only the surface and not the heart of the matter. Those who see nothing in the Arab Near East but its geography and geopolitics, its overland commercial routes, its principal airfields, its strategic location and its rich oil fields are making a grievous error. Failure to comprehend the human element in this area has been one of the major causes of the failure of the West in the Arab Near East. To evaluate correctly the situation in this part of the world, one must understand the source from which spring the motives and actions of the vast majority of its inhabitants, namely, the religion of Islam; without this it will be impossible to grasp the deeper issues at stake. Many political, economic, and social problems in this part of the world are interwoven with religion. The force of Islam is still much greater than the force of politico-secular nationalism. This basic truth should neither be ignored nor underestimated.

It is also time for Western historians to abandon some of their long cherished misconceptions about Arab-Turkish relations. Taking the latter part of the nineteenth and the beginning of the twentieth centuries as their observable starting points, at a time when corruption in the Ottoman administration was reaching its nadir and Arab-Turkish relations were strained severely both because of the short-sightedness of the Turks themselves and because of the political machinations of the Western Powers, they have projected this picture into the previous 350 years of Turkish rule in Arab lands and have reached the conclusion that the Arabs "suffered" for four hundred years under the yoke of Turkish misgovernment and despotism! Nothing is further from the truth than this assertion.

It is true that the Ottoman Empire was composed of a mosaic of races, nationalities and religions which the Turks did not attempt either to unite by force or to "Turkify." But it must be remembered that during the greatest part of Turkish rule the Arabs did not consider the Turkish rule a "foreign" rule. The word "foreign" did not have in those days the twentieth-century political connotation of a nationally alien and, often, politically "undesirable" person. The world in which the Arabs and the Turks lived together was, before the end of the nineteenth century, *politically* a non-national world. The vast majority of the Muslim Arabs did not show any nationalist or separatist tendencies except when the Turkish leaders themselves, after 1908, asserted their own nationalism and ceased to be considered, in Arab eyes, as good Muslims and as brothers in the Faith. It is, thus, unjustifiable to regard the Turks as the oppressors of the Arabs, except in the last years of Turkish rule during which time the Turks suffered, at least, as much as the Arabs from Turkish misgovernment. Numerous facts and accounts support the conclusion that the Turkish government, before its decline and fall, was, on the whole, orderly and reasonable in the treatment of its subjects.

On the other hand, while the Ottoman Empire was rapidly declining in the nineteenth century, the Western world was going through a great transition and growing in military and economic power as a result of revolutionary developments in industrial capitalism and in the progress of technology. There was also a process of secularization which had gained momentum in the social and governmental institutions of Western countries and which had contributed greatly to the growth of militant nationalism. This brings us to the third factor: the impact of the West on Arab lands.

For many years, prior to World War I, the Arab knowledge of the West was through the medium of trade and was limited by what the Arabs had read and heard about it. A few had a first hand knowledge of the West through their travels or studies abroad. Their attitude towards that West was, on the whole, one of respect for its military might, adminiration for its material progress and achievements and for its honesty in business transactions. The "word of an Englishman" was proverbial for its integrity and reliability. A European — a *Franji* — was, in general, considered as a civilized and superior being. "When I first heard the East a-calling to me, now, I regret to say, nearly fifty years ago," wrote

Sir Valentine Chirol, "the enduring supremacy of the Occident over the Orient was almost universally assumed as a matter of course. The Western nations claimed it in virtue of their superior civilization and were able to enforce it by their superior material and economic equipment...."[1]

It is regrettable that when the Arabs came in actual contact with the West in their own lands, during and at the end of the First World War, it was with a military and political West. Although the Arabs in Egypt and Palestine had seen and heard the guns of Napoleon I from 1899 to 1801, it was a short-lived occasion with short-lived results. In the twentieth century, however, the situation was vastly different. The great shock the Arabs had was their awakening to that kind of a West which, by the very nature of the circumstances of the time, was primarily and inevitably colored by the Machiavellian spirit of power-politics. At first,they were jubilant at the liberation of their countries from the horrors of war. Later, they became disillusioned and disheartened at the failure of their national aspirations and the lack of success which accompanied the political experiments which were tried in their lands. New political systems and philosophies were imported into the Near East under the general term of democracy and grafted, artificially, onto a society which was feudal in nature and theocratic in spirit. The results were not happy, and were often disappointing. The strain and stress produced by maladjustments and by lack of understanding, and sometimes of appreciation, of the new political institutions, discredited democracy in the eyes of many Easterners. It is too often forgotten that democracy is not an article of export, and there is no automatic guarantee that, just because the outward symbols of democracy are created in an alien soil, democracy itself will suddenly prevail.

It is true, of course, that Westernization in its material, technological aspects could not be stopped nor was it, probably, desirable to stop it. Indeed, there seemed nothing wrong in improving the physical conditions of life whether in building new roads, improving health conditions, constructing better houses, riding in cars, using telephones, enjoying the blessings of electricity and of better means of communication and transportation. But the cultural-spiritual heritage of the West was not wanted — except by a small

1. Sir Valentine Chirol and others, *Reawakening of the Orient and other Essays* (New Haven, 1925), p. 3.

group of "Westernized" Easterners. The Arab-Muslim reformers while admitting the necessity of improving the internal conditions in Arab lands had no intention of introducing a Western pattern of culture nor did they believe in its superiority. To them and to the vast majority of the masses behind them, the return to the purity of Islam and Muslim institutions was the answer to all the evils which surrounded them. They were, indeed, opposed to "spiritual Westernization" and preached against it as "dangerous" and "heretical." For they saw in it a double danger to their lands and to their peoples: the political danger of Western imperialism encroaching upon the Arab provinces and the spiritual danger of either Western Christian culture imposing itself upon Islam or the Western materialistic philosophy of the Machine Age submerging the new and future generations of Arab youth in its agnosticism and in its secularism. The reaction and protest of the Arabs against the ascendency of the West, against its partition of the Near East into mandates and zones of influence, found expression more and more violently in the most potent of all the new forces generated recently in this part of the world, namely the force of Arab political nationalism. Neither the speed nor the scale of this force had been foreseen.

It has often been said that the Arabs experienced a national *awakening* towards the end of the nineteenth and the beginning of the twentieth centuries, their nationalism having been submerged by nearly four hundred years of Ottoman domination. There is no satisfactory historical evidence for this contention. If by Arab awakening be meant the awakening of Arab *consciousness* and Arab *identity*, i.e., *al-'Urūbah*, then the term "awakening" is a misnomer. Throughout the four centuries of Ottoman rule, the Muslim Arabs never ceased to think of themselves as Muslims and as Arabs and they, certainly, did not forget their Arabic language. Indeed the vehemence with which the Arabs opposed the "Turkifying" policy of the Young Turks is, in itself, a proof that their Arab consciousness was wide awake. Had Arab consciousness been submerged and destroyed by the Turks, as is commonly asserted, the Young Turks would have had very little difficulty in "Turkifying" the Arab lands. Nationalism has undergone several changes in meaning during the course of its evolution in various States. But if we take into consideration, basically, the racial, cultural and spiritual elements of nationalism, we find that Arab nationalism is one of the oldest nationalisms in the world.

The true birth of Arab nationalism took place with the rise of Islam. Even as a generalization, there is no support for the contention that Arab nationalism was born as an "intellectual movement" in literary circles and secret societies and especially through the fiery poems of Arab poets. Islam was revealed by an Arabian Prophet, in the Arabic language, in Arabia. We read in the Qur'an: "A Messenger has now come to you from among yourselves...."[2] There is a tradition that the Prophet said one day: "I am an Arab, the Qur'an is in Arabic and the language of the denizens of Paradise is Arabic." And according to another tradition he is reported to have stated: "He who loves the Arabs loves me, and he who hates them hates me." The Arabs could not help feeling that they were a "chosen race." It was the Muslim Arabs of Arabia that the Prophet glorified in these words : "Ye are the best people (*Ummah* or "nation") that hath been raised up unto mankind."[3] One of the basic aims of Islam was to replace the narrow blood and tribal ties existing among the Arabs in pagan days or the "Days of Ignorance" by a broader and a wider "religious patriotism" found in Islam itself. The Arabs were to be united into one great community, the Community of the Faithful — the *Ummah* or the "nation" of Islam. "Verily, you are one *Ummah* and I, your Lord; therefore, worship me,"[4] and "Verily, the believers are brethren."[5] The Arab nation, *al-Ummah al-'Arabiyyah* was, thus, a nation originally born out of Islam. Islam was the prime creator of the national life and political unity to the Muslim Arabs.[6] This,

2. Sura 9, *Al-Tawbah* ["Repentance"], v. 128.
3. Sura 3, *Al-'Imrān* ["The family of 'Imran"], v. 106.
4. Sura 21, *Al-Anbiā'* ["The prophets"], v. 91.
5. Sura 49, *Al-Ḥujarāt* ["The apartments"], v. 10.
6. The following references are to some of the works which have appeared since 1958 on the subject of Arab nationalism and Arab unity. They were all written by Muslim authors and maintain very emphatically that Arab nationalism in its genesis and growth has been inseparable from Islam.

Idrīs al-Kattānī, *Al-Maghrib al-Muslim Ḍid al-Lādiniyyah* [Muslim Morocco opposes atheism] (Casablanca, 1958), pp. 171, 173-74; Muḥammad al-Mubārak, *Al-Ummah al-'Arabiyyah fi Ma'rakat Taḥqīq al-thāt* [The Arab *Ummah* in the struggle to establish its identity] (Damascus, 1959), pp. 64, 67, 100, 131, 160; Aḥmad Amīn, *Yawm al-Islām* [Day of Islam] (Cairo, 1958), p. 49; Aḥmad Ḥasan al-Baqurī, *'Urūbah wa Dīn* [Arabism and religion] [Cairo, n.d.], p. 66; 'Alī Ḥasanī al-Kharbutli, *Muḥammad wa'l-Qawmiyyah al-'Arabiyyah* [Muhammad and Arab nationalism] (Cairo, 1959), pp. 49, 67, 115, 121, 123; Muḥammad al-Ghazālī, *Kifāḥ Dīn* [The religious struggle] (Cairo, 1959), pp. 6, 11, 212;

"religious nationalism" remains an indelible part of the hearts and minds of the Arabs.

When Islam became the religion of such non-Arabs as the Persians and the Indians, the Arabs felt still more conscious of their Arabism (*'Urūbah*) and continued to consider themselves supreme over the nations of their "clients." The Arab Muslims believed that they had "conferred" a great favor upon the "foreign" Muslims by "having rescued them from unbelief," During the Umayyad Caliphate (A.D. 661-750), Arab national consciousness and Arab prestige were, perhaps, at their peak. "The Arabs... believed themselves at this time to be superior to all other nations, whether clients or members of tolerated creeds. In his own opinion, the Arab was born to rule, and everyone else to serve; whence, at the commencement of Islam, the Arabs occupied themselves only with governing and politics; all other occupations, especially arts and crafts, were relinquished by them to non-Arabs. An Arab and a client had a dispute in the presence of 'Abdallah ibn 'Āmir, governor of Iraq, when the client said to the Arab: 'God give us few like thee!' The Arab retorted: 'God give us many like thee!' Being asked why he blessed in answer to the other's curse, he replied: 'Do not these people sweep our streets, patch our shoes, and weave our garments?' [7] As late as the middle of the nineteenth century, an "Oriental Student" observed that "Damascenes consider themselves, on the double ground of being Moslems and Arabs, as the noblest race in the world, and that the government of the

idem, *Ḥaqīqat al-Qawmiyyah al-'Arabiyyah* [The truth about Arab nationalism] (Cairo, 1961-69), pp. 9-10; 'Abd al-'Azīz al-Dūrī, *Al-Judhūr al-Ta'rīkhiyyah li'l Qawmiyyah al-'Arabiyyah* [The historical roots of Arab nationalism] (Beirut, 1960), pp. 12-14; idem, *Muqaddamah fi Ta'rīkh Ṣadr al-Islām* [Introduction to the history of the early days of Islam], 2nd. ed. (Beirut, 1961), pp. 37-38,41, 44, 46; Muḥammad Aḥmad Bashmīl, *Sīra' ma' al-Bāṭil* [Struggle with falsehood] (Beirut, 1960), pp. 65, 74, 129, 210; idem, *Al-Qawmiyyah fi Nazar al-Islām* [Nationalism from the viewpoint of Islam] (Beirut, 1960), p. 46; Ṭāha 'Abd-al-Bāqī, Surūr, *Dawlat al-Qur'ān* [The government of the Qur'an] (Cairo, 1961), Maḥmūd Shaltūt, *Al-Islām: 'Aqīdah wa Sharī'ah* [Islam: belief and law] (Cairo, n.d.), pp. 445-47. See also A. Bint al-Shāṭi', "Al-Tafsīr al-Dīnī Li Tārīkhina"]The religious interpretation of our history], *Al-Ahrām* (Cairo), 9 August 1963, p. 13, and Mudaththir 'Abd al-Raḥīm, "Al-Islām wa'l Qawmiyyah fi'l Sharq al-Awsaṭ" [Islam and nationalism in the Middle East], *Ḥiwār* (Beirut), vol. 1, no. 6 (September-October 1963): 5-13.

7. Jurji Zaidan, *Ta'rīkh al-Tamaddun al-Islāmi* [A History of Muslim Civilization], trans. D. S. Margoliouth under the title *Umayyads and Abbasids* (London, 1907), pp. 71-72.

Sultan is the first in rank, not because he is *Malek er-Roum*, or sovereign of the Greek Empire, but the Caliph, or successor of Mohammed."[8]

Arab national consciousness survived throughout the centuries, in spite of all the vicissitudes of the Arabs during their long history, because two of the strongest ties of national unity, in the broad sense of the term, were never destroyed: the linguistic and the religious. The Arabs continued to feel as Arabs, because they continued to speak one language and believe in one religion. Their cultural and spiritual ties remained far stronger than either territorial unity or geographical separation. Hence, the Arabs never lost or "forgot" their "nationalism" under the Turks, especially as the Turk made no attempt, except at the eleventh hour to "Turkify" the Arabs. All that the Arab leaders wanted at first — the masses were still indifferent — was that the Arab provinces within the Ottoman Empire should have an autonomous Arab government. They believed that the best form of government for the multi-national, multi-racial Ottoman Empire was a decentralized government. Some had in mind visions of an Ottoman "Commonwealth of Nations." As to complete separation from the Ottoman Empire, the idea was only in the minds of few extremists among the Muslims, before the Turkish Revolution of 1908. Its exponents and real supporters in the Near East were primarily the Christians of Mount Lebanon. But even after 1908, separation was almost forced upon some Muslim Arab leaders by the shortsightedness and chauvinistic Pan-Turanian policy of the Young Turks. The despotic policy of Djemal Pasha, Commander-in-chief of the Fourth Army in Syria, during the first World War, when he ordered the hanging of prominent Arabs in Beirut and Damascus, in 1915 and 1916, widened, still further, the breach between the Arabs and the Turks and greatly intensified the Arab leaders' desire to break away completely from the Ottoman Empire. Finally, the promises of the Allies, again during that War, to "liberate" the Arabs from the Turks and to give them their "independence" led to the Arab Revolt which started in Mecca on 10 June 1916, under the leadership of Sharīf Ḥusain.

Thus, if by Arab awakening be meant the desire of the Arabs to separate themselves from the Turks and establish an independent, sovereign Arab State, similar to European states, this certainly was

8. An Oriental Student, *The Modern Syrians* (London, 1844), p. 202.

not so much an awakening as it was a desire for self-determination and political independence. What the educated and enlightened Arabs were waking up to was not to Arab consciousness which had never "slept" but to an independent political life. This was part of the general political awakening which had occurred in Europe two hundred years earlier and more recently in Asia. The moving and motivating force was a demand by the Arabs for their political rights, for social justice, and for liberty. It was essentially man's eternal quest for freedom and justice. This "political nationalism" which marks the second stage in the development of Arab nationalism was primarily a product of political and social conditions prevailing during the last years of Turkish rule in Arab lands. But even then, religion was not divorced from Arab nationalism. Not only the vast majority of the Arabs were Muslims, but together with the goal of self-determination and self-government went the further aim of rising to the defence of Islam, restoring its past glories and raising the Arabs — "the race by means of which God had led the peoples (of the world) from darkness to light ' — to their righful place under the sun, the glorious place which God had destined for them, as His own "chosen *Ummah*."[9]

The first leaders of Arab political nationalism, particularly Sharīf Ḥusain of Mecca, envisaged, immediately before and during the first World War, an Arab State rising out of the dissolution of the Ottoman Empire, built around an Arab Muslim King and on Muslim foundations. In a Memorandum submitted to the Peace Conference on 1 January 1919, the Emīr Faiṣal wrote : "The country from a line Alexandretta - Persia, southward to the Indian Ocean is inhabited by 'Arabs' — by which we mean people of closely related Semitic stock, all speaking the one language, Arabic.... The aim of the Arab nationalist movements (of which my father became the leader in war after combined appeals from the Syrian and Mesopotamian branches), is to unite the Arabs eventually into one nation...."[10]

And again, in a second memorandum to the Peace Conference, on 29 January 1919, the Emir wrote: "As representing my father, who, by request of Britain and France, led the Arab rebellion

9. See 'Abdullah, *Mudhakkarati*, p. 121, and *Al-Manār* (Cairo), vol. 16, pt. 10, pp. 735-54.

10. D. H. Miller, *My Diary at the Peace Conference of Paris, 1918-1919* (New York, 1924), vol. 4, Document 250, pp. 297-99.

against the Turks, I have come to ask that the Arabic-speaking peoples of Asia, from the line Alexandretta - Diarbekr southward to the Indian Ocean, be recognized as independent sovereign peoples under the guarantee of the League of Nations...."[11]

The Sykes-Picot Agreement of 16 May 1916 was transformed into a Mandates system by the Allied Supreme Council meeting at San-Remo, from 19 to 25 April 1920, as a result of which, Mesopotamia (Iraq) and Syria were recognized as "two independent countries", under the tutelage of Great Britain (for Iraq) and France (for Syria) as Mandatory Powers, "until such time when they would be able to stand alone." The presence of the Mandatory Powers intensified the struggle for self-determination and political independence, gave birth to a number of political parties and consolidated opposition to the West. This post-war period may be considered as the third stage in the evolution of Arab nationalism. It is a period of frustration and disappointment in the Western promises of independence which the Arab leaders had, unfortunately, interpreted literally, and is marked with a great mistrust and lack of confidence in the policies of the Western Powers in the Near East, leading even to hostility and open revolts against those policies. Arab opposition was now directed against the Western "liberators" of the Near East and not towards the Turks whose Empire had ceased to exist. Western political and economic rivalries in this area helped further to aggravate the situation.

Since the Second World War a complex process of secularization and consolidation of regional nationalisms has ushered in a fourth stage in the evolution of Arab nationalism. The roots of various regional and territorial nationalisms have been strengthened and certain Arab countries have adopted the socio-economic principles of socialism. The political independence and sovereignty of the Arab countries, with all their administrative regalia and state machinery, have inevitably accentuated and consolidated regional nationalism. There is, for instance, an Iraqi nationalism distinct from a Saudi Arabian nationalism; and both are different from Lebanese nationalism. The distinctness and particularism of the various Arab nationalities may in the long run be a negation of the dream of the universalists.

11. Ibid., Document 251, p. 300.

It is of much interest to note that as late as the middle of the nineteenth century, to be precise in 1856, the word "nationality" is not found in an English-Turkish dictionary published at that time.[12] And at the same date, the word *Qawm* is translated as "a people" in a Turkish-English dictionary of that time.[13] It was only in 1869 that the Ottoman law of nationality was issued. But this law concerned itself only with Ottoman nationality for all the subjects of the Ottoman Empire, including, of course, the Arabs — and not with nationalism in that Empire. A year later, in 1870, the word *Qawmiyyat* was suggested as a possible Turkish equivalent for the French word *nationalité*.[14]

However, before the twentieth century, the word *Qawm* had no political or patriotic connotation; it simply denotes "a number of men." In several passages of the Qur'an there are references to *qawm Nuh*, "the people of Noah," *qawm Musa*, "the people of Moses," and *qawm Ibrahim*, "the people of Abraham." It is only in the second half of the twentieth century that this word as used in the expression *al-Qawmiyyah al-'Arabiyyah*, has acquired a nationalistic significance in the Arab world, embracing all the Arabic-speaking or Arab peoples and disregarding, in principle, the geographical and political boundary lines which separate the Arab states.

It may be of interest to record that in the modern Turkey of today the word *millet* is used for nation and *milliyet* for nationality, going back to the use of this word as far back as the fifteenth century.[15]

In speaking about Arab nationalism, Arab unity, or Arab federation, the undefinable word *Ummah* has also become, in the last few years, part of the vocabulary of Arab leaders. The latest use of this word occurs in the Preamble to the Constitution of the Federation of Arab Republics. The three Arab leaders of Egypt, Syria, and Libya who signed this Constitution in Damascus on

12. See J. W. Red House, *An English and Turkish Dictionary*, 2 pts., *English and Turkish* and *Turkish and English* (London, 1856).

13. Ibid.

14. See Ottacar Maria Schlecta von Wschehrd, *Manuel Terminologique Français-Ottoman* (Vienna, 1870), 239. For a discussion of what should be the identity of the Arabs living in the Arab provinces of the Ottoman Empire, i.e., whether it should be the "Arab race" (*al-Jinss al-'Arabī*) or an Arab "nation" (*al-Waṭan al-'Arabī*) or an Arab *Ummah* (*al-Ummah al-'Arabiyyah*), see article by Salim al-Bustani in *Al-Jinan,* (Beirut), vol. 1, no. 21 (October 1870): 641-48, and vol. 1, no. 22 (October 1870): 673-77.

15. See pp. 31-32, above.

20 August 1971, declared that the "Arab people" (*Al-Sha'b-al-'Arabī*) in the three Republics believe that they are an inseparable part of the "Arab-Ummah" (*Al-Ummah al-'Arabiyyah*).

The Preamble gives us another generalization about Arab nationalism. It states: "Arab nationalism (*Al-Qawmiyyah al-'Arabiyyah*) is a call to liberation, to construction, to justice and to peace; it is the path of the Arabs to an all-embracing unity, and the building up of a democratic and socialist order which will protect the rights of the individual, safeguard his fundamental liberties and buttress the sovereignty of law."[16]

This new term *al-Qawmiyyah al-'Arabiyyah* stands, today, not only for Arab nationalism but also for Arab unity, and is considered by many of its adherents as a shield and protection against imperialism and as an instrument of victory over Israel. They also regard it as a movement of emancipation — political, social and even religious emancipation — from the political interference of Western Powers, whether visible or invisible, from the feudal spirit and mentality of the indigenous society and from the religious bond which has been the determinant factor in all political concepts in Muslim countries. It also serves as a rallying point of Arab unification: Its appeal is to Pan-Arabism, reminding one of the Pan-Slavic and Pan-Germanic movements of the nineteenth century.

Meanwhile, the "socialization" of Arab nationalism seems to be the latest trend in some Arab countries, the claim being that socialism is the best solution for their economic problems. It must be remembered that the awakening of the masses in the Arab lands, their desire to have the opportunity to "live the good life" and their rebellion against the old notion that such an opportunity was the privilege of a "capitalist" minority, have made social and economic justice an imperative necessity in these lands. It has also been suggested that socialism (especially when supported by communism) is the only way, at present, through which secularism may invade the fortress of Islam.

Advocates of secular Arab nationalism base their concept of nationalism on the "Community (*the Ummah*) feeling" of the Arabs and their "natural cohesion" as Arabs. They emphasize the

16. For the full text of the Constitution and its Preamble, see the daily paper *Al-Anwār* (Beirut), no. 3879 (20 August 1971): 6-7, or "Document: The Constitution of the Federation of Arab Republics (FAR)," *Middle East Journal*, vol. 25, no. 4 (Autumn 1971): 523-29.

"humanistic" aspect of such a nationalism which aims primarily at raising the social and economic standards of the workers and the peasants and at creating a new "Arab personality," freed from his social and religious past, emancipated politically and militarily from the West and united with his fellow Arabs in all Arab lands.

It is often argued by many Westerners that because the Arab countries have adopted Western standards of progress such as industrialization and technological education, they have become, therefore, secularized. What has actually happened and is happening is that modern economic, social and political ideologies imported from the West and the East are slowly undermining the Islamic basis of Muslim-Arab culture. Hence, the emphasis on the "Arabism" (*'Urūbah*) of the Arabs, on Arab socialism (*al-Ishtirākiyyah*) and on Arab unity (*al-Wiḥdah al-'Arabiyyah*) — Arab ideals which are trying to fill at least part of the spiritual void in the Arab youth and to replace the spiritual values of the new generation of the Arabs.

The trend towards an alliance between Arab nationalism and socialism seems to be receiving its greatest support from the educated youth and the urban masses in general. In every national crisis in recent years, this trend has been strengthened with the inevitable result that, whenever possible, the Left has taken advantage of it and has, consequently, tried to assert itself as the custodian of Arab national interests. The national feeling has become, in turn, more vigorous, and ruthless, rapidly making it very difficult for any government to form a national policy without the support of the "nationalism of the masses."

It must not be assumed from the above classification that any clear or definite lines can be drawn between the various stages of Arab nationalism. There is a great deal of overlapping. The exponents of secular nationalism are still confined to a small class. Religion continues to be the dominating factor. A Muslim polity provides, at present, a higher potential of unity than any of the political divisions into which the Arab Near East has been split. Indeed, Arab nationalism, today, defies any definition for no single definition can include all its diverse and apparently contradictory aspects. Arab nationalism is both a political movement and a religious revival; it is both secular and theocratic; both a positive, constructive force aiming at the ideal of uniting all the Arab countries and a negative, uncompromising attitude towards the West. Much of the present uncertainty and confusion in thinking about this subject could be removed if there were a consensus of agreement in the Arab world on one definition of Arab nationalism and on one common goal for all the Arab countries.

It must be remembered, however, that Arab political nationalism is still in the early stages of its development. Political nationalism in the West was part of the process of the secularization of Christian civilization — a secularization which had, at least, some of its roots in the great cultural revolution known as the Renaissance. In the struggle between this nationalism and Christianity, the former won the day. It was a new god raised on the pagan altar of the State by men who thought they could find their salvation in a rational, man-made, social and political order. In the Arab East, in the nineteenth century, Islam was still too deeply rooted to be shaken by the nationalist ideas of the West and until the first quarter of the twentieth century, successfully resisted any attempt at secularization. The few Christians, and still fewer Muslims, who dreamt of establishing an Arab State on territorial, secular lines, as distinct from a Muslim State based on the theocratic, religious principles of the Qur'an, could not get any support from the vast majority of the inhabitants of these lands. Hence, Islam and Arab nationalism could not be divorced from each other. Thus, the new political nationalism was not the result of spiritual conflicts and tensions within the Muslim-Arab culture of the Muslim Arabs themselves. There has never been a Renaissance or a Reformation in Arab lands, in the European sense of those two terms.

In spite of the ideologies which have invaded the Arab lands, the power of Islam and attachment to it are reasserted every time a crisis threatens an Arab land. Also, the Muslims always find an impetus in their memory of the glorious past of Islam. The late President Gamal 'Abd al-Nāṣir himself admitted that he could not ignore the Muslim world "to which we are tied with a religious faith." And he added that when his imagination roamed over the hundreds of millions of Muslims throughout the world, he got a strong feeling that cooperation among all these Muslims had tremendous potentialities. This cooperation would not, of course, deprive them of their loyalty to their original countries but will guarantee for them and for their brethren in the Faith unlimited power."[17] Other Arab leaders, also, in most of the Arab countries

17. Gamal 'Abd al-Nāṣir, *Falsafat al-Thawrah* [Philosophy of the revolution] (Cairo, 1954), pp. 79-80.

have declared their unequivocal attachment and allegiance to Islam, at one time or another, in recent years.

Originally, Islam was the inspiration of the Arabs and the creative source of their power and greatness. Its dynamism as a spiritual ideal, indeed, as a divine pattern of life, was the strongest unifying force of all those who embraced it. The defeat and fall of the Ottoman Empire in 1918 disrupted the political unity of the Muslim Arab lands of the Near East. It may well be that one of the main causes of restlessness, turbulence and instability in these lands, today, is that they also lost the symbol of their spiritual sovereignty and unity when the Caliphate was finally abolished by Ataturk in 1924.

Goethe one said that "he who would lift a great weight must find its center." Will the center of gravity of a renewed, rejuvenated and united Arab society be Islam or will it be a secular and socialized Arab nationalism? It remains to be seen whether an entirely secularized nationalism based only on territorial allegiance and loyalty is possible or even desirable in Arab Muslim lands — i.e., whether political and social institutions can be or should be completely divorced from Islam. No amount of logical argument or of clever analogy with the rise of nationalism in Western Europe, can indicate in which direction Arab nationalism will finally develop. To what extent will Islam be able to adjust itself successfully to all secular and material forces, to all economic and political ideologies which have invaded its lands in a thousand and one different forms, is the key question of all the questions asked, today, about the Arab Near East.

Hence, the real crisis of the Near East, today, is essentially a spiritual crisis, in its fundamentals, as that which Christianity had to face in the sixteenth and seventeenth centuries and which led to the rise of the European State-systems and the destruction of the unity of the medieval church. All human crises are, in the last analysis, spiritual in essence, if we believe in the existence of a spititual order to which man should belong. It is the contention of the author that the major conflicts between the East and the West and indeed within the East and the West are of a spiritual nature. No political or economic panaceas exist to provide a solution for the basic problems of the Near East, if such a solution be divorced from the moral law and from spiritual vision. It is one of the tragedies of the present situation that so few have been able to grasp this fundamental truth.

APPENDIX A

THE OTTOMAN EMPIRE
AREA, POPULATION, RACES, RELIGIONS IN 1844 [1]

The total area of the empire, including the tributary provinces, is estimated at 1,836,478 square miles, and the extent and population of the several grand divisions in Europe, Asia, and Africa are as follows:

Divisions	*Area sq. m.*	*Population*	*Pop./sq. m.*
Turkey in Europe	203,628	15,500,000	76.1
Turkey in Asia	673,746	16,050,000	23.8
Turkey in Africa	959,104	3,800,000	3.9
TOTAL	1,836,478	35,350,000	19.2

POPULATION

The total population, estimated according to the census taken in 1844 at 35,350,000, is distributed as follows, in the different divisions of the empire:

	Turkey in Europe	
Thrace	1,800,000	
Bulgaria	3,000,000	
Roumelia and Thessaly	2,700,000	
Albania	1,200,000	
Bosnia and the Hersegovina	1,100,000	
The Islands	700,000	
Moldavia	1,400,000	
Wallachia	2,600,000	
Serbia	1,000,000	
TOTAL		15,500,000

1. J. Lewis Farley, *The Ressources of Turkey*, pp. 2, 3.

Turkey in Asia

Asia Minor, or Anatolia	10,700,000	
Syria, Mesopotamia, and Kurdistan	4,450,000	
Arabian	900,000	
TOTAL		16,050,000

Turkey in Africa

Egypt	2,000,000		
Tripoli, Fez, and Tunis	1,800,000		
TOTAL		3,800,000	
TOTAL			35,350,000

RACES

The various races of which the population is composed may be thus classified:

Races	*In Europe*	*In Asia*	*In Africa*	*Total*
Ottomans	2,100,000	10,700,000	......	12,800,000
Greeks	1,000,000	1,000,000	......	2,000,000
Armenians	400,000	2,000,000	......	2,400,000
Jews	70,000	80,000	......	150,000
Slavs or Slavonians	6,200,000	......	......	6,200,000
Roumains	4,000,000	......	......	4,000,000
Albanians	1,500,000	......	......	1,500,000
Tartars	16,000	20,000	......	36,000
Arabs	......	885,000	3,800,000	4,685,000
Syrians and Chaldeans	......	200,000	......	200,000
Druses	......	80,000	......	80,000
Kurds	......	1,000,000	......	1,000,000
Turkomans	......	85,000	......	85,000
Gipsies	214,000	......	......	214,000
TOTAL	15,500,000	16,050,000	3,800,000	35,350 000

RELIGIONS

The classification according to religions is as follows:

Religion	*In Europe*	*In Asia*	*In Africa*	*Total*
Mussulmans	4,550,000	12,650,000	3,800,000	21,000,000
Greeks and Armenians	10,000,000	3,000,000	......	13,000,000
Catholics[2]	640,000	260,000	......	900,000
Jews	70,000	80,000	......	150,000
Other sects	240,000	60,000	......	300,000
TOTAL ...	15,500,000	16,050,000	3,800,000	35,350,000

2. Includings 140,000 Maronites (with a Patriarch at Kanobin in Mount Lebanon).

APPENDIX B

THE OTTOMAN EMPIRE IN 1914
AREA AND POPULATION [1]

Summary:

	Area sq. miles	*Population*
Turkey in Europe	10,882	1,891,000
Turkey in Asia Minor, including Armenia and Kurdistan	271,262	12,657,800
The Arab Provinces in the Near East:		
Mesopotamia:		
Mosul	35,130	500,000
Baghdad	54,540	900,000
Basra	53,580	600,000
TOTAL	143,250	2,000,000
Syria:		
Aleppo	33,430	1,500,000
Zor (Independent sanjak)	30,110	100,000
Syria	37,020	1,000,000
Beirut	6,180	533,500
Jerusalem (Independent sanjak)	6,600	341,600
Lebanon	1,190	200,000
TOTAL	114,530	3,675,100

1. E. G. Mears, *Modern Turkey*, pp. 580-81, citing *Statesman's Yearbook*, 1921 edition.

APPENDIX C

RÉSOLUTIONS VOTÉES PAR LE CONGRÈS ARABE

"Le Congrès arabe, réuni à Paris, 184, Boulevard Saint-Germain, a adopté dans sa séance du 21 Juin 1913 les résolutions suivantes:

1. Des réformes radicales et urgentes sont nécessaires dans l'Empire Ottoman.

2. Il importe d'assurer aux Arabes ottomans l'exercice de leurs droits politiques en rendant effective leur participation à l'administration centrale de l'Empire.

3. Il importe d'établir dans chacun des vilayets syriens et arabes un régime décentralisateur approprié à ses besoins et à ses aptitudes.

4. Le vilayet de Beyrouth, ayant formulé ses revendications dans un projet spécial voté le 31 Janvier 1913 par une Assemblée générale ad hoc et basé sur le double principe de l'extension des pouvoirs du conseil général du vilayet et de la nomination de conseillers étrangers, le Congrès demande la mise en application du susdit projet.

5. La langue arabe doit être reconnue au Parlement Ottoman et considérée comme officielle dans les pays syriens et arabes.

6. Le service militaire sera régional dans les vilayets syriens et arabes, en dehors des cas d'extrême nécessité.

7. Le Congrès émet le vœu de voir le Gouvernement Impérial Ottoman assurer au Liban les moyens d'améliorer sa situation financière.

8. Le Congrès affirme sa sympathie pour les demandes réformistes des Arméniens ottomans.

9. Les présentes résolutions seront communiquées au Gouvernement Impérial Ottoman.

10. Il sera fait également communication des mêmes résolutions aux Puissances amies de l'Empire Ottoman.

11. Le Congrès exprime ses chaleureux remerciements au Gouvernement de la République pour sa généreuse hospitalité."

ANNEXE AUX PRÉCÉDENTES RÉSOLUTIONS

"1. Aussi longtemps que les résolutions votées par le présent Congrès n'auront pas été dûment exécutées, les membres des comités réformistes Arabes Syriens s'abstiendront d'accepter toute fonction dans l'Empire Ottoman, à moins d'une autorisation expresse et spéciale de leurs comités respectifs.

"2. Les présentes résolutions constitueront le programme politique des Syriens et Arabes ottomans. Aucun candidat aux élections législatives ne sera appuyé s'il ne s'est engagé au préalable à défendre le susdit programme et à en poursuivre l'exécution.

"3. Le Congrès remercie les émigrés arabes de leur patriotisme et du concours qu'ils lui ont prêté, et leur transmet ses salutations par les soins de leurs délégués."[1]

1. See Al-Lujnah al-'Ulyā Li-Ḥizb al-Lāmarkaziyyah, *Al-Mu'tamar al-'Arabī al-Awwal*, pp. 132-34.

APPENDIX D

A PROGRAM OF REFORMS BASED ON ADMINISTRATIVE DECENTRALIZATION

"Une grosse question commerce à se poser: la question arabe. Toutes les personnes en contact avec les milieux arabes la prévoyaient depuis longtemps. Dès le mois de novembre dernier une personnalité syrienne et musulmane, qui exerce en Syrie une grande influence et qui est remarquable par son intelligence et sa connaissance des choses de l'Europe, me disait:

'Aucun sentiment séparatiste n'existe chez nous. Nous tenons au contraire essentiellement à faire partie de l'Empire Ottoman, afin qu'un bloc solide, capable de résister aux appétits possibles de l'Europe, soit constitué. Mais nous considérons comme une condition *sine qua non* de notre loyalisme que le gouvernement ottoman nous accorde un régime administratif acceptable.'

"Successivement les conseils des vilayets de Beyrouth, d'Alep, de Tripoli, de Syrie, viennent de faire l'exposé de ce régime réclamé par les Arabes. Il s'agit d'une décentralisation poussée à l'extrême, confinant à l'autonomie. Les principaux points réclamés sont en effet:

"1° La reconnaissance de la langue arabe comme langue officielle de la province dans tous les bureaux et tribunaux, la langue turque restant langue officielle pour la correspondance avec Stamboul.

"Dans le projet rédigé par le Conseil du vilayet de Beyrouth, on demande même que l'usage de la langue arabe soit admis à la Chambre des Députés et au Sénat.

"2° Comme corollaire, seront nommés en Syrie des fonctionnaires connaissant la langue arabe. Provisoirement, une exception pour les valis; elle prendra fin au bout d'une période de six ans, à dater de la promulgation de la loi;

"3° Les autorités locales seront consultées pour nommer les fonctionnaires civils et judiciaires, les officiers de la gendarmerie;

"4° Une haute cour sera instituée pour juger en cassation, les jugements rendus dans les provinces de Jérusalem, Damas, Beyrouth et Alep, etc. Actuellement, toute cassation se fait à Constantinople;

"5º En temps de paix, le service militaire sera régional;

"6º Les revenus provinciaux seront divisés en deux catégories:

(*a*) Revenus des douanes, de postes et télégraphes et des impôts militaires à la disposition du gouvernement central;

(*b*) Toutes autres recettes à la disposition du gouvernement local, pour être appliquées aux besoins de la province.

"7º Des conseils de vilayet seront créés; ils auront des pouvoirs administratifs et, dans une certaine mesure, des pouvoirs législatifs étendus;

"Toutes les questions, autres que celles de politique générale et de défense nationale abandonnées au gouvernement central, seront de leur compétence;

"8º Des conseillers étrangers seront nommés pour réorganniser la gendarmerie, la police, la justice, les finances. Ils seront nommés pour quinze ans et choisis parmi les spécialistes européens connaissant les usages locaux, la langue arabe ou turque.

"Certaines personnalités arabes m'ont déclaré dans leurs conversations qu'à titre de garantie elles désiraient quelque chose de plus encore: la présence d'un nombre minimum d'Arabes au conseil des ministres.

"Ces mêmes personnalités, auxquelles j'ai demandé si elles ne croyaient pas que le gouvernement central trouverait ces demandes bien radicales, m'ont répondu:

'Nous considérons ces demandes comme la simple application aux provinces Arabes des concessions faites aux Malissores, au printemps de 1911, et ensuite aux Albanais en général, durant l'été de 1912.'

"Le Gouvernement de Ghazy Moukhtar Pacha a déclaré que ces réformes seraient étendues à toutes les populations de l'Empire. Le présent Gouvernement se prêtera-t-il à ces demandes?"[1]

1. *L'Echo de Paris*, 24 February, 1913, which in turn had reproduced this article from the *Daily Telegraph* (London) of the previous day. Cited in Ludovic de Contenson, *Les Réformes en Turquie d'Asie. La Question Arménienne et la Question Syrienne*, pp. 63-67.

APPENDIX E

EXTRACT FROM THE ANNUAL REPORT ON TURKEY FOR THE YEAR 1908 [1]

The Constitutional Movement

"For some years past, in and out of Turkey, it was generally known that a revolutionary movement set on foot by Young Turks was proceeding, but it was also generally thought that, thanks to the very complete system of espionage established by the Sultan, the development of the idea was surrounded by almost insuperable difficulties...

"A Council of Ministers was called on the 23rd July. There were but two alternatives—to surrender to the demand, or to fight the rebels. It must have indeed, appeared incomprehensible to His Majesty that, with the immense army he had always maintained, a handful of rebels could not be suppressed. But the Ministers realized that things had gone too far to turn back, and on the suggestion of Said Pasha they declared that their advice to the Sultan must be to grant the Constitution...

"On the 31st July, at the Selamlik, in the presence of all the foreign Representative, the Sultan declared his firm resolve to uphold the Constitution, and a favourable impression was generally made by the freedom allowed to the people in the neighbourhood of the Palace to approach within the immediate proximity of the Sultan.

"The early stages of the revolution were distingushed by a remarkable community of enthusiasm on the part of all races and religions throughout the Empire. It was impossible to view, without some scepticism, the picture of Greek and Moslem embracing one another and Moslem and Armenian flaunting their affection for one another. But after the first doubts that were felt in the more remote districts as to whether the movement was sincere, and whether it was not some trick on the part of the Sultan, had passed away, the sense of relief from the autocratic rule of the last thirty years became evident in every corner of the Empire...

"In the meantime, the idea of the Constitution was being gradually assimilated throughout the country. Amongst the Arabs

1. Enclosure in Despatch from Sir G. Lowther to Sir Edward Grey, No. 105, of 17 February, 1909.

it produced but little impression, they seemed sceptical of reform, tolerating Turkish rule as a Moslem rule, and harbouring some veneration for the Sultan as the religious head of the Ottoman Empire. There were whispers of reaction, but in most cases it could be explained by the hesitation of those, who were not convinced of the future success of the movement, declining to throw themselves into the movement with enthusiasm...

"It was at the end of October that the first tendency towards reaction made itself sufficiently felt to require notice in despatches. The Arabs wondered how far the Constitution was in accordance with the principles of Holy Law. The apathy of the Syrians towards the Constitution was complained of by the members of the League..."[2]

2. G. P. Gooch and Harold Temperley, eds., *British Documents on the Origins of the War*, 1898-1914. Vol. 5: *The Near East*, 1903-9 (London, 1928), pp. 249-58.

APPENDIX F

THE OTTOMAN SULTANS

		Date of accession
1.	Uthman ("Osman")	1299
2.	Orkhan	1326
3.	Murad I	1360
4.	Bayezid I	1389
	(Interregnum—struggle for the Sultanate by Bayezid's three sons: Sulaiman, Muhammad, and Musa).	1402-1413
5.	Muhammad I	1413
6.	Murad II	1421
7.	Muhammad II	1451
8.	Bayezid II	1481
9.	Sélim I	1512
10.	Sulaiman I ("The Magnificent")	1520
11.	Sélim II	1566
12.	Murad III	1574

THE OTTOMAN SULTANS (CONT'D.)

13. Muhammad III, 1595

14. Ahmad I, 1603 15. Mustafa I, 1617

16. 'Uthman II, 1618 17. Murad IV, 1623 18. Ibrahim, 1640

19. Muhammad IV 1648 20. Sulaiman II 1687 21. Ahmad II 1691

22. Mustafa II, 1695 23. Ahmad III, 1703

24. Mahmud I, 1730 25. 'Uthman III, 1754

26. Mustafa III, 1757 27. 'Abdul Hamid I, 1774

28. Selim III, 1789

29. Mustafa IV, 1807 30. Mahmud II, 1808

31. 'Abdul Mejid, 1839 32. 'Abdul 'Aziz, 1861

33. Murad V, 1876 34. 'Abdul Hamid II, 1876 35. Muhammad V, Reshad, 1909 36. Muhammad VI, Vahid-ud-Din, 1918 (In 1922, Caliph only)

37. 'Abdul Mejid II, 1922-1924 (Caliph only)

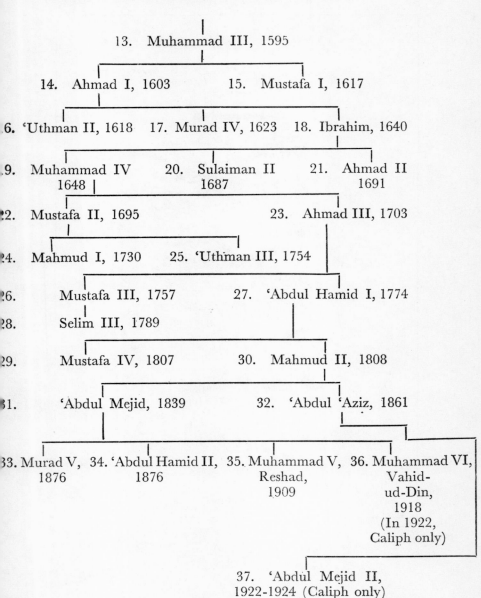

APPENDIX G

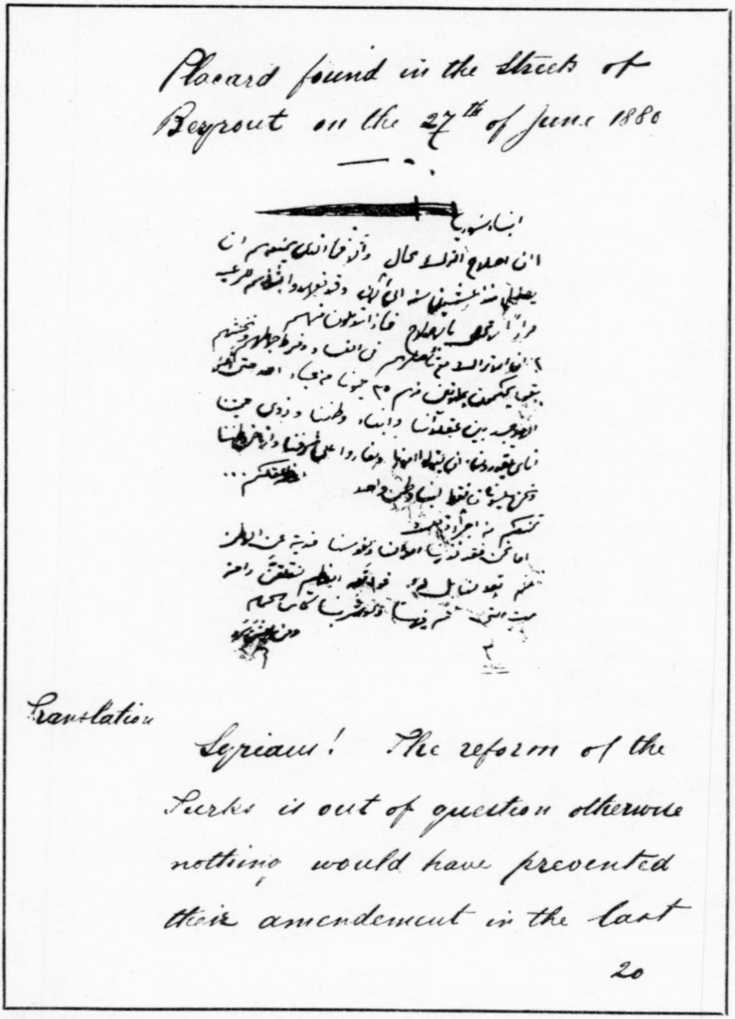
Placard found in the Streets of Beyrout on the 27th of June 1880

ابناء سورية

Translation

Syrians! The reform of the Turks is out of question otherwise nothing would have prevented their amendement in the last

20

FIG. 1. F. O. 195/1306, enclosure in Despatch No. 47, "Confidential," dated "Beyrout, July 3, 1880." Reproduced by permission of the Keeper of Public Records, Public Record Office, London.

APPENDIX H

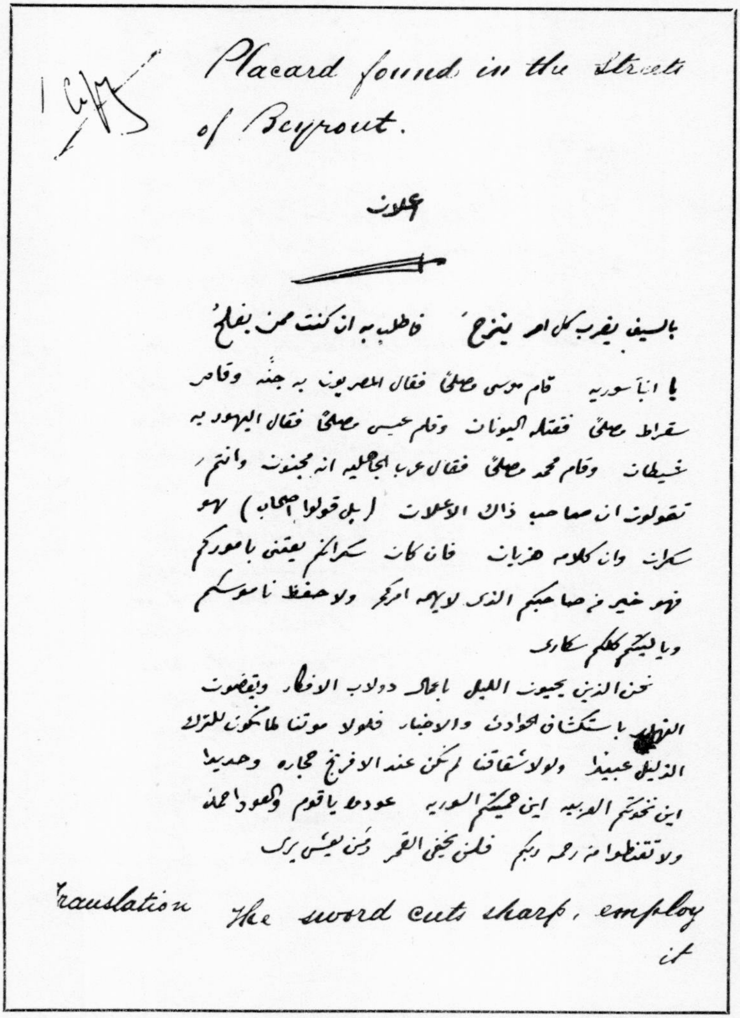

Placard found in the streets of Beyrout.

اعلان

بالسيف يقرب كل امر ينزح فاطلب به ان كنت ممن يفلح

يا ابنا سوريه قام موسى مصلحاً فقال المصريون به جنة وقام
سقراط مصلحاً فقتله اليونان وقام عيسى مصلحاً فقال اليهود به
شيطان وقام محمد مصلحاً فقال عرب الجاهليه انه مجنون وانتم
تقولون ان صاحب ذلك الاعلانات (بل قولوا اصحاب) لهم
سكرات وان كلامه هذيان فان كان سكرانا يعتني باموركم
فهو خير من صاحبكم الذي لا يهمه امركم ولا حفظ ناموسكم
ويا ليتكم كلكم سكارى

نحن الذين يجوبون الليل باجالة دولاب الافكار ويتقصون
النوازل باستكشاف الحوادث والاخبار فلولا موتنا لما نكون للترك
الذليل عبيداً ولولا شقاقنا لم تكن عند الافرنج حجارة وحديداً
اين نخوتكم العربيه اين حميتكم السوريه عودوا يا قوم وكونوا حملة
ولا تقنطوا من رحمة ربكم فلن يخفى القمر ومن يعش يرى

Translation The sword cuts sharp, employ it

FIG. 2. F. O. 195/1306, enclosure in Despatch No. 47, "Confidential," dated "Beyrout, July 3, 1880." Reproduced by permission of the Keeper of Public Records, Public Record Office, London.

APPENDIX I

نسخة

الويل

يا اهل الوطن قد علمتم بجور الاتراك وظلمهم وان فئة منهم قد تحكمت في
رقابكم واستعبدتكم وانهم قد درسوا شريعتكم وانتهكوا حرمة كتبكم حتى انهم شتتوا نظامات
نقضوا بملاشاة لغتكم الشريفة وسدوا دونكم ابواب النجاح واتخذوكم ارقاء كأن ليس من شعائر
الانسانية عندكم وقد ما كنتم اصحاب الحل والعقد ومنكم ظهر اولو العلم والفضل وبكم اصلحت
البلاد واتسعت الفتوحات وعلى قواعد لغتكم بنيت اصول الخلافة التي اختلسها منكم الاتراك
انظروا الى ابنائكم كيف تقادوا الى الحرب عند الشدة وكيف يعرضون الى القتل وباية معاملة
يعاملون وانظروا الى اوقافكم كيف وباية طريقة تصرف. اما الان فعندنا الاستمرار
مع اخواننا في اقطار البلاد على القرار ومقصدنا طلب ما ياتي قبل انتقاض الاسم الشريف
فان حصلتم عليه اتفقنا الى تدبير امورنا والا فانا:

سنطلبن بحد السيف مأربنا — فلا يخيبن لنا في جنبه ارب
ونتركن علوج الترك تندب ما — قد قدمته ايديها وتنتحب

اما المقصد التي مقصدنا في مجلس بطلبه فهي اولاً استقلال نشترك به مع
اخواننا اللبنانيين بحيث تضمنا جميعاً المصالح الوطنية ثانياً ان تكون اللغة العربية
رسمية في البلاد وان يحق لجرائدنا الحرية التامة في نشر افكارهم ومؤلفاتهم ومعارفهم
بحسب حاجات الانسانية ومقتضيات التقدم والعمران. ثالثاً ان تنحصر عساكرنا في
خدمة الوطن وتتخلص في عبودية الرديف الاتراك وهناك بعض تنقيحات واستبدالات
اخرى لا بد منها يترك البحث فيها الى اوقاتها.

تنبهوا واستفيقوا ايها العرب — فقد طمى الخطب حتى غاصت الركب
فيم التعلل بالآمال تخدعكم — وانتم بين راحات القنا سلب
لا دولة لكم يشتد ازركم — بها ولا ناصر للخطب ينتدب
أليس فيكم دم يهتاج انفة — يوماً فيدفع هذا العار اذ يثب
ومن يعش ير والايام مقبلة — يلوح للمرء في احداثها العجب

Traduction

Le Malheur

FIG. 3. F. O. 195/1368, enclosure in Despatch No. 2, dated "Beyrout, January 14, 1881." Reproduced by permission of the Keeper of Public Records, Public Record Office, London.

1. The following four documents (Appendixes J-M) belong to the private library of Dr. Salah Munajjid, author, historian, internationally-known authority on Arab Muslim manuscripts and the former Director of the Institute of Arabic manuscripts at the Arab League in Cairo. They have been reproduced here by his kind permission.

APPENDIX J

The revolutionary leaflet reproduced on pages 157 and 158 is a "Proclamation (*Balāgh*) to the Arabs, the Sons of Qaḥṭan." (Figs. 4, 5). It was put out sometime in 1913 by *al-Jam'iyyah al-Thawriyyah al-'Arabiyyah* [the Arab Revolutionary Society]. The name of the society is found in the centre of the seal at the top, right-hand corner, of the first page, encircled by the words *Comité Révolutionnaire Arabe*.

This revolutionary society was one of the offshoots of *al-Qaḥṭāniyyah* founded in Istanbul towards the end of 1909. It was established by 'Azīz 'Alī al-Miṣrī when he returned to Cairo in April 1914, after his arrest and release from prison in Istanbul during the same year. His other associates in this organization were Ḥaqqī al-'Azīm, at one time the Secretary General of *al-Ḥizb al-Lāmarkaziyyah* (the Decentralization Party), Fuād al-Khaṭīb, and fellow Arab army officers who had run away from Istanbul and sought refuge in Egypt.

The Proclamation attacks vehemently and passionately the Young Turks and particularly the leading members of the Committee of Union and Progress — "Jāwīd, Ṭal'at, Aḥmad Riḍā, Jamāl, Anwar" and others — as being the oppressors, persecutors and despoilers of the Arabs. They are accused of being chauvinistic Turks who have decided to replace the Arabic language — the language of the Qur'ān — by Turkish. Their Government is not a Muslim Government. Indeed, they are the enemies of Islam and of the Arabic language.

The Armenians, claims the Proclamation, have obtained administrative autonomy, although their number is smaller than the Arabs. The Turks respect them because they are strong but the Turks do not respect the Arabs. The Arabs are weak, submissive and are continuously humiliated and plundered by this Turkish Government.

The Proclamation, then, appeals to the Arabs, Muslims Christians and Jews in the *vilayets* of Syria and Iraq to unite: "You live on the same land, work on the same land and speak the same language; be also united in one '*Ummah*'." The Arab Muslims are brothers in the same '*waṭan*' ("nation") of Arab Christians and of Arab Jews. They should lay aside their religious prejudices and fanaticism. They are all the people of God and religion belongs to God alone. It ends by announcing to the Arabs, in general, that a society called "*Jam'iyyah Fidā'iyyah*[2]" has been formed to kill those who kill Arabs and to oppose Arab reforms on the basis of decentralization which will be subservient to the "Slaves of Constantinople." The reforms should be based on the principle of complete independence and the establishment of a decentralized Arab State restoring to the Arabs their past glory and ruling the country on the principle of autonomy for its various provinces.[3]

2. *Jam'iyyah Fidā'iyyah* is a society the members of which are ready to sacrifice themselves, i.e., to be killed, if necessary, in order to achieve their goal.

3. See also *Iḍāḥāt*, published anonymously (by Djemal Pasha) in Constantinople, A.H. 1334 (A.D. 1916), pp. 16-30. Djemal Pasha wanted the *Iḍāḥāt* to be a "clarification of the political questions which were investigated by the Court Martial in 'Aley" (Lebanon), as its full Arabic title indicates. This book was also published, simultaneously, in Turkish and in French. Its French title is *La Vérité sur la Question Syrienne.*

Djemal Pasha included the text of the "Proclamation" in his *Iḍāḥāt* as evidence of the "evil intentions" of some Arab "independence seekers living in Egypt" to rebel against the Ottoman Government and to sow discord and enmity between Arabs and Turks.

APPENDIX J[1]

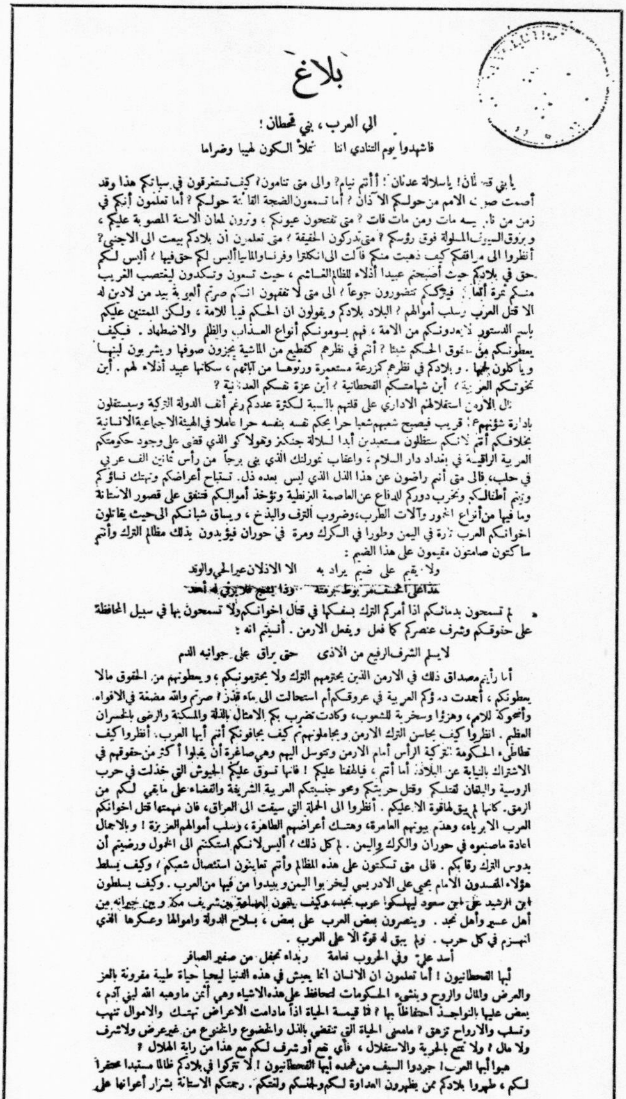

بلاغ

الي العرب ، بني قحطان !

فاشهدوا يوم التنادي اننا   نملأ الكون لهيبا وضراما

يابني قحطان! ياسلالة عدنان ! أأنتم نيام؟ والى متى تنامون؟ كيف تستغرقون في سباتكم هذا وقد
أصمت صوت الامم من حولكم الآذان ؟ أما تسمعون الضجة القائمة حولكم ؟ أما تعلمون أنكم في
زمن من نام فيه مات ومن مات فات ؟ متى تفتحون عيونكم ، وترون لمعان الاسنة المصوبة عليكم ،
وبروق السيوف المسلولة فوق رؤوسكم ؟ متى تدركون الحقيقة ؟ متى تعلمون أن بلادكم بيعت الى الاجنبي؟
أنظروا الى مراقكم كيف ذهبت منكم فآلت الى انكلترا وفرنسا والمانيا أليس لكم حق فيها ؟ أليس لكم
حق في بلادكم حيث أصبحتم عبيدا أذلاء للظالم الغاشم ، حيث تسعون وتكدون ليغتصب الغريب
منكم ثمرة ألعابكم فيتركم تتضورون جوعاً ؟ الى متى لا تفقهون انكم صرتم ألعوبة بيد من لادين له
الا قتل العرب وسلب أموالهم ؟ البلاد بلادكم ويقولون ان الحكم فيها للامة ، ولكن المتمنين عليكم
باسم الدستور لايعدونكم من الامة ، فهم يسومونكم أنواع العذاب والظلم والاضطهاد . فكيف
يعطونكم من حقوق الحكم شيئا ؟ أنتم في نظرهم كقطيع من الماشية يجزون صوفها ويشربون لبنها
ويأكلون لحمها . وبلادكم في نظرهم كزرعة مستعمرة ورثوها من آبائهم ، سكانها عبيد أذلاء لهم . أين
نخوتكم العربية ؟ أين شهامتكم القحطانية ؟ أين عزة نفسكم العدنانية ؟

نال الارمن استقلالهم الاداري على قلتهم بالنسبة لكثرة عددكم رغم أنف الدولة التركية وسيستقلون
بادارة شؤونهم عن قريب فيصبح شعبهم شعبا حرا يحكم نفسه بنفسه حرا عاملا في الهيئة الاجتماعية الانسانية
بخلافكم أنتم لانكم ستظلون مستعبدين أبدا لسلالة جنكيز وهولاكو الذي قضى على وجود حكومتكم
العربية الراقية في بغداد دار السلام ، واعقاب تيمورلنك الذي بنى برجاً من رأس ثمانين الف عربي
في حلب، فالى متى أنتم راضون عن هذا الذل الذي ليس بعده ذل . تستباح أعراضكم وتهتك نساؤكم
وتيتم أطفالكم وتخرب دوركم للدفاع عن العاصمة البزنطية وتؤخذ أموالكم فتنفق على قصور الاستانة
وما فيها من أنواع الخمور وآلات الطرب، وضروب الترف والبذخ ، ويساق شبانكم الى حيث يقاتلون
اخوانكم العرب تارة في اليمن وطورا في الكرك ومرة في حوران فيؤيدون بذلك مظالم الترك وأنتم
ساكتون صامتون مقيمون على هذا الضيم :

ولا يقيم على ضيم يراد به   الا الاذلان عير الحي والوتد
هذا على الخسف مربوط برمته   وذا يشج فلا يرثي له أحد

لم تسمحون بدمائكم اذا أمركم الترك بسفكها في قتال اخوانكم ولا تسمحون بها في سبيل المحافظة
على حقوقكم وشرف عنصركم كما فعل ويفعل الارمن . أنسيتم انه :

لا يسلم الشرف الرفيع من الاذى   حتى يراق على جوانبه الدم

أما رأيتم مصداق ذلك في الارمن الذين يحترمهم الترك ولا يحترمونكم ، ويعطونهم من الحقوق مالا
يعطونكم ، أجمدت دماؤكم العربية في عروقكم أم استحالت الى ماء قذر ؟ صرتم والله مضغة في الافواه،
وأضحوكة للامم، وهزؤا وسخرية للشعوب، وكادت تضرب بكم الامثال بالذلة والمسكنة والرضى بالخسران
المظلم . انظروا كيف يجاسن الترك الارمن ويجاملونهم ثم كيف يجافونكم أنتم أيها العرب . أنظروا كيف
تطاطىء الحكومة التركية الرأس أمام الارمن وتتوسل اليهم وهي صاغرة أن يقبلوا أكثر من حقوقهم في
الاشتراك بالنيابة عن البلاد . أما أنتم ، فيالهفنا عليكم ! فانها تسوق عليكم الجيوش التي خذلت في حرب
الروسية والبلقان لتقتلكم وتقتل حريتكم وتمحو جنسيتكم العربية الشريفة والقضاء على ما بقي لكم من
الرمق . كأنها لم يبق لها قوة الا عليكم . أنظروا الى الحملة التي سيقت الى العراق، فان مهمتها قتل اخوانكم
العرب الابرياء، وهدم بيوتهم العامرة، وهتك أعراضهم الطاهرة ، وسلب أموالهم العزيزة ! وبالاجمال
اعادة ماصنعوه في حوران والكرك واليمن . لم كل ذلك ؟ أليس لانكم استكنتم الى الخمول ورضيتم أن
يدوس الترك رقابكم . فالى متى تسكتون على هذه المظالم وأنتم تعاينون استئصال شعبكم ؟ وكيف يسلط
هؤلاء المفسدون الامام يحيى على الادريسي ليخربوا اليمن ويبيدوا من فيها من العرب . وكيف يسلطون
ابن الرشيد على ابن سعود ليهلكوا عرب نجد وكيف يلقون الخصومة بين شريف مكة وبين جيرانه من
أهل عسير وأهل نجد . وينصرون بعض العرب على بعض ، بسلاح الدولة وأموالها وعسكرها الذي
انهزم في كل حرب . ولم يبق له قوة الا على العرب .

أسد علي وفي الحروب نعامة   ربداء تجفل من صفير الصافر

أيها القحطانيون ! أما تعلمون ان الانسان انما يعيش في هذه الدنيا ليحيا حياة طيبة مقرونة بالعز
والعرض والمال والروح وينشىء الحكومات لتحافظ على هذه الاشياء وهي أثمن ماوهبه الله لبني آدم ،
يعض عليها بالنواجذ احتفاظاً بها ؟ فما قيمة الحياة اذاً مادامت الاعراض تهتك والاموال تنهب
وتسلب والارواح تزهق ؟ مامعنى الحياة التي تنقضي بالذل والخضوع والخنوع من غير عرض ولا شرف
ولا مال ؟ ولا تمتع بالحرية والاستقلال ، فأي نعم أو شرف لكم مع هذا من راية الهلال ؟

هبوا أيها العرب ! جردوا السيف من غمده أيها القحطانيون ! لا تتركوا في بلادكم ظالما مستبدا محتقراً
لكم ، طهروا بلادكم ممن يظهرون العداوة لكم ولجنسكم ولغتكم . رحتكم الاستانة بشرار أعوانها على

FIG. 4. "Proclamation to the Arabs, the Sons of Qaḥṭān."

APPENDIX J[2]

الاستبداد كعارف المارديني الذي يدعي انه منكم، وليس منكم من رضي أن يكون سوط عذاب لاعدائكم عليكم ، وحسبكم من تاريخه انه كان شريك سليم فارس في جريدة القاهرة ، وبكر سامي الذي كان يحرس غرفة جاويد اليهودي العرق عندما كان واليا على طرابزون ، وجاويد باشا قائد حملة العراق وغيرهم من أحفاد جنكيز وهلاكو الذين ذبحوا أجدادكم الطيبين الطاهرين ودمروا مدنيتهم الزاهرة ، وسدوا دجلة بمؤلفاتهم النافعة، وداسوها بسنابك خيولهم ، ثم أتلف أحفادهم، ما أبقاه أجدادهم ، فمنعوا المدنية العربية أن تلم شعثها وتسترجع مجدها

أيها العرب ! حذروا أهل اليمن وعسير ونجد والعراق من كيد أعدائكم ، واتفقوا في الولايات السورية والعراقية مع أبناء جنسكم ووطنكم، ليكن المسلمون والنصارى واليهود منكم يدا واحدة في العمل لمصلحة الامة والبلاد . انكم تقطنون أرضا واحدة وتستثمرون أرضا واحدة وتتكلمون بلغة واحدة فكونوا أيضاً أمة واحدة ويداً واحدة، ولا تتفرقوا تبعاً لمقاصد وغايات المفسدين الذين يتظاهرون بالاسلام والاسلام بريء منهم ، وقد انطبق عليهم قول الشاعر العربي :

اذا رام كيداً بالصلاة مقيمها فتاركها منه الى الله أقرب

فساعدوا واتحدوا وتعاضدوا ولا تقولوا : أيها المسلمون هذا نصراني وهذا موسوي فكلكم عيال الله، والدين لله وحده . وقد أمرنا الله بكتابه العزيز العربي وعلى لسان رسوله العربي العدناني صلى الله عليه وسلم بالعدل والمساواة، وأن نبر كل من لا يحاربنا وان خالفنا في ديننا، وأن نقاتل من يبغي علينا فقط فمن هم البغاة على العرب الآن ؟ هل جرد نصارى العرب أو غيرهم عسكرا على اليمن أو نجد أو العراق ؟ أم جماعة الاستانة هم الذين يقاتلونكم ويسعون ليبيدوا بعض العرب بالسيف والنار ، وبعضهم الآخر بالخلاف والشقاق ، عملا بالمثل القائل (فرق تسد)

أيها العرب المسلمون تخطئون خطأ عظيما اذا ظننتم أن هذه الحكومة الظالمة الغاشمة اسلامية والله يقول في كتابه العزيز (والكافرون هم الظالمون) كل حكومة ظالمة فهي عدو وخصم للاسلام فكيف اذا كانت تهدم الاسلام، وتستحل سفك دماء قوم نبي الاسلام! وتسعى لاماتة لغة الاسلام! باسم حكومة الاسلام! وخلافة الاسلام ! فمن أحب الشواهد على هذا نحيله بكتاب (قوم جديد) تأليف عبيد الله صنيعة الاتحاديين، الذي جعلوه من جملة التمهيدات لهدم هذا الدين. فكل من يعضد هؤلاء الاتحاديين ، باعتبار انهم من المسلمين ، فهو في ضلال مبين ، فليس لاحد منهم في الاسلام عمل صالح ، وليس لاكثرهم في التركية الذين يحاربون القرآن لاجلها أصل ثابت ، فجاويد من اليهود وطلعت من نور (غجر) أدرنه وأحمد رضا اللاديني المتمذهب بمذهب أوكوست كونت من أصل أوربي . وهؤلاء أفضل من جاهد وجمال ومدحت وناظم وأنور وأمثالهم الذين لا يعرفون لانفسهم نسبا كما تعرف العرب أنسابها ، وانما هم ترك بهذه اللغة الملفقة التي أحسن ما فيها مسروق من اللغة العربية المقدسة والفارسية العذبة ، وهم لاجل عصبيتها يحاربون القرآن ، وسنة النبي العربي عليه الصلاة والسلام ، فهل هذا هو الاسلام ، الذي يجب لهم به الاحترام ؟ أليس من المشهور عنهم أنهم يريدون اماتة اللغة العربية، ألم يؤلفوا الكتب في وجوب تركها والصلاة والاذان باللغة التركية، فاذا ماتت اللغة العربية فكيف يبقى القرآن والسنة ، واذا جهل الكتاب والسنة فماذا يبقى من الاسلام ؟

وأنتم أيها العرب من النصارى والموسويين ! ضعوا يدكم في يد اخوانكم المسلمين العرب ولا تتبعوا خطوات من يقول لكم منكم أو من غيركم (ان العرب المسلمين متعصبون تعصبا دينيا أعمى لذلك تفضل الاتراك اللادينيين عليهم) فهذا قول هراء لا يصدر الا من جاهل لا يعرف مصلحة نفسه وشعبه ، فان العرب المسلمين اخوانكم في الوطنية واذا كان يوجد فيهم من يتعصب تعصبا ذميما ففيكم أنتم أيضا أمثال هؤلاء المتعصبين . وكل من الفريقين تعلمها من الاعاجم ، فان أجدادنا لم يكونوا متعصبين بهذا المعنى ، بل كان اليهود والنصارى يتلقون العلوم في مساجد الاندلس وبغداد كالاخوة فليكن رائد الطرفين التساهل والسعي في ازالة هذه التعصبات الذميمة . واعلموا أن هؤلاء الاجانب عن لغتكم أضر عليكم من متعصبي العرب الجهلاء ، لانكم يمكنكم التفاهم مع العرب وهم اخوانكم في الوطنية والجنسية ، ولكن يصعب عليكم التفاهم مع العلوج الذين هم أعداؤكم وأعداء العرب المسلمين في آن واحد. ارجعوا الى كتاب عبيد الله المار ذكره لتروا ما يثبت لكم قولنا . ها أنتم تحاسنونهم وهم يسيئون اليكم ويحتقرونكم ويهضمون حقوقكم . اتفقوا مع بني وطنكم وجنسكم واعلموا ان التعصب الذميم زائل البتة . وسيأتي يوم لا يبقى فيه للتعصب أثر في بلادنا . وهذا اليوم هو الذي تكون فيه أمورنا في أيدينا وعلومنا وأعمالنا وأحكامنا بلغتنا ، وما ذلك ان اتفقت كلمتنا ببعيد

أيها العرب عموماً : اعلموا انه تأسست جمعية فدائية تقتل كل من يقاتل العرب ويقاوم الاصلاح العربي ، وما هو الاصلاح على مبدأ اللامركزية الذي يطلبه البعض مع التابعية للمدان الاستانة، بل على مبدأ الاستقلال التام ، وتأليف دولة عربية لامركزية ، تعيد سالف مجدنا الغابر وتحكم البلاد بالحكم الذاتي في كل مقاطعة بما يليق بها. وتبدأ عملها بازالة وجود بعض الثعالب المتزلفين من العرب الذين كانوا ولا يزالون سببا لدوس حقوق العرب تحت أقدام أولئك المدان السفاكين. وسيرى العالم ذلك عند مايشرعون في تنفيذ ما أعدوه لنا من المهالك. فهذا بلاغ لقوم يعقلون :

أبلغ ربيعة من مرو واخوتهم فليغضبوا قبل أن لا ينفع الغضب

ولينصبوا الحرب ان القوم قد نصبوا حربا يحرق في حافاتها الحطب

ما بالكم تلقحون الحرب بينكم كأن أهل الجماعة رأيكم عزب

وتتركون عدوا قد أظلكم مما تأشب لا دين ولا حسب

قدماً يدينون دينا ما سمعت به عن الرسول ولم تنزل به الكتب

فمن يكن سائلا عن أصل دينهم فان دينهم أن تقتل العرب

FIG. 5. Overleaf of Fig. 4. (Reduced from original size, 43×41 cms.)

APPENDIX K

الصرخة الاولى

الى اولياء الامور في العاصمة

انا عصبة العرب نمد ايدينا اليكم نصافحكم مصافحة الكريم للكريم ونغضي عما اصاب المللة على ايديكم فانا الحديد يفنيه الحديد
انا بما جبلنا عليه من العزة والاباء نفخر بما قد جعلنا من شرف الآباء فقد اثبتنا وجودنا في هذه الجامعة العثمانية بأن قد حمينا وصارنا
مدة خمسة عشر شهراً امام دولة اوروبية عظيمة لم تستطع ان تنفذ الينا بشر او ان تسومنا بعذاب فحق لنا ان نطالبكم بما هو لازم لحقنا ونشاطركم سياسة
المملكة فيما هو خاص بشأننا فالعرب قاعدة جامعتكم من قبل ومن بعد

Fig. 6. "The First Call to the Authorities in the Capital." (Reduced from original size, 33×25 cms.)

The leaflet reproduced on page 159 (Fig. 6) is entitled "The First Call (*al-Sarkhah al-Ūlā*) to the Authorities in the Capital (Constantinople)." The "Call" begins by stating: "We, a group of Arabs (*'Uṣbah al-'Arab*) stretch our hand to you, greeting you the greeting of one generous people for another." But after this greeting, the tone becomes critical and the anonymous authors of this leaflet present the Ottoman Government with a number of demands. Concerning the general policies of the Government, they ask that the new Ministries be composed of Ottomans and not of Turks. The Arabs have been and continue to be the foundation of Ottoman society. "We," says the leaflet, "and the Armenians together with you (Turks) guarantee to protect our country and yours. Therefore, your partners (in the Government of the country) should have the same right as you have to the (new) Ministry."

As to the internal administration of the country, the Authorities should adopt the type of administration existing in "civilized countries": there should be a Legislative Power, a Parliament and a Senate. The Legislative Power will be headed by His Majesty, the Sultan, and will be composed of the Prime Minister and his Cabinet, the Shaikh al-Islam, the Ministries of Foreign Affairs, the Army, the Navy, Justice, Finance, Railways and Customs. The country will be divided into three regions composed of Turkish *vilayets*, Arab *vilayets* and Armenian *vilayets*. Every region will have a small Cabinet headed by a Minister appointed by the Sultan-Caliph from among the inhabitants of that region. It will be composed of the Ministries of Interior, Education, "*Awqāf*" (religious endowments), Public Works, Agriculture, Police and "Public Assistance." There will also be, in every region, a Chamber of Deputies elected by the people of that region as the Ottoman Parliament is elected... Thus, the internal Government of the three regions of the Empire will be placed in the hands of their own inhabitants because the latter are better acquainted with their own needs and problems.

This is the kind of administrative independence that the Arabs are asking for — following the example of the governments of the Great Powers and for the sake of their own survival... and the survival of their brethren, the Turks and the Armenians...

As to the strength of this Arab Group (*'Uṣbah*) which has put out this "First Call", "only God knows it." "We," the 'Call' concludes, "are the protecting force of the Arabs... A fine link joins us with the Arab lands. Should we send out a call for help, they would be our strongest shield..."

APPENDIX L

FIG. 7. "Second Call to all the Sons of the Arabs." (Reduced from original size, 33×25 cms.)

The document reproduced[1] on page 161 (Fig. 7) is the "Second Call to all the Sons of the Arabs." The "First Call" having addressed itself to "the wisemen in Istanbul," the "Second Call" pleads with the Arabs everywhere not to be subservient slaves with the yoke of tyranny in their necks but to stand in line with the living nations of the world. It would be a great pity if this Arab-Ottoman Union (*al-Jāmi'ah al-'Arabiyyah al-'Uthmāniyyah* were to be destroyed by the Central Administration (of the Young Turks).

It is true that the Arabs will not benefit if they break away from the Ottoman State or if they ignore the Turkish "*Ummah*". But the Arabs in the Arabian Peninsula ought to know the truth of their present history: the Ottoman Government has reached a state when it cannot protect them anymore from the attacks of (foreign) invaders. It is, therefore, necessary for the Arabs, henceforth, to depend only on themselves for their survival. To rely on centralized power in Istanbul is to fall into a political abyss, an abyss which will engulf, in the near future, what remains of the Ottoman State.

"We appeal to you, Sons of the Arabian Peninsula," says this "Second Call," "to join the 'holy Movement' in Syria. Greet its organizers with the sincere greeting of a brother, for they have learned that religion belongs to God alone and they have decided that differences in religion should not lead to disagreement about the Fatherland (*al-Waṭan*). Consequently, let all the Christians in this Movement remain united in their 'nationalism' (*al-Jinsiyyah*) with the Jews and the Muslims; and let all the Muslims and the Jews stand together with the Christians. For 'nationalism' (*al-Jinsiyyah*) gave them their being before the existence of religion. Their religions are only paths which branched out from their original 'Union' (*Jāmi'ah*). In all their national demands let them work together with tolerance and forgiveness in the service of the Arab Union (*al-Jāmi'ah al-'Arabiyyah.*")

The anonymous authors of this "Second Call" praise the Syrians for the "Movement" which they have started in their country but this "Movement" is not sufficient to protect their land. Much more must be done to establish decentralization. For the guidance of the Syrians, two examples of decentralized governments are given: Germany and the United States of America, adding that Austria-Hungary, Switzerland and countries in South America and North America follow the example of Germany and the United States. And so they appeal for the establishment of a decentralized government in the full sense of that word as explained in the "First Call." They warn the Arabs not to be deceived but to strengthen themselves by themselves and to reform the administration by their own initiative, otherwise the danger to their dignity and honour is great. The Arabs do not refuse to acknowledge their association with the Turks but should the Turks be unjust to the Arabs, then the Turks must be ready to take the consequences.

* * *

The "First Call" and the "Second Call" are both remarkable in that they contain positive and concrete proposals for administrative reforms in the Ottoman Empire. They, also, specifically refer to the Armenians and ask for them the same rights — autonomy and self-government — as for the Arabs. The anonymous authors, apparently imbibed with the ideas of the French Revolution, take a very broad-minded view of religion. Indeed, they consider the homeland (*al-Waṭan*), a stronger link than religion, uniting the Arabs whether Muslims, Christians or Jews. Moreover, these two "Calls" are further testimonies — for Arab-Turkish relations — that inspite of all the grievances the Arabs had against the Turkish Government before the First World War, they did not desire to break away completely from the Ottoman Empire but all that they wanted was complete autonomy within that Empire on the basis of decentralization.

A point of further interest about these two anonymous leaflets is the seal they carry. The two Arabic letters of *Jīm* and *'Ain* are in the middle of the seal surrounded by an ear of wheat on the left and a palm leaf, on the right with the Christian and Muslim dates of A.D. 1909 and A.H. 1327, below them. From the texts of these two "Calls," it appears that those two initials stand for "*al-Jāmi'ah al-'Arabiyyah*" [The Arab Union], although before the discovery of these two "Calls" — which are being published, now, for the first time —, no Arab secret society had been known to have existed with such a name. (The possibility that the letters "*Jīm*" and "*'Ain*" may also refer to "*al-Jāmi'ah al-'Uthmāniyyah*" [The Ottoman Union] cannot be entirely excluded). The seal is also the only known seal of an Arab secret society to have used symbols for Arab lands: an ear of wheat for the Province of Syria and a palm leaf for the Arabian Peninsula. The contents of these two documents suggest that they were written sometime in 1913.

APPENDIX M[1]

دعوة

«الى أبناء الامة العربية»

نحن الجالية العربية في باريس قد أوقفتنا مناظرات الجرائد الأوربية ومغامز الساسة في الاندية العمومية على استقراء مايجري من المخابرات الدولية بشأن البلاد العربية ، وأخصها زهرة الوطن سوريا ، ولم يبق بين جمهور الناطقين بالضاد من لايعلم أن ذلك نتيجة سوء الادارة المركزية

فحدا بنا الامر الى الاجتماع ـ وعددنا ينيف عن الثلثمائة في هذه المدينة ـ لنجري البحث عن التدابير الواجب اتخاذها لوقاية الارض (المترعة بدم الآباء العظام ورفات الاجداد الاباة) من عادية الاجانب وانقاذها من صبغة التسيطر والاستبداد واصلاح أمورنا الداخلية على ما يتطلبه أهل البلاد من قواعد اللامركزية حتى يشتد بها ساعدنا وتستقيم قناتنا فينقطع بذلك خطر الاحتلال أو الاضمحلال وتنفى مذلة الرق وتخفت نأمة الاستعباد ويظهر للاعبين بحياة الشعوب أننا أمة عيوف الضيم لاتستنيم لذل ولا تستكين لمسكنة

وبعد المداولة تقرر عقد مؤتمر للعرب يقوم به السوريون في أواخر شهر ايار القادم فنهد اليه وفود أكابر من البلاد العربية وعقلاء أفاضل من السوريين المهاجرين لمصر وأميركا الجنوبية وأميركا الشمالية والبلاد الأوربية فتتمثل فيه الامة العربية المنتشرة في أقطار الارض وتحق كلمة التضامن الاجتماعي والسياسي لهذه الامة في هذا المؤتمر حيث نبسط للامم الأوربية أننا أمة مستمسكة ذات وجود حي لاينحل ومقام عزيز لاينال وخصائص قومية لاتنتزع ومنزلة سياسية لاتفرع . ونصارح الدولة العثمانية بأن اللامركزية قاعدة حياتنا وأن حياتنا أقدس حق من حقوقنا وأن العرب شركاء في هذه المملكة ، شركاء في الحربية ، شركاء في الادارة ، شركاء في السيا. وأما في داخلية بلادهم فهم شركاء أنفسهم .

FIG. 8. "Invitation to the Sons of the Arab *Ummah*." (Reduced from original size, 40.5×28 cms.)

APPENDIX M²

ومن ثم انتخبت الجالية لجنة ادارية (وهي الموقعة على هـذا) لتقوم بالعمل فوضعت خطة المؤتمر وما سيجري فيه من المباحث على مشهد من أبناء الوطن المجيد وبعض من كبار الاوربيين وممثلي الصحف الاوربية والاميركية . وهذه هي المسائل التي ستكون أساس المذاكرات :

١ ـ الحياة الوطنية ، ومناهضة الاحتلال

٢ ـ حقوق العرب في المملكة العثمانية

٣ ـ ضرورة الاصلاح على قاعدة اللامركزية

٤ ـ المهاجرة من سوريا والى سوريا

ومتى تمت المناقشات حمل المؤتمر قراراته الى حيث يحتم عليها التصديق ويحق التنفيذ

*
* *

وبعد فاننا ندعو كل من يخفق قلبه لأمة العرب صغيراً أو كبيراً أن يلبي داعي الوطن ـ لاسيما أرباب الزعامات في مقاعد الجمعيات فعليهم نعتمد واليهم نتجه ، فاما أن يتضاموا الى وفود المؤتمر وإما أن يبعثوا اليه بالرسائل البرقية أوالكتابية يظهرون فيها ارتياحهم لنيل الغاية واشتراكهم في شريف المقصد حتى يدلي المؤتمر لدى الامم بحجته وتستوثق قوته بقوة أمته . وهنالك ينشق اليقين فيطل على هذه الامة فجر الحياة من بين أنساق الغسق وركام الظلمات

وسلام على من تلقى هذا النور فما أغشاه ، ومن عرف واجبه فأداه

(لجنة المؤتمر العربي السوري)

عوني عبد الهادي	ندرة مطران	عبد الغني العريسي	شكري غانم
جميل معلوف	محمد محمصاني	شارل دباس	جميل مردوم بك

المراسلات تكون باسم كاتب اللجنة ، وهذا عنوانه :

Abdul-Gani Araïssi, 17 Rue Claude Bernard
Paris

FIG. 9. Overleaf of Fig. 8.

The document reproduced on pages 164-165, (Fig. 8, 9) is an "Invitation to the Sons of the Arab *Ummah*" from the Arab Community (*al-Jāliyah al-'Arabiyyah*) in Paris. It informs them that this Community, the members of which exceed three hundred, has met and discussed the necessary measures to be taken to protect its Fatherland from the threats of the foreigners, save it from domination and tyranny and introduce reforms in it on the basis of decentralization.

It has, consequently, been decided to hold an Arab Congress towards the end of May[1] in which the whole Arab *Ummah* will be represented (including the Arab communities in Egypt, South America, North America and the European countries). "We shall demonstrate in this Congress," says this 'Invitation,' "to the European nations that we are an *Ummah* with a living identity... and with national characteristics which cannot be destroyed... We shall also tell the Ottoman Government, frankly, that decentralization is the basis of our existence... and that the Arabs are partners in this (Ottoman) Kingdom, partners in the army, partners in the administration and partners in its policies; but, inside their own lands they are partners with themselves only."

The following agenda for discussion at the Congress has been drawn up by an Administrative Committee elected by the Paris Community:

1. "National life and opposition to (foreign) occupation.
2. The rights of the Arabs in the Ottoman Kingdom.
3. Necessity of reforms on the basis of decentralization.
4. Emigration from Syria and immigration to Syria."

The Arabs, everywhere, are invited to cooperate with and to support the forthcoming Congress. The "Invitation" bears the seal of "the Committee of the Arab Syrian Congress" dated "Paris, 1913" and the following names of the members of the Administrative Committee : 'Awnī 'Abd al-Hādī, Nadrā Muṭrān, 'Abd al-Ghanī al-'Araisī, Shucrī Ghānem, Jamīl Ma'lūf, Muḥammad Maḥmaṣānī, Charles Debbas and Jamīl Mardam Bey[2].

For purposes of correspondence, it gives the name of its Secretary and his Paris address: "Abdul-Ġanī Araīssī, 17 Rue Claude Bernard, Paris."

1. This Arab Congress was actually held 18-23 June, 1913, in the Hall of the Geographic Society at Boulevard Saint-Germain, in Paris. For the resolutions which were voted at the Congress, see Appendix C.

2. See also *Iḍāḥāt*, pp. 49-51.

APPENDIX N

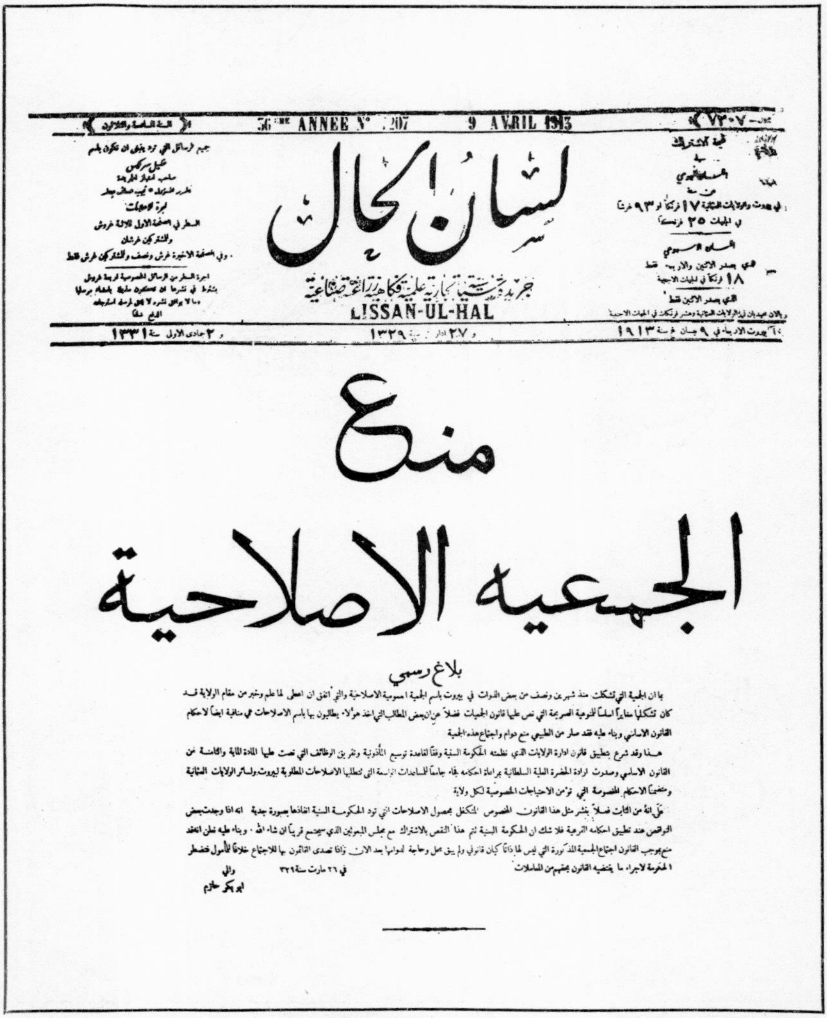

56me ANNEE N° 7207 9 AVRIL 1913

لسان الحال

جريدة سياسية تجارية علمية فكاهية زراعية صناعية

LISSAN-UL-HAL

منع

الجمعية الاصلاحية

بلاغ رسمي

بما ان الجمعية التي تشكلت منذ شهرين ونصف من بعض الذوات في بيروت باسم الجمعية العمومية الاصلاحية والتي اتفق ان اعطي لها علم وخبر من مقام الولاية قد كان تشكلها مغايراً اساساً للنوعية الصريحة التي نص عليها قانون الجمعيات فضلاً عن ان بعض المطالب التي اخذ هؤلاء يطالبون بها باسم الاصلاحات هي منافية ايضاً لاحكام القانون الاساسي وبناء عليه فقد صار من الطبيعي منع دوام واجتماع هذه الجمعية

هذا وقد شرع بتطبيق قانون ادارة الولايات الذي نظمته الحكومة السنية وفقاً لقاعدة توسيع المأذونية وتفريق الوظائف التي نصت عليها المادة المائة والثامنة من القانون الاساسي وصدرت ارادة الحضرة العلية السلطانية بمراعاة احكامه فجاء جامعاً للمساعدات الواسعة التي تتطلبها الاصلاحات المطلوبة لبيروت ولسائر الولايات العثمانية ومتضمناً الاحكام المنصوصة التي تؤمن الاحتياجات المخصوصة لكل ولاية

على انه من الثابت فضلاً بنشر مثل هذا القانون المخصوص المتكفل بحصول الاصلاحات التي تود الحكومة السنية انفاذها بصورة جدية انه اذا وجدت بعض النواقص عند تطبيق احكامه الفرعية فلا شك ان الحكومة السنية تتم هذا النقص بالاشتراك مع مجلس المبعوثين الذي سيجتمع قريباً ان شاء الله. وبناء عليه فلن انفذ منع بموجب القانون اجتماع الجمعية المذكورة التي ليس لها ذاتاً كيان قانوني ولم يبق محل وحاجة لدوامها بعد الآن. واذا تصدى القائمون بها للاجتماع خلافاً للأصول فخطر الحكومة لاجراء ما يقتضيه القانون بحقهم من المعاملات

في ٢٦ مارت سنة ٣٢٩

والي

ابو بكر حازم

FIG. 10. The official proclamation of the *Valī* of Beirut, Abū-Bakr Ḥāzim, forbidding the meetings of the Beirut Reform Society (*al-Jam'iyyah al-Iṣlāḥiyyah*), published in "*Lissan ul-Ḥāl*," 9 April, 1913. Reproduced by permission of Nami Jafet Memorial Library, American University of Beirut, Lebanon.

APPENDIX O

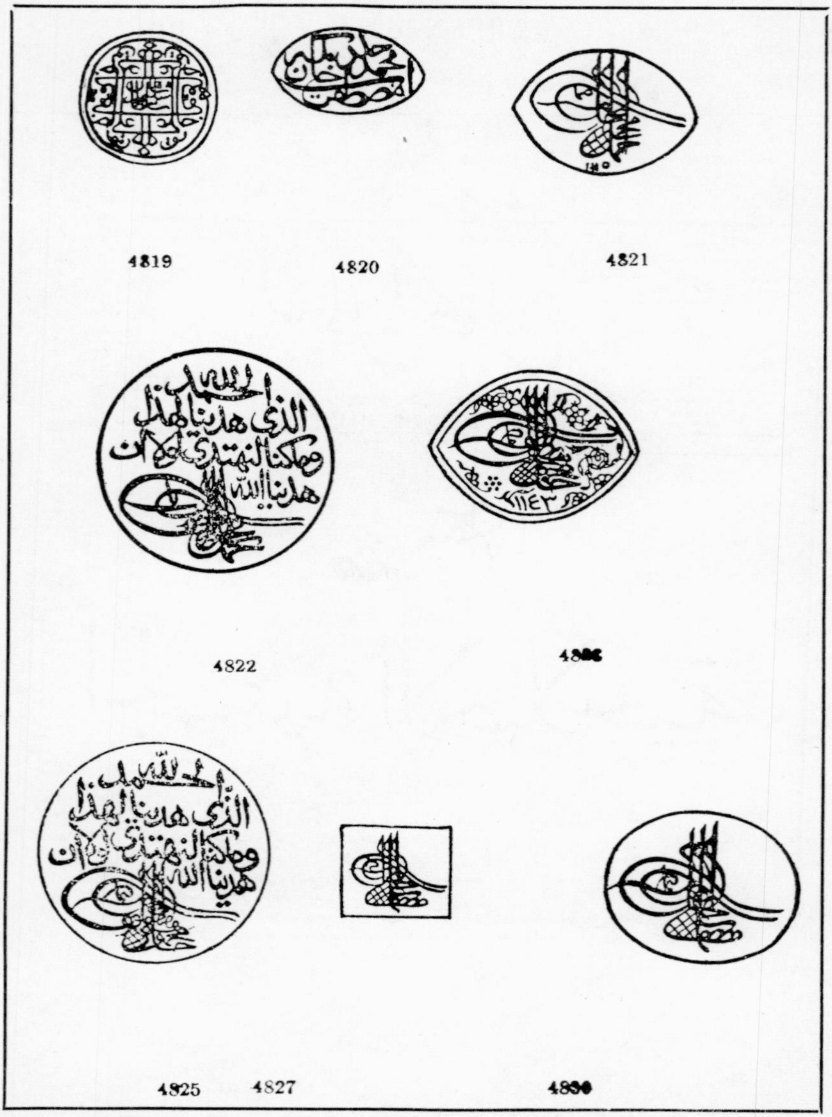

FIG. 11. Reproductions of the Imperial Seals of Ottoman Sultans with Arabic engravings. No. 4819 is the seal of Sultan Selim I (1512-1520); No. 4822 is that of Sultan Aḥmad III (1703-1730) and No. 4825 is one of the seals of Sultan Maḥmud I (1730-1754). See Isma'il Ḥakki Uzunçarşilli, *Topkapi Sarayi Mühürler Seksiyounu Rehberi* [A guide to the Seals Section in the Topkapi Saray Museum] (Istanbul, 1959).

APPENDIX P

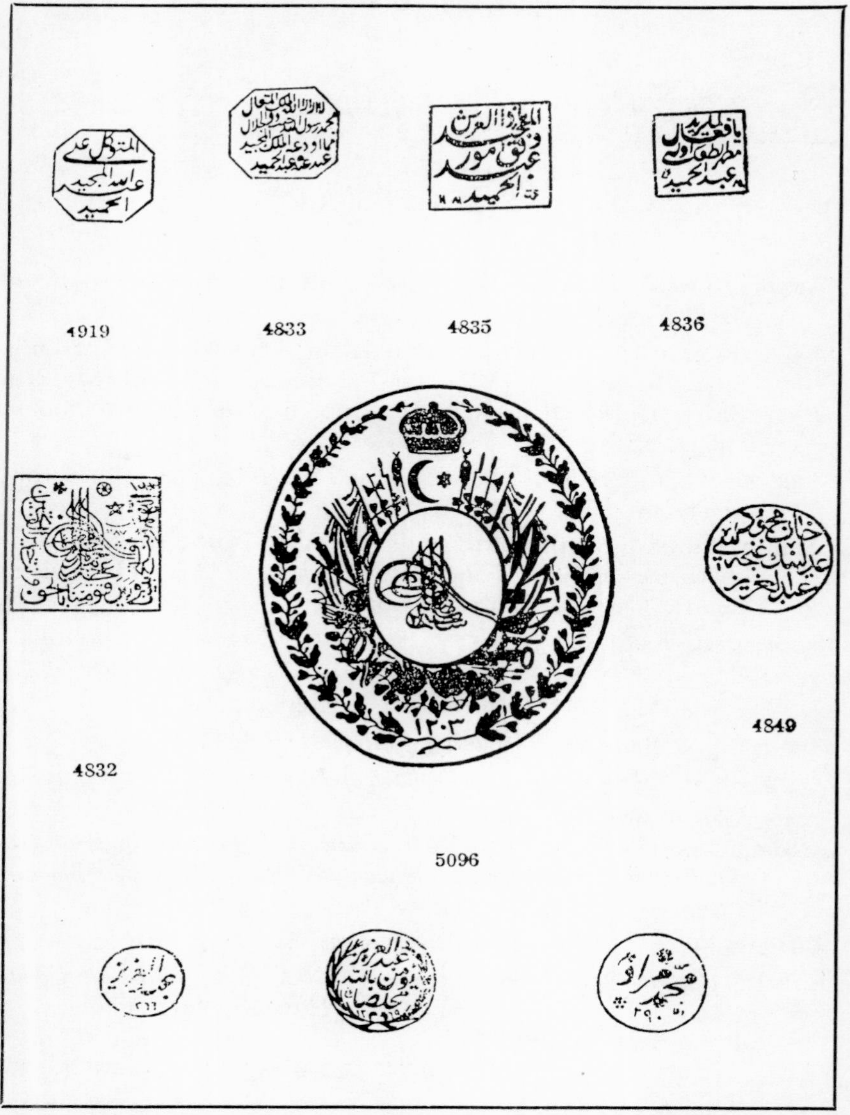

FIG. 12. Reproductions of the Imperial Seals of Ottoman Sultans with Arabic engravings. Nos. 4919, 4832 and 4833 are the seals of Sultan 'Abdul-Ḥamīd I (1774-1789). See Uzonçarşili, *Topkapi Sarayi Muzesi Muhurler Seksiyonu Rehberi.*

BIBLIOGRAPHY

BOOKS AND ARTICLES

'ABADI, AKRAM. *Miḥnat al-Qawmiyyah al-'Arabiyyah* [The ordeal of Arab Nationalism]. Beirut, 1962.

'ABD AL-RAḤĪM, MUDDATHIR. "Al-Islām wa'l Qawmiyyah fi'l Sharq al-Awṣat", [Islam and nationalism in the Middle East], *Ḥiwār* (Beirut), vol. 1, no. 6 (September-October 1963): 5:13.

'ABD AL-RĀZIQ, 'ALĪ. *Al-Islām wa Uṣūl al-Ḥukm* [Islam and the principles of government]. Cairo, 1925.

'ABDUH, SHAIKH MUḤAMMAD, and AFGHĀNĪ, JAMĀL AL-DĪN AL-. *Al-'Urwa al-Wuthqā Lā Inqisāma Lahā* [The indissoluble bond]. Cairo, A.H. 1328 [A.D. 1910].

'ABDULLĀH, KING OF JORDAN. *Amālī al-Siyāsiyyah* [My political hopes].

———. *Mudhakkarātī* [My memoirs]. Jerusalem, 1945.

ABOUSSOUAN, BENOÎT. *Le problème politique Syrien.* Paris, 1925.

ABU ZAHRAH, MUḤAMMAD. *Al-Waḥdah al-Islāmiyyah* [Muslim unity]. Cairo, 1958.

ADAMS, CHARLES C. *Islam and Modernism in Egypt: A Study of the Modern Reform Movement Inaugurated by Muḥammad 'Abduh.* London: Oxford University Press, 1933.

A DIPLOMATIST. *Nationalism and War in the Near East.* Oxford, 1915.

ADIVAR, HALIDÉ EDIB. *Turkey Faces West: A Turkish View of Recent Changes and their Origin.* New Haven: Yale University Press, 1930.

———. *Conflict of East and West in Turkey.* 2d ed. Lahore: S.M. Ashraf, n.d. [1935?]

AFSHĀR, IRAJ, and MAHDAVI, ASGHAR, eds. *Documents Inédits Concernant Seyyed Jamāl al-Dīn Afghānī.* Publication no. 841. Tehran: Tehran University Press, 1963.

A German Diplomat. *The Near East from Within*. London, 1915.

Aḥmed, Jamāl Moḥammad. *The Intellectual Origins of Egyptian Nationalism*. London: Oxford University Press, 1960.

Akçuraoglu, Yusuf. *Uç Terzi Siyaset* [Three types of policy]. Cairo, 1903; Istanbul, A.H. 1327 [A.D. 1909].

'Alamī, Shaikh 'Abdullāh. *A'zam Tidhkār li'l-'Uthmāniyyīn al-Aḥrār, aw al-Ḥurriyyah w-al Musāwāt wa'l Mab'uthan* [The greatest memorial for the free Ottomans: liberty, equality, and the Ottoman parliament]. Beirut, A.H. 1326 [A.D. 1908].

'Alāyili, 'Abdullāh al-. *Dustūr al-'Arab al-Qawmī* [The national constitution of the Arabs]. Beirut, 1941.

Amīn, Aḥmad. *Yawm al-Islām* [Day of Islam]. Cairo, 1958.

———. *Zu'amā' al-Iṣlāḥ fī-l-'Aṣr al-Ḥadīth* [Leaders of reform in the modern age]. Cairo, 1948.

An Oriental Student. *The Modern Syrians*. London, 1844.

Antonius, George. *The Arab Awakening: The Story of the Arab National Movement*. London: Hamish Hamilton, 1938.

'Arabī, Muḥammad 'Abdullah. *Dimuqrātiyyat al-Qawmīyyah al-'Arabiyyah* [The democratic nature of Arab nationalism]. Cairo, 1959.

Arminjon, Pierre. *De la Nationalité dans l'Empire Ottoman*. Paris, 1903.

Arnold, Sir Thomas W. *The Caliphate*. London, 1924.

———, and Guillaume, Alfred, eds. *The Legacy of Islam*. Oxford: Clarendon Press, 1931.

A'zamī, Aḥmad 'Izzat al-. *Al-Qaḍiyyah al-'Arabiyyah* [The Arab question]. Baghdad, 1831.

'Azm, 'Uthmān al-, ed. *Majmū'at Athār Rafīq Bey al-'Azim* [A collection of the writings of Rafiq Bey al-Azm]. Cairo, A.H. 1344 [A.D. 1925].

'Azīz Bey. *Sūrīyyah wa Lubnān fī'l-Ḥarb al-'Ālamiyyah* [Syria and Lebanon during the world war], trans. Fuad Maydani. Beirut, 1933.

Azoury, Négib. *Le réveil de la nation arabe dans l'Asie turque, en présence des intérêts et des rivalités des puissances étrangères, de la Curie romaine et du Patriarcat œcuménique*. Paris, Plon, 1905.

Stoddard, Lothrop. *The New World of Islam*. London, 1921.

'AZZĀM PASHA, 'ABD AL-RAḤMAN. *Al-Risālah al-Khālidah* [The eternal message]. Cairo, 1946.

BĀHĪ, MUḤAMMAD AL-. *Al-Fikr al-Islāmī al-Ḥadīth wa Ṣilātahū bi'l Isti'mār al-Gharbī* [Contemporary Islamic thought and its connections with Western imperialism]. Cairo, 1957.

BAIHUM, MUḤAMMAD JAMĪL. *Al-'Arab wa'l Turk* [The Arabs and the Turks]. Beirut, 1957.

BAILEY, FRANK EDGAR. *British Policy and the Turkish Reform Movement: A Study in Anglo-Turkish Relations, 1826-1853.* Cambridge: Harvard University Press, 1942.

BĀQŪRĪ, AḤMAD ḤASAN AL-. *'Urūbah wa Dīn* [Arabism and religion]. [Cairo, n.d.].

BARKER, EDWARD B. B. *Syria and Egypt Under the Last Five Sultans of Turkey, Being Experiences During 50 Years of Mr. Consul-Gen. Barker.* 2 vols. London: Tinsley, 1876.

BARTHOLD, VASILI VLADIMIROVICH. *Histoire des Turcs d'Asie Centrale*, trans. Mme. M. Donskis. Paris: Adrien-Maisonneuve, 1945.

BASHMĪL, MUḤAMMAD AḤMAD. *Lahīb al-Ṣarāḥah yaḥriq al-Mughālaṭāt* [The fire of frankness burns all errors]. Beirut, 1961.

———. *Ṣirā' ma' al-Bāṭil* [Struggle with falsehood]. Beirut, 1960.

———. *Al-Qawmiyyah fī Nazar al-Islām* [Nationalism from the viewpoint of Islam]. Beirut, 1960.

BELL, GERTRUDE LOWTHIAN. *Amurath to Amurath.* London: Heinemann, 1911.

———. *Syria, The Desert and the Sown.* London: Heinemann, 1907.

BERRO, TAWFĪQ 'ALĪ. *Al-'Arab wa'l-Turk fī 'Ahd al-Dastūr al-'Uthmānī, 1908-1914* [The Arabs and the Turks under the Ottoman Constitution, 1908-1914]. Cairo, 1960.

———. *Al-Qawmiyyah al-'Arabiyyah fi'l Qarn al-Tāsi' 'Ashar* [Arab nationalism in the nineteenth century]. Damascus, 1965.

BINT AL-SHĀTI'. ['Ā'isha 'Abd al-Raḥmān] "Al-Tafsīr al-Dīnī Li-Tārīkhinā" [The religious interpretation of our history], *Al-Ahrām* (Cairo), 9 August 1963, p. 13.

BLISS, DANIEL. *The Reminiscences of Daniel Bliss*, ed. Frederick J. Bliss. New York: Fleming H. Revell, 1920.

BOWEN, HAROLD. *British Contributions to Turkish Studies.* London: Longmans, Green & Co., for the British Council, 1945.

BRÉMOND, GEN. ÉDOUARD. *Le Hedjaz dans la guerre mondiale.* Paris: Payot, 1931.

BROCKELMANN, CARL. *History of the Islamic Peoples,* trans. Joel Carmichael and Moshé Perlmann. New York: G.P. Putnam's Sons, 1947.

BUSTĀNĪ, SULAIMĀN AL-. *Al-Dawlah al-'Uthmāniyyah Qabl al-Dustūr wa Ba'dahu* [The Ottoman Empire before and after the Constitution]. Beirut, 1908.

CAHUET, ALBÉRIC. *La question d'Orient, dans l'histoire contemporaine (1821-1905).* Paris: Dujarric, 1905.

CAHUN, LEON. *Introduction à l'histoire de l'Asie: Turcs et Mongols des origines à 1405.* Paris: Colin, 1896.

CHEVRILLON, ANDRÉ. *Conférence sur la Syrie.* Rouen, 1897.

CHIROL, SIR VALENTINE, AND OTHERS. *Reawakening of the Orient and Other Essays.* New Haven: Yale University Press, 1925.

CHURCHILL, COL. CHARLES HENRY. *The Druzes and the Maronites Under the Turkish Rule from 1840-1860.* London: Quarith, 1862.

CONTENSON, BARON LUDOVIC DE. *Les réformes en Turquie d'Asie: la question arménienne, la question syrienne.* 2d ed. Paris: Plon, 1913.

COULSON, NOEL J. *A History of Islamic Law.* Islamic Surveys 2. Edinburgh: Edinburgh University Press, 1964.

CREASY, EDWARD S. *History of the Ottoman Turks From the Beginning of their Empire to the Present Time.* rev. ed. London: Richard Bentley and Son, 1878.

CUINET, VITAL. *Syrie, Liban et Palestine.* Paris: Leroux, 1896.

CUMMING, HENRY H. *Franco-British Rivalry in the Post-War Near East: The Decline of French Influence.* London: Oxford University Press, 1938.

DĀGHIR, AS'AD. *Mudhakkarātī* [My memoirs]. Cairo, n.d.

DARWAZAH, AL-ḤAKAM, AND JABBŪRĪ, ḤAMĪD AL-. *Ma' al-Qawmiyyah al-'Arabiyyah* [Arab nationalism]. Cairo, 1958.

DAVID, WADE DEWOOD. *European Diplomacy in the Near Eastern Question, 1906-1909.* Illinois Studies in the Social Sciences, vol. 25, no. 4. Urbana: University of Illinois Press, 1940.

DAVISON, RODERIC H. *Reform in the Ottoman Empire, 1856-1876.* Princeton: Princeton University Press, 1963.

DAWĀLĪBĪ, MA'RŪF. *Al-Qawmiyyah al-'Arabiyyah fī Ḥaqīqatihā* [The truth about Arab nationalism]. Cairo, 1959.

DE TARRAZI, VICOMTE PHILIP. *Tārīkh al-Ṣaḥāfah al-'Arabiyyah* [History of the Arabic press]. Beirut, 1913.

DIEHL, CHARLES, AND MARÇAIS, GEORGES. *Histoire générale : Histoire du moyen âge.* 3 vols. Vol. 3, *Le monde oriental de 395 à 1081.* Paris: Presses Universitaires de France, 1944.

DIMASHQĪ, MIKHĀ'ĪL AL-. *Ta'rīkh Ḥawādith al-Shām wa Lubnān* [A history of the events in Syria and Lebanon]. Beirut, 1912.

DJEMAL PASHA, AḤMAD. *La Vérité sur la Question Syrienne.* Constantinople, 1916. [This book was also published simultaneously in Turkish and in Arabic.]

———. *Memories of a Turkish Statesman, 1913-1919.* London: Hutchinson, 1922.

DJUVARA, TRAUDAFIL G. *Cent projets de partage de la Turquie* (*1281-1913*). Paris: Alcan, 1914.

DODWELL, HENRY H. *The Founder of Modern Egypt: A Study of Muhammad 'Ali.* Cambridge: At the University Press, 1931.

DŪRĪ, 'ABD AL-'AZĪZ AL-. *Al-Judhūr al-Tārīkhiyyah li'l-Qawmiyyah al-'Arabiyyah* [The historical roots of Arab nationalism]. Beirut, 1960.

———. *Muqaddamah fī Tārīkh Ṣadr al-Islām* [Introduction to the history of the early days of Islam]. 2d ed. Beirut, 1961.

DUWAYHĪ, MĀR IṢTIFĀN AL-. *Ta'rīkh al-Ṭā'ifah al-Mārūniyyah* [A history of the Maronites]. Beirut, 1890.

———. *Tārīkh al-Amīr Ḥaidar Aḥmad Shihāb* [History (written) by Amir Ḥaidar Aḥmad Shihāb]. Cairo, 1900.

ENGELHARDT, EDOUARD PHILIPPE. *La Turquie et le tanzimat: ou histoire de réformes dans l'Empire ottoman depuis 1826 jusqu'à nos jours.* 2 vols. Paris: Cotillon, 1882-84.

FAHMĪ, MĀHIR ḤASAN. *Al-Qawmiyyah al-'Arabiyyah wa'l-Shi'r al-Mu'āṣir* [Arab nationalism and contemporary poetry], Ma' al-'Arab, no. 6. Cairo, 1960.

FAIḌĪ, SULAIMAN. *Fī Ghamrat al-Niḍāl: Mudhakkarāt Sulaiman Faiḍi* [In the throes of the struggle: memoirs of Sulaiman Faiḍi]. Baghdad, 1952.

FALLS, CAPT. CYRILL BENTHAM. *Military Operations: Egypt and Palestine, from June 1917, to the end of the War. History of the Great War Based on Official Documents.* London: H.M.S.O., 1930.

FARLEY, J. LEWIS. *Modern Turkey.* London: Hurst, 1872.

———. *The Resources of Turkey, Considered with Special Reference to the Profitable Investment of Capital in the Ottoman Empire.* London: Longman, 1863.

———. *Turks and Christians.* London, 1876.

FRANCE, Bibliothèque Nationale, Archives du Ministère des Affaires Étrangères, *Turquie.*

———. *Documents Diplomatiques, 1860.* Paris, 1861.

FREYCINET, CHARLES DE. *La question d'Egypte.* 2d ed. Paris: P. Brodard, 1904.

FYZEE, ASAF ALI ASGHAR. *Outlines of Muhammadan Law.* Calcutta: Oxford University Press, 1949.

GEORGES-GAULIS, BERTHE. *La question arabe: de l'Arabie du Roi Ibn Saoud à l'indépendance syrienne.* Paris: Berger-Levrault, 1930.

GHALI, PAUL. *Les nationalités détachées de l'Empire Ottoman à la suite de la guerre.* Paris: Domat-Montchrestiens, 1934.

GHAZĀLĪ, MUḤAMMAD AL-. *Kifāḥ Dīn* [A religious struggle]. Cairo, 1959.

———. *Ḥaqīqat al-Qawmiyyah al-'Arabiyyah* [The truth about Arab nationalism]. Cairo, 1961-69.

GHRĀYBAH, 'ABD AL-KARĪM MAḤMŪD. *Al-'Arab wa'l-Atrāk* [The Arabs and the Turks]. Damascus, A.H. 1381 [A.D. 1961].

———. *Muqaddamat Ta'rīkh al-'Arab al-Ḥadīth, 1500-1918* [An introduction to the modern history of the Arabs, 1500-1918]. Damascus, 1960.

GIBB, HAMILTON A.R. *Modern Trends in Islam.* Chicago, 1947.

———. *Studies on the Civilization of Islam,* ed. Stanford J. Shaw and William R. Polk. Boston: Beacon Press, 1962.

———, AND BOWEN, HAROLD. *Islamic Society and the West: A Study of the Impact of Western Civilization on Moslem Culture.* 1 vol. in 2. London and New York: Oxford University Press, 1950-57.

GIBBONS, HERBERT ADAMS. *The Foundation of the Ottoman Empire: A History of the Osmanlis up to the Death of Bayezid I (1300-1403).* Oxford: Clarendon Press, 1916.

GOODELL, REV. WILLIAM. *Forty Years in the Turkish Empire,* ed. E. D. G. Prime. New York, 1876.

GOUILLY, ALPHONSE. *L'Islam devant le monde moderne.* Paris, 1904.

Graves, Sir Robert Windham. *Storm Centres of the Near East: Personal Memories, 1879-1929.* London: Hutchinson, 1933.

Great Britain. Admiralty. *A Handbook of Syria (including Palestine).* Prepared by the Geographical section of the Naval Intelligence Division, Naval Staff. London, H.M.S.O., 1919.

———. Foreign Office. *British Documents on the Origins of the War: 1898-1914*, ed. G.P. Gooch and Harold W.V. Temperley. 11 vols. Vols. 5, *The Near East, 1903-9.* Vol. 10, pt. 1, *The Near and Middle East on the Eve of War*; pt. 2; *The Last Years of Peace.* London: H.M.S.O., 1926-38.

———. Foreign Office. *Correspondence Relating to the Affairs of Syria 1860-61.* London, 1861.

———. Foreign Office. Despatches, *Turkey*, *Egypt.*

———. Foreign Office. *Further Correspondence Respecting the Affairs of Asiatic Turkey and Arabia.*

———. Foreign Office. *Further Correspondence Respecting the Affairs of Egypt, 1902.*

———. Foreign Office. *Handbooks Prepared Under the Direction of the Historical Section of the Foreign Office.* No. 88, *Turkey in Asia.* No. 96 a & b, *The Rise of Islam and the Caliphate*; *The Pan-Islamic Movement.* No. 96 c & d, *The Rise of the Turks*; *The Pan-Turanian Movement.* London, H.M.S.O., January-March 1919.

Guys, Henri. *Esquisse de l'état politique et commercial de la Syrie.* Paris, 1862.

Haim, Sylvia G. *Arab Nationalism: An Anthology.* Berkeley & Los Angeles: University of California Press, 1962.

Ḥakīm, Yusuf al-. *Beirut wa Lubnān fī 'Ahd Āl-'Uthman* [Beirut and Lebanon during the Ottoman period]. Beirut, 1964.

Ḥalīm, Ibrahim Bey. *Kitāb al-Tuḥfa al-Ḥalīmiyyah fī Tārīkh al-Dawlah al-'Aliyyah* [A history of the Ottoman Empire]. Cairo, 1950.

Hamilton, Angus. *Problems of the Middle East.* London: Nash, 1909.

Hammer-Purgstall, [Joseph] Freiherr von. *Histoire de l'Empire Ottoman, depuis son origine jusqu'à nos jours*, trans. J.J. Hellert. 18 vols. Paris: Bellizard, 1835-41.

Hanotaux, Gabriel. *Etudes diplomatiques: La politique de l'équilibre, 1907-1911.* Paris, 1914.

Ḥatatah, Yusuf Kamāl. *Mudhakkarāt Midḥat Pasha* [Memoirs of Midhat Pasha]. Cairo, n.d.

Hayes, Carlton J.H. *The Historical Evolution of Modern Nationalism.* New York: Richard R. Smith, 1931.

Herbert, Aubrey. *Ben Kendim: A Record of Eastern Travel.* London, 1924.

Heyd, Uriel. *Foundations of Turkish Nationalism: The Life and Teachings of Ziya Gökalp.* London: Luzac and Harvill Press, 1950.

Hinckley, Frank Erastus. *American Consular Jurisdiction in the Orient.* Washington: Lowdermilk, 1906.

Hitti, Philip K. *Lebanon in History, from the Earliest Times to the Present.* London: Macmillan, 1957.

Homsy, Msgr. Basile. *Les capitulations et la protection des chrétiens au Proche-Orient, au XVIe, XVIIe et XVIIIe siècles.* Harissa, Lebanon: Imprimerie St. Paul, 1956.

Hostler, Charles W. *Turkism and the Soviets: The Turks of the World and their Political Objectives.* London: Allen, 1957.

Hourani, Albert H. *Arabic Thought in the Liberal Age, 1798-1939.* London: Oxford University Press, 1962.

———. *Minorities in the Arab World.* London: Oxford University Press, 1947.

———. *Syria and Lebanon: A Political Essay.* London: Oxford University Press, 1946.

Hoard, Harry N. *The Partition of Turkey: A Diplomatic History, 1913-1923.* Norman: University of Oklahoma Press, 1931.

Husri, Sāti' al-. *Nushū' al-Fikrah al-Qawmiyyah* [The emergence of the idea of nationalism]. Beirut, 1951-59.

———. *Al-Bilād al-'Arabiyyah wa'l Dawlah al-'Uthmāniyyah* [The Arab countries and the Ottoman Empire]. Cairo, 1957; Beirut, 1960.

Ibn Iyās, Abū al-Barakāt Muḥammad ibn Aḥmad. *Badā'i' al-Zuhūr fī Waqā'i' al-Duhūr* [Wondrous flowers called from the annals of time]. 3 vols. Cairo, A.H. 1312 [A.D. 1894].

Ireland, Philip W., ed. *The Near East: Problems and Prospects.* Chicago: University of Chicago Press, 1945.

Jessup, Henry Harris. *Fifty-three Years in Syria.* 2 vols. New York: Fleming H. Revell, 1910.

JOUPLAIN, M. [pseud. for PAUL NUJAYM]. *La question du Liban: Étude d'histoire diplomatique & de droit international.* Paris: A. Rousseau 1908.

JOWETT, REV. WILLIAM. *Christian Researches in the Mediterranean from 1815-1820.* London: Watts, 1822.

JUNG, EUGÈNE. *Les puissances devant la révolte arabe: la crise mondiale de demain.* Paris: Hachette, 1906.

———. *La Révolte Arabe.* 2 vols. Paris: Colberts, 1924.

KARAL, ENVER ZIYA. *Osmanli Tarihi* [History of Turkey]. 18 vols. Vol. 6, *Islahat fermani devri, 1856-1861* [The period of reform decrees, 1856-1861]. Vol. 8, *Birinci Meşrutiyet ve Istibdat Devirleri, 1876-1907*]The first Constitutional period and despotism, 1856-1907]. Ankara, 1954, 1956.

KATTANĪ, IDRIS AL-. *Al-Maghrib al-Muslim ḍid al-Lādiniyyah* [Muslim Morocco opposes atheism]. Casablanca, 1958.

KAWĀKIBĪ, 'ABD AL-RAḤMĀN AL.- *Umm al-Qurā* [Mecca]. Cairo, 1931; Aleppo, 1959.

———. *Ṭabā'i' al-Istibdād wa Maṣāri' al-Isti'bād* [The nature of tyranny and the struggle against enslavement]. Cairo, n.d.

KAZAMZADEH, FIRUZ. *The Struggle for Transcaucasia, 1917-1921.* New York and London: Oxford University Press, 1952.

KEMAL, ISMAIL. *The Memoirs of Ismail Kemal Bey.* London, 1920.

KHADDURI, MAJID. "Aziz 'Alī Misrī and the Arab Nationalist Movement," St. Antony's Papers, no. 17, in *Middle Eastern Affairs,* no. 4, ed. Albert Hourani. London: Oxford University Press, 1965.

KHAIRALLAH, IBRĀHĪM AS'AD. *The Law of Inheritance in the Republics of Syria and Lebanon.* Beirut: American Press, 1941.

KHAIRALLAH, K.T. *Le problème du Levant: Les régions arabes libérées.* Paris, 1919.

KHĀLID, KHĀLID MUḤAMMAD. *Min Hunā Nabda'* [From here we start]. Cairo, 1950.

———. *From Here We Start,* trans. Ismai'l R. al-Faruqi. 3d ed. Washington: American Council of Learned Societies, 1953.

KHALĪL, YĀSIN, *Al-idiologiyyah al-'Arabiyyah* [The Arab Ideology]. Baghdad: Ministry of Culture and Guidance, 1966.

KHĀLIDĪ, M.R. AL-. *Al-Inqilāb al-'Uthmānī wa Turkiyya al-Fatāt* [The Ottoman revolution and the Young Turks]. Cairo, A.H. 1326.

KHĀRBUTLĪ, 'ALĪ ḤASANĪ AL-. *Muḥammad wa'l-Qawmiyyah al-'Arabiyyah* [Muhammad and Arab nationalism]. Cairo, 1959.

———. *Al-Ta'rikh al-Muwaḥḥad li'l Ummah al-'Arabiyyah* [A unified history of the Arab *Ummah*]. Cairo, 1970.

KIRK, GEORGE EDWARD. *A Short History of the Middle East, from the Rise of Islam to Modern Times.* London: Methuen, 1948. New ed. London, 1955.

KNIGHT, EDWARD F. *The Awakening of Turkey: A History of the Turkish Revolution.* London: Milne, 1909.

KOHN, HANS. *A History of Nationalism in the East*, trans. Margaret M. Green. New York: Harcourt, Brace, 1929.

———. *The Idea of Nationalism: A Study in its Origins and Background.* New York: Macmillan Co., 1944.

KURAN, AHMED BEDEVI. *Inkilāp tarihimiz ve Jön Türkler* [A history of the revolution and the Young Turks]. Istanbul: Tan Matbaasi, 1945.

———. *Inkilāp Tarihimiz ve Ittihad ve Terakki* [A history of the revolution and the Union and Progress]. Istanbul, 1948.

KURD 'ALĪ, MUḤAMMAD. *Khiṭaṭ al-Shām.* 6 vols. Vols. 2, 3, 4. Damascus, 1925-28.

LAWRENCE, T.E. *The Seven Pillars of Wisdom: A Triumph.* London and Toronto: J. Cape, 1935.

LEWIS, BERNARD. *The Middle East and the West.* Bloomington: Indiana University Press; London, 1964.

LONGRIGG, STEPHEN HEMSLEY. *Four Centuries of Modern Iraq.* Oxford: Clarendon Press, 1925.

———. *'Iraq, 1900 to 1950: A Political, Social and Economic History.* London: Oxford University Press for Royal Institute of International Affairs, 1953.

LUJNAH AL-'ULYĀ LI-ḤIZB AL-LĀMARKAZIYYAH, AL- [The Higher Committee of the Decentralization Party]. *Al-Mu'tamar al-'Arabī al-Awwal* [The First Arab Congress]. [Held in Paris, 18-23 June 1913.] Cairo, 1913.

LYBYER, ALBERT HOWE. *The Government of the Ottoman Empire in the time of Suleiman the Magnificent.* Harvard Historical Studies, vol. 18. Cambridge: Harvard University Press, 1913.

MADDEN, RICHARD ROBERT. *The Turkish Empire in its Relation with Christianity and Civilization.* London: Newby, 1862.

MAHMAṢĀNĪ, SUBḤĪ. *Al-Awḍā' al-Tashri'iyyah fi'l Duwal al-'Arabiyyah, Māḍīhā wa Ḥāḍiruhā* [Legal conditions in the Arab states, past and present]. Beirut, 1957-62.

———. *Falsafat al-Tashrī' fi'l-Islām* [The philosophy of legislation in Islam]. Beirut, 1946.

MAJDHUB, MUḤAMMAD AL-. *Al-Qawmiyyah al-'Arabiyyah Amām Taṣāru' al-Aḍḍād* [Arab nationalism face to face with contradictory struggles]. Beirut, 1960.

MAKHZŪMĪ, MUḤAMMAD AL-. *Khāṭirāt Jamāl al-Dīn al-Afghānī al-Ḥusainī* [Mémoirs of Jamal al-Din al-Afghani al-Husaini]. Beirut, 1931.

MANDELSTAM, ANDRÉ NIKOLAIEVICH. *Le sort de l'empire ottoman.* Lausanne: Payot, 1917.

MANTRAN, ROBERT, and SAUVAGET, JEAN, comps. *Règlements fiscaux ottomans: Les Provinces syriennes.* Beirut: Imprimerie Catholique, 1951.

MAQDISĪ, JIRJUS AL-KHŪRĪ AL-. *A'zam Ḥarb fi'l-Tārīkh*] The greatest war in history]. Beirut, 1928.

MAQDISĪ, RUḤĪ KHĀLIDĪ AL-. *Al-Inqilāb al-'Uthmānī wa Turkiyya al-Fatāt* [The Ottoman revolution and the Young Turks]. N.p., n.d.

MARRIOT, JOHN A.R. *The Eastern Question: A Historical Study in European Diplomacy.* 4th ed. Oxford: Clarendon Press, 1940.

MAS'AD, BULOS. *Al-Dawlah al-'Uthmāniyyah fī Lunbān wa Sūriyya, 1517-1916* [Ottoman rule in Lebanon and Syria, 1517-1916]. Cairo, 1916.

———. *Lubnān wa Sūriyyah Qabl al-Intidāb wa Ba'duh* [Lebanon and Syria before and after the establishment of the Mandates]. Cairo, 1929.

MAS'ŪD, JUBRĀN. *Lubnān wa'l-Nahḍah al-'Arabiyyah al-Ḥadīthah* [Lebanon and the Modern Arab renaissance]. Beirut, 1967.

MEARS, ELIOT GRINNEL. *Modern Turkey: A Politico-Economic Interpretation, 1908-1923.* New York, 1925.

MIDḤAT BEY, 'ALI ḤAYDAR. *The Life of Midhat Pasha: A Record of His Services, Political Reforms, Banishment, and Judicial Murder, Derived from Private Documents and Reminiscences, by His Son Ali Haidar Midhat Bey....* London: J. Murray, 1903.

MILLER, WILLIAM. *The Ottoman Empire and its Successors, 1801-1922.* Cambridge: At the University Press, 1923.

MONTAGNE, ROBERT. *L'Evolution moderne des pays arabes.* Paris, 1935.

MORRIS, ROBERT. *Freemasonry in the Holy Land; or, Handmarks of Hiram's Builders.* 5th ed. New York: Masonic Publishing Co., for the author, 1873.

MUBĀRAK, MUḤAMMAD AL-. *Al-Ummah al-'Arabiyyah fī Ma'rakat Taḥqīq al-thāt* [The Arab *Ummah* in the struggle to establish its identity]. Damascus, 1959.

MUWAILIHĪ, MUḤAMMAD AL-. *Ma Hunālik* [What is there]. Cairo, 1896.

NAPIER, LT. COL. EDWARD D.H.E. *Reminiscence of Syria, and the Holy Land.* 2 vols. London: Parry, 1847.

NĀṢIR AL-DĪN, 'ALĪ. *Qaḍiyyat al-'Arab* [The Arab cause]. Beirut, 1963.

NAWFAL, 'ABD AL-RAZZĀQ. *Al-Islām Dīn wa Dunyā* [Islam: temporal and spiritual power]. Cairo, 1959.

NERVAL, GÉRARD DE. *Voyage en Orient.* 3 vols. Paris: Bossard, 1927.

NIYĀZI, AḤMAD. *Khawāṭir Niyāzi* [Memoirs of Niyazi], trans. Wālī-al-Dīn Yakan. Cairo, 1909.

NŪRĪ BEY, JALĀL. *Tārīkh al-Mustaqbal* [A history of the future]. N.p., n.d.

NUSEIBEH, HĀZEM ZAKĪ. *The Ideas of Arab Nationalism.* Ithaca: Cornell University Press, 1956.

NUSŪLĪ, ANĪS ZAKARIYYA. *Asbāb al-Nahḍah al-'Arabiyyah fī'l Qarn al-Tāsi'-'ashar* [The Causes of Arab Renaissance in the Nineteenth Century]. Beirut, 1926.

OSMANOGLU, AYŞE. *Babam Abdülhamid* [My father 'Abdul Hamid]. Istanbul, 1960.

PEARS, SIR EDWIN. *Life of Abdul Hamid.* New York: Henry Holt, 1917.

PICHON, JEAN. *Le partage du Proche-Orient.* Paris: Peyronnet, 1938.

PORTER, J.L. *Five Years in Damascus, Including an Account of the History, Topography, and Antiquities of that City; with Travels and Researches in Palmyra, Lebanon and the Hauran.* London: Murray, 1855.

QAL'AJI, QADRI. *Jeel al-Fidā* [A generation that was sacrificed]. Beirut, 1968.

RAMSAUR, ERNEST E., JR. *The Young Turks: Prelude to the Revolution of 1908.* Princeton: Princeton University Press, 1957.

RAUSAS, G. PELISSIÉ DU. *Le régime des capitulations dans l'Empire Ottoman.* 2 vols. Paris, 1902-05.

RAZZĀZ, MUNĪF AL-. *The Evolution of the Meaning of Nationalism.* New York: Doubleday & Co., 1963.

RIḤĀNĪ, AMĪN AL-. *Mulūk al-'Arab* [The kings of the Arabs]. 2 vols. Beirut, 1929.

RUSTUM, ASAD J. *The Royal Archives of Egypt and the Origins of the Egyptian Expedition to Syria, 1831-1841.* Beirut: American Press, 1936.

SA'AB, ḤASSAN. *Arab Federalists of the Ottoman Empire.* Amsterdam: Djambatan, 1958.

SABA, JEAN S., *L'Islam et la nationalité.* Paris Librairie de Jurisprudence Ancienne et Moderne, 1931.

SA'ID, AḤMAD. *Al-Qawmiyyah al-'Arabiyyah* [Arab nationalism]. Cairo, 1959.

SA'ID, AMĪN. *Al-Thawrah al-'Arabiyyah ak-Kubrā* [The great Arab revolts]. 3 vols. Cairo, 1934.

SA'ID, NŪRĪ AS-. *Arab Independence and Unity.* Baghdad: Government Press, 1943.

SALMON, W.H. *An Account of the Ottoman Conquest of Egypt in the Year A.H. 922 (A.D. 1516).* London: Royal Asiatic Society, 1921.

SAMNÉ, GEORGES. *La Syrie.* Paris: Brossard, 1920.

SARKIS, SALIM. *Sirr Mamlakah* [The secret of a kingdom]. Cairo, 1895.

SĀYIGH, ANĪS. *Taṭawwur al-Mafhūm al-Qawmī 'ind al-'Arab* [The evolution of the meaning of nationalism among the Arabs]. Beirut, 1961.

SETON-WATSON, ROBERT WILLIAM. *Disraeli, Gladstone and the Eastern Question: A Study in Diplomacy and Party Politics.* London: Macmillan, 1935.

———. *The Rise of Nationality in the Balkans.* London: Constable, 1917.

SHAHBANDAR, 'ABD AL-RAḤMĀN. *Al-Thawrah al-Waṭaniyyah* [The national revolution]. Damascus, 1933.

SHAIBĀNĪ, AḤMAD AL-. *Al-Qawmiyyah al-'Arabiyyah fī' l-Nazariyyah wa'l-Taṭbiq* [The theory and practice of Arab nationalism]. Beirut, 1966.

SHĀKIR, AMĪN; 'IRYĀN, SA'ĪD AL-.; and 'ATĀ, MUḤAMMAD MUṢTAFA. *Turkiyyah wa'l Siyāsah al-'Arabiyyah* [Turkey and Arab politics]. Ikhtarna Laka, no. 10. Cairo, 1954.

SHALTŪT, MAḤMŪD. *Al-Islām : 'Aqidah wa Sharī'ah* [Islam: belief and law]. Cairo, n.d.

SHARAF, 'ABD AL-RAḤMAN. *Ta'rikh-i Dawlat-i-Osmaniyyeh* [Ottoman History]. Istanbul, A.H. 1309 [A.D. 1893].

SHIHĀBĪ, AL-AMĪR MUSTAFA AL-. *Muḥāḍarāt 'an al-Qawmiyyah al-'Arabiyyah* [Lectures on Arab nationalism]. Cairo, 1959.

SKELTON, MRS. GLADYS [PRESLAND, JOHN]. *Deedes Bey : A Study of Sir Wyndham Deedes, 1883-1923.* London: Macmillan, 1942.

STITT, GEORGE. *A Prince of Arabia: The Emir Shereef Ali Haidar.* London: Allen & Unwin, 1948.

STRIPLING, GEORGE W.F. *The Ottoman Turks and the Arabs 1511-1574.* Illinois Studies in the Social Sciences, vol. 26, no. 4. Urbana: University of Illinois Press, 1942.

SULḤ, 'ĀDIL. *Suṭūr min al-Risālah* [A brief message]. Beirut, 1966.

SURŪR, ṬĀHA 'ABD-AL-BĀQĪ. *Dawlat al-Qur'ān* [The government of the Qur'an]. Cairo, 1961.

SUSA, NASĪM. *The Capitulatory Regime of Turkey: Its History, Origin, and Nature.* Johns Hopkins University Studies in History and Political Science, n.s. no. 18. Baltimore: Johns Hopkins Press, 1933.

TAḤSĪN PASHA. *Abdulhamid ve Yildiz Hatirlari* [Abdul Hamid and the Memories of Yildiz]. Istanbul, 1921.

ṬAḤṬĀWĪ, SHAIKH RIFĀ'A RĀFI' AL-. *Takhlīṣ al-Ibrīz fī Talkhīṣ Bārīz* [The quintessence of Paris]. Cairo, A.H. 1250 [A.D. 1905].

Thawrat al-'Arab [The Arab revolution by DĀGHIR, AS'AD ?]. Cairo, 1916.

Topkapi Sarayi Müzesi Arşivi Kilavuzu [A guide to the archives of the Topkapi Saray Museum]. 2 vols. Istanbul, 1940.

TUNAYA, TARIK Z. *Turkiyede Siyasi Partiler, 1859-1952* [The political parties in Turkey, 1859-1952]. Istanbul, 1952.

TÜTSCH, HANS E. *Facets of Arab Nationalism.* Detroit: Wayne State University Press, 1965.

URQUHART, DAVID. *The Lebanon (Mount Souria) : A History and a Diary.* 2 vols. London: Newby, 1860.

———. *The Spirit of the East.* 2 vols. London, 1839.

Us, Hakki Tarik. *Meclis-i-Meb'usan, A.H. 1293 (1877 A.D.)* [The Ottoman parliament]. 2 vols. Istanbul, 1954.

Uzunçarşili, Isma'il Hakki. *Topkapi Sarayi Müzesi Mühürler Seksiyonu Rehberi* [A Guide to the Seals Section in the Topkapi Saray Museum]. Topkapi Sarayi Müzesi Yazinlari, no. 8. Istanbul, 1959.

Vámbéry, Ármin. "Personal Recollections of 'Abdul Hamid II and His Court," *The Nineteenth Century and After*, June-July 1909, pp. 69-88.

Van Dyck, Edward A. *Report of Edward A. Van Dyck, Consular Clerk of the United States at Cairo, Upon the Capitulations of the Ottoman Empire Since the Year 1150.* 2 pts. Washington: G.P.O., 1881-82.

Volney, Constantin-François Chasseboeuf. *Travels in Syria and Egypt During the Years 1783, 1784 and 1785, Containing the Present Natural and Political State of Those Countries, Their Productions, Arts, Manufactures, and Commerce; With Observations on the Manners, Customs, and Government of the Turks and Arabs*, trans. from the French. 2 vols. London: Robinson, 1787.

Wittek, Paul. *The Rise of the Ottoman Empire.* Royal Asiatic Society Monographs, vol. 23. London: Royal Asiatic Society of Great Britain and Ireland, 1938.

Wortabet, Gregory M. *Syria and the Syrians; or, Turkey in the Dependencies.* 2 vols. London: James Madden, 1856.

Yalman, Ahmet Emin. *Turkey in the World War.* New Haven: Yale University Press, 1930.

Young, George. *Nationalism and War in the Near East*, ed. by Lord Courtney of Penwith. Oxford: Clarendon Press, 1915.

———. ed. *Corps de Droit Ottoman; recueil des codes, lois, règlements, ordonnances, et actes les plus importants du droit intérieur, et d'études sur le droit coutumier de l'Empire Ottoman.* 7 vols. Oxford: Clarendon Press, 1905-06.

Ziādeh, Nicolā, and others. *Dirāsāt fi'l Thawrah al-'Arabiyyah al-Kubrā* [Studies in the great Arab revolt]. Amman, 1967.

PERIODICALS

Afkār (*Amman*). 1966.
Ahrām, Al- (Cairo). 1963.
Daily Mail, The (London). 1914.
Daily News, The (London). 1914.
Echo de Paris, L'. 1913.
Eqdam (Constantinople). 1913.
Hilāl, Al- (Cairo), 1908, 1914.
Ḥiwār (Beirut). 1963.
Illustrated London News, The. 1908.
Jinān, Al- (Beirut). 1870.
Lisān-ul-Ḥāl (Beirut) 1878, 1913.
Manār, Al- (Cairo). 1913-14.
Mokaṭṭam, Al- (Cairo). 1913.
Muqtabas, Al- (Damascus). 1909.
Tesvir-i-Efkar (Constantinople). 1913.
Times, The (London). 1911, 1914.
Osmanli, The (Geneva). 1898.

INDEX

Abbasids, 5, 9, 12n
'Abd al-Nāsir, Gamāl, 138
'Abduh, Shaikh Muḥammad, 61-62, 62n
'Abdul Hamīd I, Sultan of Turkey (1774-1789), 9, 15
'Abdul Hamīd II, Sultan of Turkey (1876-1909), 10, 45, 46-50, 65-66, 66n, 68n, 69, 69n, 70, 70n, 71, 71n, 72, 73n, 75, 84, 88n
'Abdul 'Azīz, Sultan of Turkey (1861-1876), 10
'Abdallah, Emir of Trans-Jordan (1921-1946), 107, 107n, 108
Acre, 26
Adana, 43n
Aden, 30
Adivar, Halidé Edib, 83, 115
Adrianople, 2, 99
Afghani, Jamal al-Din al-, 61n, 62, 62n, 88 n
Afghanistan, 2, 2n
Ahl al-Kitāb, 26
'Aintūra, 40, 52n
Akcuraoglu, Yūsuf Bey, 79
'Akkār, 22
Albania, 22n, 69n
Albanians, 65
Aleppo, 6, 9, 23, 25, 25n, 26, 40, 48n, 54, 56n, 60n, 74n, 97, 123
Allenby, Gen. Edmund, 123
Alp, Tekin, 79, 80
Ammān, 27
American University of Beirut (see Syrian Protestant College).
'Ammūn, Iskandar, 91n, 92
'Ammūn, Salīm, 52n
Anatolia, 4, 5, 6, 51, 84, 99
'Anbar, Sulaimān, 92n
Anglo-Russian Convention of 1907, 106
Antonius, George, 83n
Arab, "Awakening," 40, 61, 129, 132; Congress (Paris, 1913), 92, 94, 97, 98; nationalism, 51, 55, 129-30, 134, 137; Question, 33, 100n; relations with Turks, 7, 8, 32, 35-36, 39, 73; Revolt, 60, 116n, 118, 132; revolutionary pamphlets and placards, 47, 55-56, 57-59; societies, 50, 50n, 52, 55, 57, 82, 83, 89; *Ummah*, 58n, 83, 92, 118, 130, 133, 135, 136; unity, 135
Arabia, 2, 22, 25, 34, 51, 104, 113n, 118, 121
Arabic (language), 9, 36, 87-88, 88n, 93, 95
Arabs, 33, 65, 73, 75, 76, 104, 106
'Araisī, 'Abd al-Ghanī al-, 91n, 108n
Aristidi Pasha, 72
Armenia, 69n, 113n, 114n, 121
Armenia, 28, 50, 74n, 75, 76, 105n
Armenian Question, 65
Armistice, 123
Ashrusnah,5
Assir, 123

Atatürk, Mustafa Kemal, 139
Athens, 2
Atrash, Nasīb Bey al-, 117
Austria, 25, 31n, 36
Azhar, University of al-, 9
Azhari, Shaikh Aḥmad Abbās al-, 41n
'Azim, Rafīq al-, 50n, 85n, 93
'Azoury, Négīb, 66, 67n

Baalbek, 92n
Bāb al-Mandib, 1
Baghdad, 3, 25, 25n, 34, 48n, 56, 56n, 58n, 94, 125
Baghdad Railway, 101, 102
Baihum, Ahmad Mukhtar, 91n, 94n
Balkan Wars, 99, 105n
Balkans, 54, 69n, 76, 98
Banu Sifas, 22
Barron, Sir Edmund, 104
Basra, 82, 94, 102, 104, 120
Bayezid I, Sultan of Turkey (1389-1403), 2
Bayezid II, Sultan of Turkey (1481-1512), 2
Beirut, 25n, 26, 28, 29, 37, 38, 40, 51, 54, 55, 56, 57, 58-59, 64, 73n, 83n, 89, 90, 91n, 97, 110, 123; Reform Society, 82, 90, 91, 91n; secret societies in, 52-54, 57, 58
Belgrade, 2
Beratli, 23
Berlin, 78n; Congress of, 55
Black Sea, 51n
Blanche, Vice-Consul, 29n
Bliss, Rev. Daniel, 45n
Bokhara, 5
Bopp, A., 97
Bourquency, Ambassador, 40n
Brémond, Lt. Col. Edouard, 116n
Buchanan, Sir G., 103
Bucharest, 99
Budapest, 3, 78n
Bulgaria, 98
Bulwer, Sir Henry, 28

Cahun, Léon, 79n
Cairo, 6, 7, 50, 52n, 69, 91
Caliph (Caliphate), 8, 12, 12n, 35, 49, 55, 73, 78, 88, 94, 94n, 98n, 106, 110, 139
Cambon, Ambassador Paul, 65, 101, 103
Capitulations, 19-21, 23, 105n
Carslaw, Rev. Dr., 38
Casimir-Perrier, M., 65
Caspian Sea, 30
Caucasus, 1
Chalderan, Plain of, 6
Charles V, Holy Roman Emperor (1519-1556), 3
Chevrillon, Andre, 28
Chirol, Sir Valentine, 127
Christian, 27, 27n, 28, 32, 36, 37, 40, 41, 41n, 42n, 52, 53, 58, 59, 61, 70, 72, 73n, 80, 105n, 110, 119, 132
Cilicia, 113n
Cohen, Albert, 79n
Constantinople, 2, 3, 10, 12n, 13, 19, 47, 48n, 54, 56, 59, 72, 72n, 73n, 76, 77, 82, 85, 89, 112, 114n, 121
Constitution (see Ottoman Constitution)
Consular Courts, 21
Contenson, Baron Ludovic de, 100
Creasy, Edward, 2
Cumberbatch, Consul-General, 90
Curry, Sir P., 65
Cyprus, 21

Dāghir, As'ad, 96
Daily Mail (London), 103
Daily News (London), 103
Damascus, 7, 9, 25, 25n, 40, 48, 53n, 54, 55, 56, 64, 85n, 97, 109, 110, 116, 118, 122, 123; Congress of, 55
Dardanelles, 112
Debbās, Charles, 91n
Decentralization Party, 72, 85-86, 93
Deedes, Sir Wyndham, 106, 119

Delaporte, 56
Dickson, John, 55, 56, 57-59
Djavid Bey, 76, 78, 105
Djemal Pasha (see Jamal Pasha)
Dufferin and Ava, Marquis of, 28

Egypt, 2, 6, 7, 8, 12, 22, 34, 51, 63n, 69, 70, 104, 128
Enver Pasha, 78, 80, 81, 94, 105, 108n, 109
Egdam (Constantinople), 99n
Ertoghrul, 4

Faidi, Sulaimān, 115n
Faḍl, Shaikh, 48n
Faiṣal, Emir, 116, 117, 118, 122, 133
Fakhr al-Dīn II, Emir of Lebanon (1592-1635), 22
Farghanah, 5
Fatāt, al-, 82-83
Fatwa (*fetva*), 72n
Federation of Arab Republics, 135-36
Firman of 1 June 1841, 36
Flourens, 64
France, 23-25, 36, 37, 63n, 116n
Francis I, King of France (1515-1547), 20
Freycinet, Charles de, 56

Galata, 20
Gallipoli, 112
Gaza, 22, 43n
Geary, A., 76
Geneva, 50, 69n, 78
Germany, 101, 105, 105n, 107
Ghānem, Shukrī, 91n
Ghawrī, Qansaw al-, Sultan of Egypt (1501-1516), 6, 7
Ghazālī, al-, Vali of Syria, 22
Ghāzī, 125
Ghazīr, 40
Gibb, Hamilton A. R., 8, 15, 62
Gibbons, H. A., 4
Gilbert, T., 60
Gökalp, Ziya Bey, 80, 84
Goschen, Ambassador G. T., 56, 59, 102
Great Britain, 25, 106, 109n, 116
Greece, 98, 99
Greeks, 26n, 28, 41n, 42n, 52, 65, 69n, 75, 89, 105n
Grey of Fallodon, Viscount, 65, 76, 95, 95n, 101, 102, 103
Grey, Sir Edward (see Grey of Fallodon)
Guillois, 64

Ḥabbalīn, Elias, 52n
Hadhramaut, 48n
Hādī, 'Awnī, 'Abd al-, 91n
Hādī, Rūḥī 'Abd al-, 72
Ḥaidar, 'Alī, Sharīf, 93, 93n
Ḥaidar, Ibrahīm, 92n
Ḥaidar, Muhammad, 92n
Haifa, 123
Hama, 7, 54
Haqq, Shaikh 'Abd al-, 77
Harborne, Ambassador William, 21
Harun al-Rashid, Caliph (786-809), 5
Hashimī, Yāsīn, al-, 117
Hatti-Hulayun of 1886, 28, 31
Hazim Bey, 90
Hejaz, 25n, 66, 107n, 108n, 118, 123; Railway, 48, 49n
Hellespont, 1
Herat, Sultan of, 2n
Heyd, Uriel, 73
Hizb al-Lamarkaziyyah al-Idariyyah al-'Uthmani, 82-83, 85, 98
Homs, 7, 23, 54
Ḥourānī, Ibrahīm al-, 52n
Huda Effendi, 'Abdul, 48
Hulussi Bey, 111n
Hulagu, 125
Hungary, 2, 3
Ḥusain, Grand Sharif of Mecca (1908-1918), 81, 105n, 106, 107, 108, 109n, 116, 116n, 118n, 119, 132, 133
Ḥusayni, Shaikh Badr al-Dīn al-, 117

Ibn Iyās, 7
Ibn Sa'ud, 109n
Iran, 6
Iraq, 70, 113n, 120
Islam, 5, 125-126, 130-31
Isma'il I, Shah of Persia (1500-1524), 6
Italy, 3, 98

Jamal Pasha, 94, 105, 108n, 109, 109n, 110, 111, 112, 113n, 114, 114n, 115, 117, 118, 132
Jam'iyyah al-'Arabiyyah 'al-Fatat, 83
Jam'iyyah al-Natiqin bi'l-Dad, 83
Jam'iyyah al-Shawra al-'Uthmani, 50n
Janissaries, 1, 60n
Jazā'irī, 'Abdu'l Qadir al-, Emir, 54, 55
Jeddah, 116n
Jerusalem, 13, 22, 26, 123
Jesuits, 40, 40n, 43n, 44
Jews, 28, 37, 72, 78, 105n
Jihād, 110, 115

Kamil Pasha, Grand Vizier, 99n
Karak, al- (Krak des Chévaliers), 22
Kawakibī, 'Abd al-Rahmān al-, 61, 62
Kazemzadeh, Firuz, 113n
Kerr, Niven, 21n
Khairy Bey, 118
Khalīl, 'Abdul Karīm al-, 94, 112n
Khan, Jenghis, 80
Kitchener of Khartoum and of Broome, Earl, Consul General of Egypt (1911-1916), 107, 108n, 118
Knolles, Richard, 4
Köprülü, Mehmed Fu'ad, 4, 5
Koran (see Qur'an)
Kossovo, 2
Kulliyah al-'Uthmaniyyah al-Islamiyyah, al-, 41n
Kurdistan, 6, 22, 113n
Kutahiya, 35
Kuwait, 104, 109

Lattakia, 26, 54
Lawrence, Col. T. E., 115n, 118, 122
Lazarists, 44, 52n
Lebanon, 22, 23, 25, 26, 34, 36, 37, 39, 43n, 47, 51, 53, 61, 70, 101, 111, 112, 123; emigres from, 92n; Protocols for, 25-26; schools in, 38, 43-44
Lesseps, E. de, Consul-General, 29n
Lewis, Bernard, 16, 100n
Libya, 98
Lichnowsky, Princes, 102
Lisān-ul-Hāl (Beirut), 50
Lloyd, Geroge, 105
London, 50, 58n, 78n, 106; Treaty of, (1841) 36, (1913) 99
Lowther, Sir Gerard, 65, 76

Macedonia, 68, 69n, 70, 72, 76
Mahdi, the (Muhammad Ahmad), 60
Mahmassani, Muhammad, 91n
Mahmud II, Sultan of Turkey (1808-1839), 30
Maḥmūd Pasha, Damad, 84
Majallah al-Ahkām al-'Adliyyah, 23, 24
Majallah Jam'iyyati, 24
Makarius, Shāhīn, 52n
Ma'luf, Jamīla, 91n
Manār, al- (Cairo), 33n, 61, 63
Mansur, al-, Caliph (745-775), 5
Maqrizi, Tagi-al-Din Ahmad al-, 9
Marash, 25n
Mardam, Jamil, 91n
Maronites, 26n, 36, 52, 52n, 67n, 89n, 119; massacres of, 36
Marriott, John A. R., 98
Masonic lodges, 53, 53n
McMahon, Sir Arthur Henry, 108, 108n, 109n, 116
Mecca, 13, 22, 34, 48n, 56n, 59n, 117
Medina, 13, 22, 48, 56n, 66, 81, 97, 118
Mehakim-i-Nizamiye, 24, 24n
Midhat Pasha, Grand Vizier of Turkey (1872, 1876-1877), 25, 31n, 47, 49, 50, 58-59, 67

Millet, 28-29, 89
Misri, 'Azīz al-, 108n
Missionaries, 40, 42, 43, 44
Mohàcs, Battle of (1526), 3
Mongols, 6
Montenegro, 98
Morgenthau, Ambassador Henry M., 73
Mosul, 3, 25, 25n, 43n, 56n
Mount Lebanon, 25-26, 36, 132
Muhammad I, Sultan of Turkey (1413-1421), 2
Muhammad II ("The Conqueror"), Sultan of Turkey (1451-1481), 10, 19, 20n
Muhammad V, Sultan of Turkey (1909-1918), 72, 83, 94, 105n
Muhammad 'Ali Pasha, Viceroy of Egypt (1805-1848), 35
Muharram Bey, Dr., 87
Mukattam, Al- (Cairo), 52n, 89, 93
Munlā Bey, Najm-al-Din, 87
Murad I, Sultan of Turkey (1359-1389), 1
Murad II, Sultan of Turkey (1421-1451), 2
Murad III, Sultan of Turkey (1574-1595), 21n
Murad V, Sultan of Turkey (1876), 10, 46
Muslim Empire, 1, 53
Muslims, 1, 26, 26n, 27, 33, 36, 41, 48, 52, 53, 58, 59, 61-62, 72, 105n, 110
Mu'tasim, al-, Caliph (833-842), 5
Mutawakkil, J'afar al-, Caliph (847-861), 12, 12n
Mutrān, Nadrah, 91n

Nablus, 26
Naples, 3
Napoleon Bonaparte, 128
Naqīb, Tālib al-, 94
Nātūr, Tawfiq al-, 83, 83n, 84
Nāzim Pasha, 71n, 79n, 99n
Nedchia Draga, 72
Nejd, 102
Nicaea, 1
Nicomedia, 1
Nicopolis, Batt. of (1396), 2, 2n
Nimr Pasha, Faris, 52, 52n, 54, 55
Nūri Bey, Jalāl, 79

Oman, Sea of, 66
Orkhan, Sultan of Turkey (1326-1359), 1, 10
Osmanli, The (Geneva), 69n
Ottawi, Consul-General, 97
Ottoman, administrators, 24-25; censorship, 44-45n; Chamber of Deputies, 77; Empire, 30, 33, 54; Commercial Code of 1850, 23; Constitution, 65, 67, 70, 72, 75, 105; government, 17-29; legal system, 17-29; Ministery of Justice, 24; minorities, treatment of, 27, 27n; nationality law of, 24, 26; Parliament, 49, 50, 71, 72, 75, 105n; Penal Code of 1840, 23; population statistics, 25; Senate, 72; Sultans, titles of, 31-32; Tribunals of Commerce, 23-24

Palestine, 26, 111, 113n, 128
Pan-Islam, 34n, 47, 49n, 61, 77, 80
Pan-Turanism, 79, 80, 80n, 81, 99
Paris, 50, 67, 69n, 78n, 83, 91, 92, 97
Peace Conference (Paris, 1919), 121n, 133
Pears, Sir Edwin, 86
Pergamum, 1
Persia, 6, 77
Persian Gulf, 30, 101, 102, 120
Petiteville, Vicomte de, 29, 43n, 64
Picot, Georges, 121n
Pinon, René, 51n
Poincaré, Raymond, 110
Poitiers, Battle of (732), 125
Protestants, 52
Prussia, 25

Qanun, 18-19, 23
Qanun alAsasi, El-, 69
Qur'ān, 87, 88, 135, 138

Ra'iyyah, 26-28, 53
Rashid Pasha, 31n
Raydaniyyah, Battle of, 7
Raymond, Jean, 34
Red Sea, 30
Reglements Organiques of 1861, 26
Rhodes, 3
Rida Bey, Ahmad, 72
Ridā, Muḥammad Rāshid, 33n, 42n, 50n, 61, 63
Rikābī, Alī Ridā Pasha al-, 117
Rifā'i, 48n
Riza, Aḥmad, 77, 78
Rodd, Renell of, Lord, 101
Romania, 99
Rome, 3
Russia, 25, 31n, 42n, 77, 101, 105n, 106, 108, 112, 113
Russo-Turkish War of 1877-78, 54, 55, 56

Sabāh al-Dīn, Prince, 68n, 69n, 84, 85, 120
Safad, 22
Sa'īd, Nūrī Pasha al-, 14
Sa'īd Pasha, Grand Vizier, 91
Sa'īd, Port, 27n
Saida, 25, 55, 56
St. John, F. R., 57
Saint-Joseph, Université, 40
Salam, Salim 'Ali, 91n, 94n
Salonika, 70, 72, 74n, 76, 78, 78n, 79n; Congress of (1911), 77
Samarkand, 5
Sanders, Gen. Liman von, 114n, 115
Sarkīs, Khalīl, 50
Sarrūf, Ya'qūb, 52n
Sa'ud, Muḥammad al-, Emir, 34
Selim I, Sultan of Turkey (1512-1520), 2, 6, 22, 23, 123
Selim III, Sultan of Turkey (1789-1808), 10, 34
Seljukids, 4, 5, 6
Serbia, 98, 99
Seton-Waston, R. W., 78
Shadhili, 48n
Shahbandar, Dr. 'Abdul-Rahmān, 86
Shaikh al-Islam, 9, 10, 10n, 14, 17, 32n, 72n
Shalan, Shaikh Nawāf al-, 117
Sharī'a, 17-18, 23, 25n, 72, 116n
Shawkat Pasha, 72
Sherīf Pasha, 77
Shevket Pasha, Mahmoud, 83
Shī'a, 52
Shī'ism, 6
Shūf, 22
Shukrī, Midhat, 92
Shawair, 38-39
Sicily, 3
Sinai, 7
Skene, J. H., 59, 60n
Solḥ, 'Adil al-, 54
Solḥ, Aḥmad al-, 54, 55
Solḥ, Kāmil Bey al-, 87
Spain, 21n
Storrs, Sir Ronald, 107n, 108, 116n
Stotzingen, Baron von, 118
Stripling, George W. F., 8
Suez, 66, 110
Sulaiman I ("The Magnificent"), Sultan of Turkey (1520-1566), 2, 2n, 11, 20, 23
Sunni, 48, 52
Sunnism, 6
Sursock, Albert, 91n
Suwaidi, Tawfiq al-, 92n
Sykes, Sir Mark, 121n
Sykes-Picot Agreement, 114n, 120, 134
Syria, 2, 6, 7, 8, 22, 23, 26, 29, 34, 35, 41, 51, 53, 54, 56, 58-59, 59n, 60, 70, 71, 89, 101, 107n, 109, 111, 111n, 113n, 114, 114n, 117, 119, 120, 121, 123

Syrian Protestant College (Amerrican University of Beirut), 40, 43-45, 45n, 52, 52n, 91

Tabbārah, Shaikh Aḥmad Ḥasan, 91n, 94, 94n
Tabriz, 6
Tahtāwī, Shaikh Rifa'a Rifa'i al-, 63n
Talaat Pasha, 70n, 76, 77, 78, 94, 97, 105, 108n
Talib Bey, Seyyed, 95, 97
Tanukhi, 22
Tanzimat, 23, 30
Temperley, Harold W. V., 32
Tesvir-i-Efkar (Constantinople), 98
Tewfiḳ Pasha, 105-6
Thābit, Dr. Ayyūb, 91n
Times, The (London), 103
Topkapi Palace Museum, 10, 11n
Torey, de, 47
Toynbee, Arnold J., 37
Transoxiana, 5
Tripoli, 9, 22, 23, 26, 29n, 55
Turkestan, 5
Turkish army, 23, 109; navy,
Turkish (language), 87-88
Turks, chauvinism of, 4; Islamization of, 5; nationalism of, 84; origin of, 4

'Ubaidullah, Shaikh, 79
Umayyad Caliphate, 131
Ummah (see Arab *Ummah*).
Union and Progress, Committee of (C.U.P.), 15, 68n, 69, 70n, 75, 76, 77, 78, 79n, 80, 84, 86, 92, 94, 95, 95n, 96, 97, 116n; League of, 67n, 68
United States of America, 63n
Urfa, 25n
Urmia, Lake, 6
'Urrabi Pasha, 60
'Uthman I (Osman), Sultan of Turkey (1288-1326), 1, 4

Varna, 2, 2n
Vienna, 1, 3, 11, 30, 78n, 125

Wadir, 'Abd al-, 56n
Wahhābīs, 34-35
Western ideas, Arab attitudes toward, 63n; influence of, 33, 36, 37, 40, 42n, 52n
Wingate, Sir Reginald, 116n, 117
Wittek, Paul, 2n
World War, First, 102, 105; Second, 134
Wortabet, Rev. Dr. Gregory, 37, 40

Yalman, Ahmet Emin, 31n
Yāzigi, Ibrāhīm al-, 52n
Yemen, 25n, 120, 123
Yildiz Palace, 65, 72
Young Turks, 9, 65, 67, 68, 72, 73, 73n, 75, 76, 83, 85, 86, 96, 98, 99, 100n, 105n, 112n, 117

Zafir, Shaikh Muhammad, 48, 48n
Zaḥleh, 40
Zahrawi, 'Abd al-Hamid, 91n
Zainiyyah, Khalīl, 91n
Zor, 25n